Asian/Oceanian Historical Dictionaries
Edited by Jon Woronoff

Asia

1. *Vietnam*, by William J. Duiker. 1989
2. *Bangladesh*, 2nd ed., by Craig Baxter and Syedur Rahman. 1996
3. *Pakistan*, by Shahid Javed Burki. 1991
4. *Jordan*, by Peter Gubser. 1991
5. *Afghanistan*, by Ludwig W. Adamec. 1991
6. *Laos*, by Martin Stuart-Fox and Mary Kooyman. 1992
7. *Singapore*, by K. Mulliner and Lian The-Mulliner. 1991
8. *Israel*, by Bernard Reich. 1992
9. *Indonesia*, by Robert Cribb. 1992
10. *Hong Kong and Macau*, by Elfed Vaughan Roberts, Sum Ngai Ling, and Peter Bradshaw. 1992
11. *Korea*, by Andrew C. Nahm. 1993
12. *Taiwan*, by John F. Copper. 1993
13. *Malaysia*, by Amarjit Kaur. 1993
14. *Saudi Arabia*, by J. E. Peterson. 1993
15. *Myanmar*, by Jan Becka. 1995
16. *Iran*, by John H. Lorentz. 1995
17. *Yemen*, by Robert D. Burrowes. 1995
18. *Thailand*, by May Kyi Win and Harold Smith. 1995
19. *Mongolia*, by Alan J. K. Sanders. 1996
20. *India*, by Surjit Mansingh. 1996
21. *Gulf Arab States*, by Malcolm C. Peck. 1996
22. *Syria*, by David Commins. 1996
23. *Palestine*, by Nafez Y. Nazzal and Laila A. Nazzal. 1997
24. *Philippines*, by Artemio R. Guillermo and May Kyi Win. 1997

Oceania

1. *Australia*, by James C. Docherty. 1992
2. *Polynesia*, by Robert D. Craig. 1993
3. *Guam and Micronesia*, by William Wuerch and Dirk Ballendorf. 1994
4. *Papua New Guinea*, by Ann Turner. 1994
5. *New Zealand*, by Keith Jackson and Alan McRobie. 1996

Historical Dictionary of Taiwan (Republic of China)

Second Edition

John F. Copper

Asian/Oceanian Historical Dictionaries, No. 34

The Scarecrow Press, Inc.
Lanham, Maryland, and London
2000

SCARECROW PRESS, INC.

Published in the United States of America
by Scarecrow Press, Inc.
4720 Boston Way, Lanham, Maryland 20706
http://www.scarecrowpress.com

4 Pleydell Gardens, Folkestone
Kent CT20 2DN, England

Copyright © 2000 by John F. Copper

British Library Cataloguing in Publication Information Available

Library of Congress Cataloging-in-Publication Data

Copper, John F., 1940-
    Historical dictionary of Taiwan (Republic of China) / John F. Copper. --
2nd ed.
        p.   cm.   -- (Asian/Oceanian historical dictionaries; no. 34)
    ISBN 0-8108-3665-3 (cloth : alk. paper)
    1. Taiwan--History Dictionaries.   I. Title.   II. Series.
DS798.96.C67   2000
951.24'9'003--dc21   99-27946
                                              CIP

⊖™ The paper used in this publication meets the minimum requirements of
American National Standard for Information Sciences—Permanence of
Paper for Printed Library Materials, ANSI/NISO Z39.48–1992.
Manufactured in the United States of America.

To Royce Wellington Copper

CONTENTS

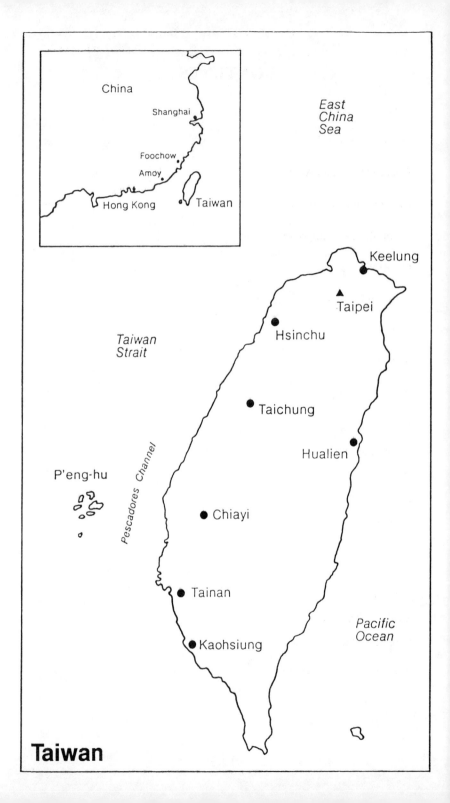

Taiwan

EDITOR'S FOREWORD

The Republic of China, often referred to as Taiwan, has long aroused interest abroad. Earlier, much attention focused on the extraordinary economic development. Observers wondered how such a small, densely populated, and initially poor country with virtually no natural resources could accomplish so much. Indeed, the media frequently portrayed Taiwan as a "miracle." Comments on Taiwan's political system were far less flattering. The Kuomintang regime was the object of criticism, as were its leaders; observers, in fact, pondered why a country that achieved so much economically could not do more to improve its politics.

The source of interest in recent years has been a political "coming of age," a transition toward a far more democratic regime, or a political "miracle" of sorts. This has greatly improved the country's image abroad. It has also dated much of the literature. That is why this second edition of the *Historical Dictionary of Taiwan* is particularly important, appearing at a time when so much has changed and when it is so necessary to understand the "new situation" in Taiwan. In addition to shedding light on the present and recent past, the author reaches much further back to an era when the island was known as Formosa. And, in an extensive bibliography, he directs the reader to other sources of information on the various subjects and historical periods.

John F. Copper is the Stanley J. Buckman Distinguished Professor of International Studies at Rhodes College in Memphis, Tennessee. Along with the first and second editions of this volume, he is the author of 22 books on China, Taiwan, and Asian affairs. His *China's Global Role* won the Clarence Day Foundation Award in 1981 for outstanding research. His most recent books on Taiwan are *Taiwan: Nation-State or Province* (second edition) (1996); *The Taiwan Political Miracle: Essays on Political Development, Elections and Foreign Relations* (1979); and *Taiwan's Mid-1990s Elections: Taking the Final Steps to Democracy* (1998). Dr. Copper, who has lived for 13 years in Asia, has contributed to many other books and has written numerous articles on Taiwan.

Jon Woronoff

Series Editor

ABBREVIATIONS AND ACRONYMS

ADB	Asian Development Bank
AIT	American Institute in Taiwan
APACL	Asian Pacific Anti-Communist League
APEC	Asia-Pacific Economic Cooperation (forum)
APPS	Association for Public Policy Studies
ARATS	Association for Relations Across the Taiwan Strait
ASPAC	Asian and Pacific Council
BCC	Broadcasting Corporation of China
CAC	Campaign Assistance Committee
CAL	China Airlines
CBC	Central Bank of China
CBS	Central Broadcasting System
CCK	Chiang Ching-kuo
CCNAA	Coordination Council for North American Affairs
CDC	China Development Corporation
CEC	Central Election Commission
CEPD	Council for Economic Planning and Development
CETDC	China External Trade Development Council
CFL	Chinese Federation of Labor
CHT	Chunghua Telecom
CKS	Chiang Kai-shek
CLA	Council of Labor Affairs
CNA	Central News Agency
CPC	Chinese Petroleum Corporation
CRC	Central Reform Committee
CSC	Central Standing Committee
CSDP	Chinese Social Democratic Party
CTOC	Chinese Taipei Olympic Committee
CTS	China Television Service
CTV	China Television Company
CYC	China Youth Corps
CYP	China Youth Party
DPP	Democratic Progressive Party
DSP	Democratic Socialist Party
EPA	Environmental Protection Administration
EPC	Economic Planning Council
EPZ	Export Processing Zone
FAPA	Formosan Association for Public Affairs
FTV	Formosa Television Corporation
GIO	Government Information Office

IDF	Indigenous Defense Fighter
ITRI	Industrial Technology Research Institute
JCRR	Joint Commission on Rural Reconstruction
KMT	Kuomintang (or Nationalist Party)
MAC	Mainland Affairs Council
MOFA	Ministry of Foreign Affairs
MSA	Mutual Security Agency
NDIPA	National Democratic Independent Political Alliance
NP	New Party
NSB	National Security Bureau
NSC	National Science Council
NSC	National Security Council
NTU	National Taiwan University
NUC	National Unification Council
OCAC	Overseas Chinese Affairs Commission
PCT	Presbyterian Church of Taiwan
PRC	Peoples Republic of China
ROC	Republic of China
SEF	Straits Exchange Foundation
TAIP	Taiwan Independence Party
TCP	Taiwan Communist Party
TECRO	Taipei Economic and Cultural Representative Office
TRA	Taiwan Relations Act
TRAPP	Tangwai Research Association for Public Policy
TTV	Taiwan Television Corporation
WTO	World Trade Organization
WUFI	World United Formosans for Independence

NOTE ON CHINESE TERMS

The system of romanizing Chinese words, terms, place names, and people's names used in this book is the Wade-Giles System. This is the system used in Taiwan and is the system employed in romanizing Chinese in most historical works published in the West. The Pinyin System used in the People's Republic of China is employed for words whose referent is a place or name in China, though older and common terms such as Peking are used if they were in use at the time. Beijing, which is the pinyin romanization of Peking, is employed after that usage became common. Sometimes words will be romanized in two systems indicating that they are spelled differently in different places. For example, some names are romanized in two ways indicating that the Republic of China and the Peoples Republic of China disagree about the spelling. In some cases, persons' names are romanized using another system or from a dialect of Chinese rather than Mandarin. In these instances, the author prefers to accept the spelling of the person's name that he or she uses, even though it is not standard. Some aboriginal words are used in this book, taking whatever spelling is used in Taiwan. The reader should note that family names come first in Chinese; given names come last and are hyphenated if there are two given names.

CHRONOLOGY OF IMPORTANT EVENTS

10,000 BC   Human life on Taiwan.

206 BC   Taiwan is referred to in Chinese records as the "Land of Yangchow."

AD 239   Chinese Emperor Wu sends an expeditionary force to Taiwan to explore the island.

607   First of three exploratory missions from China are sent to Taiwan.

c. 1000   Chinese settlements are present in southern Taiwan.

c. 1350   Mongol Dynasty ruling China sends a mission to the Pescadores, where a base is established.

1517   Portuguese vessels sailing to Japan spot Taiwan and refer to it as Ilha Formosa (beautiful island). This is the first mention of Taiwan in Western history.

1622   Dutch forces capture the Pescadores and build a base from which Dutch ships can control traffic through the Taiwan Strait.

1624   Dutch reach an agreement with the Chinese government to evacuate from the Pescadores in return for establishing settlements on Taiwan. This marks the beginning of Dutch colonial rule of Taiwan.

1626   Spanish forces seize Keelung and from there expand to control northern Taiwan.

1628   Japanese settlers leave Taiwan under orders from the Tokugawa Shogunate, Japan's military leader, as part of Japan's isolationist policies.

1642   Dutch forces capture major Spanish settlements in northern Taiwan, thereby consolidating control over the island.

1659   Cheng Ch'eng-kung's forces almost capture Nanking in an effort to overthrow the Manchu Dynasty and reestablish the Ming Dynasty.

1662   Cheng Ch'eng-kung, also known as Koxinga, defeats Dutch forces, marking the end of Dutch rule and the beginning of the "Cheng Dynasty" in Taiwan.

1683   The end of the Cheng family rule of Taiwan and the beginning of China's governance of Taiwan under the Manchu Dynasty.

1729   Emperor of China forbids immigration to Taiwan under penalty of death.

1786   Major rebellion in Taiwan against Chinese rule.

1860   Opening of several ports in Taiwan to Western trade.

1874   Japanese punitive expedition is sent to Taiwan in response to aborigines killing Japanese sailors.

1884   Liu Ming-chuan becomes governor of Taiwan. French naval vessels attack port of Keelung.

1887   Taiwan is made a province of China.

1895   Treaty of Shimonoseki concludes Sino-Japanese War; Taiwan is ceded to Japan "in perpetuity." Unsuccessful attempt is made to form the Republic of Taiwan.

1924   Lin Hsien-tang presents 12-point grievances to Japanese colonial government.

1928   First university is established in Taiwan.

1935   Taiwan witnesses its worst earthquake; more than 3,000 die.

1938   Chiang Kai-shek announces his intention to take Taiwan back from Japan.

1941   Taiwan serves as a base for Japanese forces that attack the Philippines.

1943   At the Cairo Conference, the United States and the United Kingdom promise Chiang Kai-shek the return of territories "stolen by Japan," meaning Taiwan, to China after the war.

1945   In July, Allied forces at Potsdam reiterate the territorial provisions of the Cairo Declaration. On October 25, Taiwan becomes part of the Republic of China as a result of Japan's defeat in World War II.

1947   February 28, a major rebellion breaks out against the rule of Nationalist Chinese Governor-General Chen Yi; it is put down with force and many Taiwanese are killed.

1948   December 29, General Chen Cheng is appointed governor of Taiwan.

1949   The government of the Republic of China flees to Taiwan after its defeat on the mainland. Taipei becomes the provisional capital of the Republic of China.

            In December, Wu Kuo-chen is named governor of Taiwan.

1950   Taipei breaks diplomatic relations with the United Kingdom after the latter establishes formal ties with Peking.

            In March, Chiang Kai-shek resumes the presidency of the Republic of China. He names General Chen Cheng president of the Executive Yuan, or premier.

            In June, as a result of the Korean War, U.S. president Harry S. Truman sends the Seventh Fleet to the Taiwan Strait, blocking a planned invasion of Taiwan by Mao.

            In July, General Douglas MacArthur meets Chiang Kai-shek in Taipei. U.S. aid to Nationalist China, now on Taiwan, is resumed.

1951   The Legislative Yuan passes the Farm Rent Reduction Act, limiting rent on farm land to 37.5 percent of the value of the crop, marking the formalization of the first stage of Taiwan's land reform program.

In September, 49 nations sign a peace treaty with Japan. China is not represented. Taiwan's status is not mentioned.

In December, the Taiwan Provincial Assembly (provisional) is established.

1952   In August, the Legislative Yuan approves the just-negotiated separate peace treaty between the Republic of China and Japan. Some interpret this to legalize the transfer of Taiwan to the Republic of China. Some say this is not the case since such was not cited in the treaty.

1953   In January, the Legislative Yuan adopts the Land-to-the-Tiller Program the second phase of land reform. First four-year economic plan is announced.

In September, Chiang Kai-shek extends the term of the National Assembly elected in 1947, until another National Assembly can be elected.

1954   In January, 14,000 Chinese captured during the Korean War who refuse repatriation to the People's Republic of China arrive in Taipei.

In March, the National Assembly approves the indefinite extension of the Temporary Provisions of the Constitution.

In March, Chiang Kai-shek is reelected president of the Republic of China for a second six-year term. Chen Cheng is reelected vice president.

In May, Chiang Kai-shek appoints Yen Chia-kan governor of Taiwan.

On September 3, after a series of statements by Chinese leaders in Peking promising to "liberate" Taiwan, Communist forces launch an artillery bombardment of Quemoy, the largest of the offshore islands held by the Republic of China. Washington pledges to help Taipei.

In December, the U.S.-Republic of China Defense Treaty is signed in Washington, D.C. Each side promises defense help to the other, but the treaty is primarily seen as a U.S. security promise to Taiwan. The treaty is a response to the Offshore Islands crisis.

1955   In January, the northernmost island of the Tachen Island group (held by Taipei) falls to People's Republic of China forces. All 720 of the Republic of China soldiers defending the island die.

In January, the U.S. Congress passes the Formosa Resolution authorizing President Dwight D. Eisenhower to use American forces to defend Taiwan, the Pescadores, and "related positions and territories." The resolution does not specifically mention the Offshore Islands but seems to make it possible for the United States to help defend them.

In February, Taipei evacuates its forces from the Tachen Islands. The United States had considered them too distant and not defensible and recommended the move, perhaps asking for this in exchange for promises to defend Quemoy and Matsu.

In March, Foreign Minister George K.C. Yeh and U.S. secretary of state John Foster Dulles exchange ratification documents for the two countries' mutual defense treaty.

In December, the Republic of China vetoes a United Nations Security Council proposal to approve the membership request by Outer Mongolia (territory claimed by the Republic of China).

1956   In July, ground is broken for the construction of the East-West Cross Island Highway, the first modern road transversing the center of the island.

1957   October 20, Chiang Kai-shek is reelected director-general of the Nationalist Party or Kuomintang (KMT).

1958   August 23, the second Offshore Island Crisis begins with forces of the People's Republic of China firing on Quemoy.

September 13, U.S. president Eisenhower declares that the attack on Quemoy is preparatory to invading Taiwan and that the Formosa Resolution passed by Congress in 1955 applies to the present situation.

October 23, President Chiang Kai-shek and U.S. secretary of state Dulles issue a joint communiqué reaffirming their solidarity and stating that Quemoy and Matsu are "closely related" to the defense of Taiwan. The communiqué also states that the use of force would not be the "principal means" to restore the freedom of the people of China.

1959   March 26, President Chiang Kai-shek issues a special message to the Tibetan people, supporting their aspirations in accordance with the principle of self-determination.

In July, the Legislative Yuan revises the Conscription Law, stipulating 19-year-olds are to be drafted for two years in the army or three years in the navy or air force.

August 7, the worst floods in more than half a century hit central and southern Taiwan.

In August, Taiwan receives Nike-Hercules missiles from the United States.

December 8, the Legislative Yuan amends Article 12 of the Organic Law of the National Assembly to allow the president to appoint an acting secretary-general when the assembly is not in session.

1960   March 11, the National Assembly adopts an amendment to the Temporary Provisions of the Constitution allowing the president and the vice president to exceed the two-term limit in Article 47 of the Constitution. This allows Chiang Kai-shek to be reelected to a third term as president and Chen Cheng a second term as vice president.

In May, the East-West Highway is open to traffic.

In June, President Eisenhower visits Taiwan. Prior to and during the visit, military forces of the People's Republic of China bombard Quemoy Island.

In August, Yang Chuan-kuang wins the Silver Medal in the Olympic games for his performance in the decathlon.

1961   In December, Taiwan's first nuclear reactor is put into operation.

1962   In February, Taiwan opens its first stock exchange.

March 14, Foreign Minister Shen Chang-huan announces that Taipei does not recognize Japan's residual sovereignty over the Ryukyu Islands.

In November, General Huang Chieh is appointed governor of Taiwan.

1963   In April, Yang Chuan-kuang breaks the world decathlon record.

August 23, ambassador to the U.S. Tsiang Ting-fu signs Nuclear Test Ban Treaty.

November 12, the 9th Party Congress of the Kuomintang opens in Taipei.

November 16, Yen Chia-kan becomes premier.

1964   June 14, Shihmen Dam is dedicated.

1965   July 1, the U.S. officially terminates its economic aid to Taiwan.

July 31, the Republic of China and the United States sign an agreement on the status of U.S. military force in Taiwan.

1966   March 22, the National Assembly elects Chiang Kai-shek to a fourth term as president.

December 3, the Kaohsiung Export Processing Zone is inaugurated, the first of Taiwan's export processing zones that subsequently facilitate economic growth through exports.

1967   February 1, the National Security Council is formed, with Huang Shao-ku as its first secretary-general.

July 1, Taipei becomes a special municipality, with Henry Kao as its mayor.

July 28, the Executive Yuan extends period of compulsory education from six to nine years.

1968   June 25, Defense Minister Chiang Ching-kuo, Chiang Kai-shek's eldest son, is named vice-premier.

In December, Taiwan opens a satellite telecommunications station.

1969   March 29, the Kuomintang holds its 10th Party Congress.

1970   Vice-Premier Chiang Ching-kuo visits the United States; an attempt is made on his life by Taiwan independence advocates.

In July, Chi Cheng breaks the women's record in the 200-meter sprint in West Germany.

1971   In August, the North-South Freeway is started.

October 25, the Republic of China is "expelled" from the United Nations after the United States lost a General Assembly vote to make the matter of the China seat an important question requiring a two-thirds majority; the China seat is given to the People's Republic of China.

1972   February 28, President Richard M. Nixon, during a visit to China, signs the "Shanghai Communiqué" which states that the United States does not challenge Peking's position that Taiwan is part of China.

March 21, Chiang Kai-shek is elected to a fifth six-year term as president by the National Assembly.

May 26, Chiang Ching-kuo becomes premier.

In August, the Taipei Little League baseball team wins the World Series.

September 29, Japan severs diplomatic relations with Taipei.

1973   In February, Taipei revalues the New Taiwan dollar to N.T. $38 to one U.S. dollar.

October 30, Tsengwen Dam and Reservoir, the largest in Taiwan, is inaugurated.

1974   October 30, the first F-5E jet fighter made in Taiwan under a joint agreement with the United States comes off the assembly line.

1975   April 5, Chiang Kai-shek dies.

April 6, Vice President Yen Chia-kan becomes president.

In May, Premier Chiang Ching-kuo is elected chairman of the Central Committee of the Kuomintang.

1976   March 26, Lin Yu-tang, Taiwan's best-known writer, dies.

In July, the Republic of China Olympic Committee withdraws from the Montreal Olympic Games to protest its being forced to compete under the name "Taiwan."

1977   October 22, the first generator of Taiwan's first nuclear power plant is put into use.

1978   March 21, Chiang Ching-kuo is elected president. Shieh Tung-min is elected vice president, the first Taiwanese to hold this office.

May 26, former stage protest outside U.S. minister of economic affairs Sun Yun-suan is appointed premier.

June 30, International Monetary Fund lists Republic of China as the world's twenty-fifth-largest trading nation.

December 8, the Legislative Yuan passes a bill unpegging Taiwan's currency from the U.S. dollar.

December 15, President Jimmy Carter announces that the United States will de-recognize the Republic of China and will establish diplomatic ties with the People's Republic of China.

December 17, 5,000 people embassy in Taipei because of the decision to move the embassy to Peking.

1979   January 1, United States grants diplomatic recognition to People's Republic of China and breaks ties with the Republic of China.

April 10, the U.S. Congress passes, by an overwhelming vote, the Taiwan Relations Act. The United States gives Taiwan security and economic guarantees and treats Taiwan as a sovereign nation-state (though it does not use the term "Republic of China"), unlike the Normalization Act signed by President Carter with the People's Republic of China, which states Taiwan is a part of China.

June 17, Charles Cross assumes the post of director of the American Institute in Taiwan, which replaced the U.S. embassy.

July 1, Kaohsiung is elevated to the status of Special Municipality.

September 6, the Cabinet announces its decision to extend the territorial waters of the Republic of China to 12 miles and to establish a 200-mile economic zone.

December 10, *Formosa* magazine supporters organize a rally and parade in Kaohsiung to commemorate Human

Rights Day, but also to protest government policies which the opposition charges have caused Taiwan to become diplomatically isolated. The "Kaohsiung Incident" follows, during which more than one hundred people are injured—mostly police. Leaders of the protest are subsequently put on trial, including a number of opposition politicians.

December 17, Tsiang Yen-si replaces Chang Pao-shu as secretary-general of the Kuomintang Central Committee.

1980   January 1, U.S.-Republic of China Defense Treaty is terminated.

January 3, the U.S. government announces that it will resume arms sales to Taiwan which had been suspended for a year.

December 6, 70 new members are elected to the Legislative Yuan and 76 to the National Assembly in supplemental national elections in what many observers say is the first competitive election in Taiwan at the national level and the beginning of open and democratic politics in the country.

1981   February 18, the government announces that it is planning to manufacture tanks, ships, and other sophisticated weapons.

March 29, the Kuomintang holds its 12th Congress.

April 3, President Chiang Ching-kuo is reelected chairman of the Kuomintang.

1982   In August, the United States and the People's Republic of China sign a communiqué in which Washington promises to decrease and ultimately end weapons sales to Taiwan.

1983   In December, Taiwan holds its second national election, which is characterized by genuine competition. The Kuomintang wins a big victory, capturing 52 of 71 contested seats in the Legislative Yuan, leaving three to the opposition and three to independents.

1984   March 20, former head of the Council for Economic Planning and Development Yu Kuo-hwa is chosen premier.

March 21, President Chiang Ching-kuo is elected to another six-year term. Lee Teng-hui is elected vice-president. June 2, Chiu Chuang-huan becomes governor of Taiwan Province.

1985   In January, the Ministry of Economic Affairs announces lower tariffs in response to an increasing foreign exchange position and a growing trade surplus.

May 23, Hsu Shui-teh and Su Nan-cheng are appointed mayors of Taipei and Kaohsiung, respectively.

In July, the Ministry of Defense announces that Taiwan has successfully tested a homemade surface-to-air missile named Sky Bow.

1986   April 1, a new value-added tax is inaugurated.

In September, the Democratic Progressive Party (DPP), made up of opposition politicians, announces its formation.

November 6, the DPP holds its first assembly and releases a draft of its charter and platform.

In December, the nation holds its first two-party election, with the Kuomintang competing against the DPP. The KMT wins.

1987   June 23, the Legislative Yuan passes the National Security Law that will replace martial law.

July 1, Lee Huan is appointed secretary-general of the Kuomintang.

July 15, the Emergency Decree, generally called martial law, is terminated. The National Security Law goes into effect.

In September, the N.T. dollar appreciates to 30 to one against the U.S. dollar.

In October, Minister of Interior Wu Poh-hsiung announces that residents of Taiwan may apply for permits to travel to China.

In October, the Legislative Yuan passes a law on assembly and parades.

November 1, Central Bank announces that Taiwan has U.S. $70 billion in foreign exchange reserves—the largest in the world.

1988   In January, new regulations go into effect allowing new newspapers to publish and all papers to increase the number of pages printed.

January 13, President Chiang Ching-kuo dies. Vice President Lee Teng-hui is sworn in as president—Taiwan's first native-born president.

January 27, President Lee Teng-hui is elected chairman of the Kuomintang.

March 9, Legislative Yuan passes bill abolishing system whereby deceased members of the National Assembly are replaced by runners-up in an election held in China more than four decades earlier.

March 9, the Council for Economic Planning and Development approves N.T. $30 billion fund for assisting developing countries.

In April, mail from Taiwan begins going to China.

July 7, the Kuomintang opens its 13th Party Congress. The ruling party democratizes many of its rules and procedures and elects a majority of Taiwanese to its powerful Central Standing Committee.

December 10, a prototype of Taiwan's first homemade jet fighter plane, called the Ching-kuo, is displayed in public.

1989   January 20, the Legislative Yuan passes the Law on the Organization of Civic Groups, which allows new political parties and organizations to form.

January 29, the Legislative Yuan passes a new election law and the law on the voluntary retirement of senior parliamentarians.

May 20, Taipei proclaims its support for the Democracy Movement in China.

May 30, Lee Huan is appointed premier.

June 4, President Lee Teng-hui issues a statement condemning the Tiananmen Massacre.

December 2, the Democratic Progressive Party wins what is called a major upset victory in the national election, gaining a sufficient number of seats in the Legislative Yuan to propose legislation and to control district and city executive offices where 40 percent of the population of the country reside. Sixteen other parties participate, but none makes a good showing. The Nationalist Party, while winning the most votes and seats, calls the results a setback because it did much more poorly than in other recent elections.

1990   March 21, President Lee Teng-hui is reelected president for a six-year term by the National Assembly in an uncontested vote—though Lin Yang-kang, a popular Taiwanese politician, and Chiang Wei-kuo, Chiang Kai-shek's second son, had challenged Lee. Shortly thereafter, Lee meets with 4,000 pro-democracy students who had occupied Chiang Kai-shek Memorial for six days and pledges democratic reform. President Lee promises, among other things, a National Affairs Conference in June to discuss issues such as the composition of elected bodies of government.

In May, President Lee, in his inauguration address (to his second term as president), announces opening channels of communication to China. President Lee appoints General Hau Pei-tsun as premier, causing opposition protest. President Lee also announces political amnesty for political prisoners.

July 4, National Affairs Conference ends after suggesting popular election of president and mayors of Taipei and Kaohsiung, and other reforms. Delegates to the Conference include members of the ruling party, the opposition Democratic Progressive Party, and academics.

August 26, baseball team from Taiwan wins Little League World Series again.

1991   In January, the Executive Yuan approves a Six-Year Development Plan aimed at improving the nation's economic infrastructure. Plan will cost over U.S.$300 billion. Premier Hau says the plan will elevate Taiwan to the top 20 nations in the world in per capita income by the end of the century.

In May, the government terminates the "Period of National Mobilization for the Suppression of the Communist Rebellion," formally ending the state of war with the People's Republic of China.

In May, government authorities in China announce that Taiwan has replaced Japan and the United States to become the number-one investor there.

In December, an election is held to pick a new National Assembly. This is the first national election that is not a supplementary election. The KMT wins and, according to some observers, gains a democratic mandate.

1992   February 28, official report of the "2-28 Incident," which occurred 45 years earlier when Nationalist soldiers killed a large number of Taiwanese, is released. The report, issued by the "2-28 Incident" Research Task Force formed by President Lee Teng-hui in December 1990, cites as causes for the incident Governor Chen Yi (or Chen I), lack of military discipline, resentment of military rule, over-expectations of the people in the Nationalist government, an imbalance in political participation in favor of mainland Chinese, an unstable economy, inflation, and poor living conditions. The report, which calls the incident tragic and one "that could have been avoided," also blames Chiang Kai-shek for failing to punish responsible officials—the first time he is criticized by any official body.

March 20, the new or Second National Assembly convenes to take up the task of amending the Constitution. Changes are made to give National Assembly members a four-year term, instead of a six-year term, and increase its powers. The Control Yuan, as of February 1, 1993, is slated to become a semi-judiciary body rather than one of the nations—three parliamentary bodies. Amendments also make the provincial governor and county magistrate positions ones to be filled by direct popular vote. Voters will also elect the president and vice-president, although a decision whether this will be by direct popular vote or not is postponed to May 1995.

May 16, Taiwan's sedition law (Article 100 of Criminal Code) is revised, making it no longer a crime to discuss Taiwan's independence or Communism.

July 7, Interior Minister Wu Poh-hsiung announces that Black List would be reduced from 282 to five names following Legislative Yuan revision of the National Security Law that redefines violations of the Constitution to exclude political activities except those advocating Taiwan independence or Communism.

July 16, Legislative Yuan passes statute decreeing that China is "one country, two areas" in regard to relations between Taipei and Peking, thereby recognizing laws in effect on the mainland and allowing Chinese Communist Party members to enter Taiwan without fear of prosecution as enemies of the state.

July 31, Taiwan Garrison Command is abolished. Coastal Patrol Command is created to assume role of control of coastline and smuggling.

August 22, South Korea breaks diplomatic relations with Taipei and establishes ties with China—the last important Asian country to do so.

September 2, U.S. president George Bush approves the sale of 150 F-16 fighter aircraft to Taiwan.

September 29, Taiwan is granted observer status in the General Agreement on Tariffs and Trade as the "Separate Customs Territory of Taiwan, Penghu, Kinmen and Matsu."

October 24, the Mainland Affairs Council approves 158 categories of service industries that can invest in China.

November 1, Peng Ming-min, known as the father of Taiwan independence, returns to Taiwan after 22 years in exile in the United States.

November 7, the military administration of Kinmen and Matsu ends after 44 years.

November 23, Formosa Plastics announces scrapping its plan to build a giant petrochemical complex in China.

November 30, U.S. trade representative Carla Hills visits Taiwan, the first such high official to do so in 13 years.

December 19, Taiwan holds its first nonsupplementary Legislative Yuan election. The opposition Democratic Progressive Party wins 50 seats, increasing its representation from 14.4 percent to 31.1 percent in what is considered a stunning victory. The KMT, while winning a large majority of 96 seats, sees its percent of seats drop from 74 to 63 percent. The KMT's "defeat" results, in part, from factionalism and disunity in the ruling party. The voter turnout is over 72 percent.

1993   January 4, President Lee Teng-hui gives the first ever state-of-the-nation address to the National Assembly. His speech is followed by shouting and fighting over the issue of Taiwan independence.

January 10, thousands march in Taipei in support of Premier Hau Pei-tsun, who is expected to leave office soon.

February 4, Premier Hau and cabinet resign ending weeks of political uncertainty while setting a precedent for cabinet dissolution following a legislative election.

February 27, Lien Chan is sworn in as premier, the first Taiwanese to hold that office.

April 9, President Lee announces that Taiwan will actively seek participation in the United Nations while calling for international support for this effort.

April 27, two days of talks between representatives of China and Taiwan begin in Singapore. The Koo-Wang talks are considered a historical breakthrough.

May 28, the Legislative Yuan passes Taiwan's largest budget cut ever, reducing spending by U.S.$1.6 billion.

June 16, the Legislative Yuan passes a—sunshine law—requiring 2,000 high government and public officials to make their financial records public.

August 6, the ROC signs an agreement with the Philippines and offers U.S.$60 million to develop Subic Bay into an industrial zone.

August 10, the New KMT Alliance breaks with the ruling party and establishes the New Party.

August 16, the 14th Congress of the KMT reelects President Lee Teng-hui chairman and Vice President Li Yuan-zu, former Premier Hau Pei-tsun, Judicial Yuan President Lin Yang-kang, and Premier Lien Chan vice chairmen.

September 16, the Mainland Affairs Council issues the publication *There Is No Taiwan Question: There Is Only a China Question* in response to Beijing's white paper *The Taiwan Question and the Reunification of China.*

November 28, Shih Ming-the replaces Hsu Hsin-liang as chairman of the Democratic Progressive Party.

1994   February 17, the first squadron of the locally made Indigenous Defense Fighters go into service.

April 12, all cultural and educational exchanges with China are temporarily terminated because of the Qiandao Lake incident during which 24 tourists from Taiwan were murdered and robbed.

September 7, the U.S. government announces that the ROC representative office in the United States can change its name to Taipei Economic and Cultural Representative Office, which is seen as an upgrading of Taipei's diplomatic status.

September 22, the UN General Assembly drops a proposal on the ROC's membership in the United Nations which seven nations supported.

December 3, the first popular election for governor of Taiwan province is held and James C.Y. Soong is elected. Elections for metropolitan city mayors are also held, after a hiatus of several years, and Chen Shui-bian is elected mayor of Taipei and Wu Den-yi mayor of Kaohsiung.

1995   China's President Jiang Zemin offers an Eight-Point Proposal urging Taiwan to hold talks that might lead to reunification.

February 28, President Lee Teng-hui issues an apology to victims of the February 28, 1947 Uprising at the Taipei New Park, where a monument memorializing the tragedy was built.

March 1, the National Health Insurance program is formally put in place.

June 7, President Lee Teng-hui arrives in the United States where he gives an address at his alma mater, Cornell University. The visit is widely reported, and Lee wins considerable favorable publicity. Beijing, however, is angered by the visit.

June 21, China begins the firing of surface-to-surface missiles at targets in the East China Sea 140 kilometers north of Taiwan in response to President Lee's trip to the United States.

July 19, the Legislative Yuan passes the Presidential and Vice Presidential Election and Recall Law, setting the stage for the first direct election of the president and vice president in March 1996.

August 17, Control Yuan President Chen Li-an announces he is a candidate for president.

August 21, Lin Yang-kang, vice chairman of the Nationalist Party, announces he will be an independent candidate for the presidency.

August 31, President Lee Teng-hui announces he will run for another term as president.

August 25, the DPP chooses Peng Ming-min as its candidate for the presidency.

August 27, Jeffrey Ku, chairman of the Chinese National Association of Industry and Commerce, leads a delegation to the Pacific Economic Cooperation Council meeting in Peking.

December 2, 164 delegates are elected to the Legislative Yuan. The KMT suffers a defeat in the polls but hangs on to a majority. The Democratic Progressive Party makes gains, but a number of its well-known candidates lose. The New Party makes big gains. Observers say the election was influenced by Peking's missile tests.

1996   March 8, China begins eight days of missile tests in the Taiwan Strait.

March 23, Lee Teng-hui and Lien Chan, respectively, are elected president and vice president with 54 percent of the vote in the Republic of China's first ever direct presidential election. The election is also dubbed the first direct election of a chief executive in 5,000 years of Chinese history. Elections are also held for the 334-member National Assembly, with the KMT losing seats and the Democratic Progressive Party and the New Party making gains.

May 20, Lee Teng-hui and Lien Chan are sworn in as president and vice president, respectively. In his inaugural address President Lee offers to make a "journey of peace" to China.

June 5, President Lee reappoints Lien Chan to serve as premier. A number of Legislative Yuan members oppose the nomination because of Lee's earlier promise to appoint a new premier.

June 15, the Democratic Progressive Party convenes its seventh national congress and elects a former chairman, Hsu Hsin-liang, its new chairman.

July 4, the National Assembly convenes and elects Fredrick Chien speaker.

July 18, the European Parliament passes a resolution backing the Republic of China's efforts to be represented in international organizations.

August 16, Formosa Plastics Group cancels project to build a U.S.$3 billion thermal power plant in China.

August 23, the U.S. Department of Defense notifies Congress that it will sell U.S.$420 million worth of ground-to-air missiles to Taiwan.

August 24, the Republic of China wins the 1996 Little League World Series in Williamsport, Pennsylvania.

September 12, the Republic of China announces its policy via-à-vis the Tiaoyutai (Senkaku in Japanese) islands that are in dispute between Japan, China, and Taiwan: absolute sovereignty, rational attitude, no need for cooperation with Beijing, and protection of fishing rights.

September 18, United Nations rejects 16-nation petition requesting discussion of Republic of China's lack of representation in the world organization.

September 24, the U.S. House of Representatives endorses European Parliament's resolution supporting the Republic of China's efforts to participate in international organizations.

October 6, the Taiwan Independence Party is formed.

November 21, Taoyuan County Magistrate Liu Pang-you and seven other politicians are shot to death at Liu's home in what is reported as a gang political assassination.

November 27, South Africa announces it will sever diplomatic relations with Taipei, marking the last important nation in the world with formal diplomatic ties with the Republic of China.

December 10, the Cabinet-level Aboriginal Affairs Commission is established.

December 15, Victor Trifonov, Russia's first envoy to the Republic of China, arrives in Taipei to set up a representative office.

December 23, National Development Conference opens.

December 31, Taiwan governor James Soong resigns after National Development Conference recommends downsizing or abolishing the provincial government.

1997   February 28 is declared a national holiday in memory of the February 28, 1947, Uprising when thousands were killed by the military following violent opposition to or a revolt against the Nationalist Chinese government.

March 2, the ship Liana Feng, owned by the People's Republic of China but registered in Panama, arrives in Kaohsiung, making it the first PRC ship to call at a port in Taiwan in more than five decades.

March 18, the Legislative Yuan passes the Statute Governing Relations with Hong Kong and Macao, defining them as "intermediate areas" before Taiwan and China unify.

March 28, the Tamsui line of the Taipei Rapid Transit System opens after ten years of construction at a cost of U.S.$2 billion.

April 2, China permits five companies to operate cross-strait shipping services.

April 14, Pai Hsiao-yen, the daughter of a famous television star, is kidnapped and U.S.$5 million is demanded in ransom; the first two of the 150 F-16 fighter planes purchased from the United States in 1992 arrive.

April 19, the container ship *Sheng Da* from China docks in Kaohsiung. The voyage marks the opening of cross-strait transshipment services.

May 4, a massive demonstration called "March for Taiwan" is held to protest the deterioration in social order following the murder of kidnapped Pai Hsiao-yen. Demonstrators ask Premier Lien Chan to take responsibility and resign from office. It is said to be the largest demonstration in Taiwan's history.

May 5, National Assembly begins discussions on new constitutional amendments, including one to eliminate or drastically downsize the provincial government.

May 6, the Republic of China lodges a protest with Japan over the Tiaoyutai (Senkaku in Japanese) Islands, that are claimed by China, Japan, and Taiwan.

May 8, Minister of State Ma Ying-jeou resigns in protest over weak Nationalist Party efforts to deal with corruption; Minister of Interior Lin Feng-cheng also quits.

May 11, the Hong Kong-based East Asia Bank opens a branch in Taipei, the first bank to use capital from China to run operations in Taiwan.

May 17, President Lee Teng-hui apologizes publicly for the upsurge in violence in Taiwan and promises action.

June 10, the Republic of China reiterates its claim to sovereignty over the Macclesfield Bank Island, Paracel Islands, Spratly Islands, and Pratas Islands in the South China Sea.

June 11, Taiwan's first private over-the-air television station, Formosa Television Corporation, begins operations in Kaohsiung.

July 1, the Mainland Affairs Council sets up a Hong Kong Affairs Bureau to handle Taiwan-Hong Kong relations on the date Hong Kong returns to the People's Republic of China.

July 3, the government calls a press conference to reiterate its refusal to accept China's "one country, two systems" formula for the reunification of Taiwan. Straits Exchange Foundation Chairman Koo Chen-fu meets with Hong Kong Chief Executive Tung Chee-hwa regarding Taiwan-Hong Kong ties.

July 16, nine nations propose that the United Nations rescind Resolution 2758, which forced Taipei out of the world organization in 1971.

August 1, the Council of Grand Justices rules that legislators who engage in violence during legislative sessions will no longer be immune from arrest and prosecution.

August 11, Ministry of Economic Affairs sells a large number of shares of China Steel Corporation in a four-day auction.

August 25, Nationalist Party holds its 15th Congress and reelects President Lee Teng-hui party chairman with more than 93 percent of the vote.

September 1, a new cabinet is sworn in with Vincent Siew the new premier.

September 30, the Committee on International Relations of the U.S. House of Representatives passes a resolution to include Taiwan in a theater missile defense system.

November 29, in elections for 23 city mayor and county magistrates, the Democratic Progressive Party wins 12 posts in a resounding victory. This puts Taiwan's main opposition party in control of the executive offices of local governments having jurisdiction over more than 70 percent of the population.

December 1, the first squadron of French-built Mirage 2000-5 jet fighters is commissioned.

December 31, the Republic of China and South Africa sever diplomatic relations because the latter wants to establish ties with Beijing.

1998   January 2, the Legislative Yuan approves a statute defining the Republic of China's territorial waters as 12 nautical miles from its shore.

January 10, five-day workweek policy begins and workers take Saturdays off.

January 10, on the eve of the 10th anniversary of President Chiang Ching-kuo's death, a poll indicates he is the most admired of the Republic of China's presidents.

January 22, Chen Chin-hsing is given five death sentences, two life terms, and 59.5 years in prison for the kidnapping and murder of Pai Hsiao-yen, daughter of television celebrity Pai Ping-ping, and a number of other crimes. Chen was Taiwan's most famous criminal in recent times.

January 24, 890 county and city councilors and 319 small-city mayors and township chiefs are elected. More than 70 percent of the elected municipality and township mayors and 55 percent of the council members represent the Nationalist Party. The opposition Democratic Progressive Party receives less than 15 percent of the seats contested. The New Party also does poorly.

January 29, the Central African Republic switches diplomatic relations to Beijing.

1998   February 21, Bishop Paul Shan of Taiwan is formally appointed a cardinal by Pope John Paul II.

March 17, the Central Bank of China announces that the faces of Sun Yat-sen and Chiang Kai-shek will no longer appear on Taiwan's currency. They will be replaced by historical figures, including Koxinga, who drove the Dutch from Taiwan in the 17th century; Liu Ming-chuan, the first governor of Taiwan Province; and Chiang Ching-kuo, who launched the nation's democratization.

March 18, the German-based Bayer AG drops a large plan to build a chemical plant in Taiwan as a result of public protest and other problems.

March 27, the Council of Grand Justices rules that the requirement that the nation's colleges and universities provide compulsory military studies is unconstitutional.

April 8, the nation's top energy official states that the government will work to complete Taiwan's fourth nuclear power plant but will build no more.

April 8, Foreign Minister Jason Hu announces Taiwan is tripling its foreign aid budget to shore up the support of its allies in the face of pressure from Beijing.

April 24, Guinea Bisseau switches diplomatic relations to Beijing.

April 30, the American Institute in Taiwan announces that there will be no "fourth communiqué" signed between Washington and Beijing that might impact Taiwan. (It had been rumored that another communiqué would be signed during President Bill Clinton's trip to the People's Republic of China in June.)

1998

May 1, more than 20,000 workers of state-run and private enterprises march in Taipei in protest of government labor practices in the largest labor rally in the country's history.

May 10, Taiwan's Air Force tests a French-made Mica missile, considered the best air-to-air missile in the world. It is the first such test outside of France.

May 21, Legislative Yuan passes a law compensating victims of "White Terror", or government oppression before martial law was terminated in 1987.

May 28, Legislative Yuan passes a bill giving compensation to victims of martial law. The maximum amount allowed is U.S.$180,000.

June 13, the Nationalist Party wins 45 percent of seats contested in nationwide election for township council members and wardens in villages and boroughs.

June 16, the Republic of China military announces a plan to cut personnel by 15 percent before June 2001.

June 30, U.S. president Bill Clinton, during a visit to China, states: "We don't support independence for Taiwan, or two Chinas, or one Taiwan, one China, and we don't believe that Taiwan should be a member in any organization for which statehood is a requirement."

July 1, Public Television Services begins broadcasting.

July 15, Minister of Science and Technology Zhu Lilan visits Taiwan, marking the first time a government minister of the People's Republic of China has visited the island.

July 23, Taiwan High Speed Rail Consortium signs a contract with the Ministry of Transportation to build an NT$430 billion 435-kilometer rail system that will be completed in 2003. The project will reportedly create 486,000 jobs.

1998

July 30, Foreign Minister Jason Hu condemns violence against Chinese in Indonesia, especially the numerous rapes of Chinese women.

July 31, Kaohsiung City Council member Lin Ti-chuan who was earlier kidnapped in China, is proclaimed dead. Incident sours Taipei-Beijing relations.

August 2, Lin Yi-hsiung is sworn in as the eighth chairman of the Democratic Progressive Party. Leftist group in the party lodges protests against outgoing party head, Hsu Hsin-liang, for advocating engagement with China.

August 4, the Ministry of Defense declares that the Republic of China will not research, develop, or produce chemical, biological, or nuclear weapons.

August 25, Taiwan's first commercial satellite is successfully launched into orbit from French Guiana by the European firm Arianespace.

August 29, the government announces the allocation of NT$110 billion to help first-time buyers of houses.

September 2, an armored car driver gets NT$49 million in the country's largest robbery.

September 4, the TAIEX (Taiwan's Stock Exchange) falls to a 10-year low as a result of the Asian economic crisis and a slump on Wall Street.

September 18, a group of pro-independence politicians form the New Nation Alliance.

1998 October 9, the Legislative Yuan passes a statute for streamlining the Taiwan Provincial Government.

October 14, Koo Chen-fu, chairman of the Straits Exchange Foundation, begins a five-day trip to the People's Republic of China, renewing the Koo-Wang talks of 1993, which were discontinued after President Lee Teng-hui's trip to the United States in 1995. Koo's counterpart, Wang Daohan, chairman of the Association for Relations Across the Taiwan Strait, agrees to visit Taipei in the future. Several agreements are signed.

October 17, President Lee Teng-hui, setting a precedent, suggests to a Japanese news reporter that he use the term "ROC Taiwan," saying, "The ROC is Taiwan."

October 18, Koo Chen-fu, meets with President Jiang Zemin of the People's Republic of China—marking the highest-level contact across the Taiwan Strait in nearly five decades.

October 22, the Grand Council of Justices rules that the Taiwan Provincial Government is a local government but has lost its local autonomy status.

November 2, Tonga breaks relations with the Republic of China to establish ties with Beijing.

November 20, the Republic of China and the Marshall Islands establish diplomatic relations.

November 26, the Air Force puts a wing of 60 French-made Mirage 2000-5 into duty.

December 5, President Lee Teng-hui uses the term "New Taiwanese" in an effort to play down ethnic differences in the context of an election campaign.

1998   December 5, elections for seats in the Legislative Yuan, the city councils of Taipei and Kaohsiung, and the mayorships of these two metropolitan cities are held. The ruling Nationalist Party is the victor, winning a healthy majority in the Legislative Yuan and taking back the mayorship of Taipei, though it loses the Kaohsiung mayorship race.

December 20, elections for the Taiwan Provincial Assembly and the governor are postponed indefinitely. James Soong's term as governor, the first elected governor, ends. This marks the significant downsizing of Taiwan's Provincial Government.

December 21, Chao Shou-pu, former minister without portfolio, is appointed Taiwan's new governor. A twenty-plus member advisory council replaces the Taiwan Provincial Assembly.

INTRODUCTION

Taiwan (meaning "terraced bay" in Chinese) refers to the island approximately 250 miles in length, and 95 miles (at the closest point) off the east coast of southern China. It is the largest piece of territory under the jurisdiction of the Republic of China, or, in the past, often called Nationalist China. Other areas under the Republic of China's control include several islands or island groups near Taiwan, such as the Pescadores (West of Taiwan); Orchid Island and Green Island (to the East); the "Offshore Islands," or the Quemoy and Matsu groups, which are just yards off the coast of China's Fukien Province; plus some islands or islets in the South China Sea.

The word "Taiwan" (actually two characters in Chinese), the origin of which is unclear (possibly a city in the southern part of the island), in recent years has been used increasingly to refer to all of the territory controlled by or under the political jurisdiction of the Republic of China. It is a word used by some to suggest that the territory controlled by the Republic of China is not really part of China (except perhaps the Offshore Islands) but rather is another China, or that the separation between China and Taiwan is, or should be, viewed as a permanent reality, and that Taiwan is a separate and sovereign nation-state. Some of those, especially radical opposition groups in Taiwan, who use the term to suggest separation, say that the Republic of China is not a legitimate government and that the name "Republic of China" should be changed to "Republic of Taiwan." Many people now use the term "Taiwan" rather than 'Republic of China" simply because it is shorter and easier to remember, or they use the two terms interchangeably. The government of the Republic of China often uses the term "Republic of China on Taiwan. "Taiwan" is also synonymous with the Western term "Formosa," which means "beautiful" in Portuguese—the Portuguese being the first Westerners to see Taiwan and who gave the island this name, based on their first impression.

For many years, the government of Taiwan or the Republic of China claimed jurisdiction over not only the territory it ruled, but all of China, as well as some territory that the government of the People's Republic of China did not control, such as Outer Mongolia. But most did not take these claims seriously. The government of the People's Republic of China claims Taiwan as a province of China, as well as all other territory under the jurisdiction of the Republic of China. Many say this claim is a myth. On the other hand, Taipei, representing one of the divided nations of the world, may someday reconcile differences with Beijing, at which time

China will be unified to include Taiwan. Government officials in Taipei and the ruling Nationalist Party (though some opposition parties do not agree) adhere to a one-China policy meaning that unification will happen. Certain trends, such as trade; investment; and people traveling between the two Chinas, between Taiwan and China, or between the Republic of China and the People's Republic of China, suggest that a peaceful resolution in the form of a "Greater China" federation or something similar may occur in the future. Political trends, meaning rapid democratization in the Republic of China and not in the People's Republic, suggest otherwise. Alternatively the People's Republic of China may decide to try to resolve the matter by force, though it is uncertain what the result of such an action might be, particularly given U. S. policy (Washington holds the key to whether an invasion would succeed or not).

Geography

Taiwan is surrounded by more than a dozen islands or island groups that are considered geologically part of Taiwan, though the Pescadores to the west of the southern part of Taiwan are the only group of significant size. The Quemoy and Matsu groups, just off the coast of the mainland, are not considered geologically part of Taiwan. The same is true of the islands controlled by Taipei in the South China Sea.

Taiwan lies between the Ryukyu Islands, which are part of Japan, to the north, and the Philippines, to the south. To the east of Taiwan is the Pacific Ocean; to the west is the Taiwan (or Formosa) Strait; to the northwest lies the East China Sea, and to the southwest, the South China Sea. The Bashi Channel separates Taiwan from the Philippines.

Some geologists say that Taiwan was once part of the mainland. Others dispute this view because of its volcanic soil (not found in China) and say that it is geologically part of a long chain of islands separate from the Asian continent that extends from Alaska through Japan and south of Taiwan to the Philippines and on further south. These geologists contend there was no mainland connection, or that such is very far removed in time. It may be that volcanic activity caused Taiwan to separate from China at some time in the distant past and that therefore, both of these views are true.

Taiwan is very mountainous. Mountains, in fact, cover more than two-thirds of the island. Yu Shan (Jade Mountain) is the highest peak, reaching more than 13,000 feet above sea level. It is part of a central range of mountains stretching from north to south, closer to the island's eastern coast than its western coast. For this reason there are few good harbors on the eastern side of Taiwan. The western part of the island is the location of a plain that is home to most of the population and most of its tilled land. Taiwan's rivers originate in the mountains, are generally short, and are not navigable. The Tamsui River, which flows past Taipei and to the Taiwan Strait, is an exception.

Rainfall is plentiful in Taiwan, averaging over 100 inches a year. The east coast receives more rain than the west, and the mountains receive more than the lowlands. October through March is the rainy season in the north; the south gets more precipitation from April to September. Winds are periodic and seasonal, not continental or strong. Taiwan experiences no cyclones or tornadoes, but witnesses very severe typhoons in the late summer and early fall. The typhoons that hit Taiwan are among the strongest in the world and do considerable damage, often causing severe flooding.

Taiwan is traversed by the Tropic of Cancer just below the middle of the island. The climate of Taiwan is therefore subtropical and, in the very southern part of the island, tropical. Proximity to the ocean also moderates the climate. On the other hand, temperatures throughout the island vary considerably with elevation. In fact, snow falls in the high mountains and occasionally at some lesser elevations to the north in the winter. Generally, however, temperatures are moderate or hot. The island's average temperature is 70 degrees Fahrenheit.

The soil in Taiwan is generally rich in the lowlands but leached and acidic at higher elevations. This, in addition to changes in elevation, accounts for the wide variety of trees and other flora on the island. Rice is the staple crop: two or three crops a year are harvested. Taiwan's farmers also produce a wide variety of vegetables and fruits, the latter having the reputation for being the tastiest in the world.

Taiwan has few natural resources. Early in its history, coal and some other minerals played some commercial role. Water power has also been important to the island's economy in the recent past. Good soil is vital to the agricultural sector of the economy; however, farming is of declining importance in Taiwan, and many say now that the nation's only resource of any consequence seems to be its human talent.

The People

The population of the Republic of China was 21.7 million in 1998. Nearly all of the nation's population resides on the island of Taiwan. The population of the Pescadores is around 150,000, Quemoy's is 50,000, and Matsu's about 8,000 (though there are an additional 200,000 to 300,000 military personnel stationed on Quemoy and Matsu). Considering its small geographic size, this makes the Republic of China the second-most-densely-populated nation in the world, after Bangladesh (excluding, of course, the city-states and ministates). There are nearly 1,500 people per square mile. Taking cognizance of the fact that most of the island of Taiwan is mountainous, the Republic of China has more people per unit of flat land than any small, mediumsized, or large nation in the world.

Although very crowded, Taiwan is not said to have a population problem because of the low rate of population growth in recent years and the nation's strong economy. The population replacement rate has been below one for about 15 years. Life expectancy for males is 71.9 and for females is 77.8. All of these figures represent dramatic changes from the recent past. In 1940, Taiwan's population was 5.8 million. An influx of people after the Nationalist Chinese regime was defeated by the Communists on the mainland and a rapid rate of increase for more than two decades after caused the population to grow rapidly. As a result, in 1964, the government established a birth control program. Subsequent years saw the population growth rate fall precipitously due to government policies and the very rapid urbanization that paralleled the nation's successful industrialization. In the 1980s, Taiwan's birthrate fell to below the world's average. The Republic of China's population is projected to peak at around 26 million about the year 2020 and decline after that.

Taiwan's population can be divided into four ethnic groups. The aborigines, or the island's earliest inhabitants, are considered to be mainly or exclusively of Malay or Polynesian origin, based on their languages and culture. Today they constitute less than 2 percent of the population. There are two groups of early Chinese immigrants or "Taiwanese." The Hakka came from south China, mainly from Kuang-tung (or Canton) Province near Hong Kong, though some came from Fukien Province. The second, the Fukienese or *min nan*, came from Fukien Province directly across the Taiwan Strait. Together they represent 85 percent of the population, with the latter outnumbering the former by two or three to one. The fourth group is made up of Chinese from various parts of China who moved to Taiwan after World War II, mostly in 1949 after the Nationalist Chinese defeat. They hail disproportionately from coastal and southern provinces of China but, in total, represent just under 15 percent of the population. They are referred to as Mainland Chinese, or "mainlanders."

The aborigines came to Taiwan in prehistoric times. Currently most live in the mountains, although originally two separate groups could be identified: mountain and lowland aborigines. There are a number of different aboriginal tribes, but there are only nine major ones. Although the aborigines speak languages or tribal dialects that resemble Malay rather than Chinese, they do not have a common language other than Chinese. Many still live by hunting and fishing, though most aborigines are now working in other occupations, especially those associated with tourism. They are poorer than the rest of the population, and their birthrate is lower.

It is uncertain when Chinese first took up residence in Taiwan. It may have been as early as the sixth century AD, but probably most Chinese on the island during those years were fishermen who stopped there to repair their boats or nets, merchants who traded with the aborigines, and pirates who used places on the island as hideouts. By AD 1000, there were a number of Chinese communities in western Taiwan. Most of the early Chinese immigrants engaged in fishing, farming, and trading. The Hakka, who probably came earlier, resided more in the southern part of the island. As the Fukien Taiwanese increased in number they pushed the Hakka out of a number of coastal areas. Today there are still Hakka-dominated areas in Taiwan, though this group of Chinese can also be found throughout the island. They speak the Hakka dialect of Chinese in addition to Taiwanese (a derivative of the Fukien dialect) and Mandarin Chinese. Hakkas are, in a number of ways, culturally distinct from other Chinese. Today, many Hakkas are in politics and many work in local police organizations and the railroads.

The Fukien Taiwanese also began to settle in Taiwan nearly a thousand years ago, but most migrated in the 14th through the 17th centuries. At that time they forced most of the Hakka population to move inland and took much of the island's best farmland. They also controlled the island politically when it was not governed by outside powers. The Fukien Chinese or Taiwanese are now dominant in agriculture, business, and local politics. Because of the years of separation from China, and as a result of greater contact with other peoples and countries and a 50-year period of Japanese colonial rule before World War II, their culture is also unique.

The Mainland Chinese are regarded as latecomers. When they came, most were government or ruling party officials and soldiers. In the early years after 1949, they monopolized government employment and jobs in education and lived primarily in the large cities, especially Taipei. Assimilation and other factors, however, have changed their status in recent years. Since they hailed from all parts of China they speak various dialects, in addition to Mandarin Chinese. Today, however, many also speak Taiwanese.

There have been "ethnic" (perhaps better called regional or provincial in the case of the three groups of Chinese) frictions between and among the four groups residing in Taiwan. The aborigines battled both groups of early-arrival Chinese when they migrated to the island and for a long time thereafter. The Hakka and Fukien Chinese have also fought and have long harbored hostilities toward each other. Both of these groups also have had illfeelings toward the Mainland Chinese. Ethnic identification and hatred, however, have waned in recent years with urbanization, prosperity, and a common outside threat from China.

In terms of religions or religious beliefs, the population of Taiwan is quite eclectic, and most people report adhering to more than one religion. The aborigines practice nature worship and various sacrifices. Most Chinese—65 percent according to a recent poll—adhere to some Chinese folk religion. But Chinese immigrants also brought Confucianism, Taoism, and Buddhism to Taiwan, and most of the population report being followers of one or all of these "religions." (Confucianism is seen by many as more an ethical system or guidelines for personal interaction rather than a religion, and Taoism is said to be a philosophy.) The Dutch introduced Protestant Christianity to Taiwan, while the Spanish brought Catholicism and the Japanese brought Shinto to the island.

Buddhism has seen an increase in followers in Taiwan in recent years, with 15 percent of the population reporting to be converts. In all, there are one million "pure" Buddhists. Taoism, being the "first" Chinese religion, has merged with the local folk religions. Though there are many Confucian temples, its main influence is in education and politics. After making gains in the 1950s and 1960s, the number of Christians has remained about the same in recent years: Protestants count their numbers at just over 420,000; Catholics number over 300,000. Among Protestants, the Methodist Church has had an advantage because Chiang Kai-shek was Methodist. The Methodist Church attracts many Mainland Chinese. The Presbyterian Church, which was active in Taiwan earlier and which is more politically involved, has, in contrast, attracted Taiwanese.

Early History

Recent studies reveal that there was human life on Taiwan at least ten thousand years ago. Whether or not these very early inhabitants were ancestors of the present aborigines is uncertain; they probably were. It has been assumed that all or most of the aborigines came to Taiwan from what is now Southeast Asia or a southern part of China which was not at that time culturally Chinese. Some recent studies suggest some may have migrated from the north—north China or possibly even Japan. The aboriginal languages are classified as Malay, as two-thirds of the words are similar to those of Malay. This is so even though there were no known cultural links of any importance in historical times.

Very little is known of Taiwan's early history because the aborigines did not develop a written language. However, anthropologists say the human population was quite evenly distributed throughout the island and that the early residents on the island lived by hunting, fishing, and shifting agriculture. Their political and social systems were tribal in structure, with land held in common. Lineage and customs varied among tribes.

There is mention of Taiwan in early Chinese historical records. However, very early Chinese records do not give a precise location, and the names used for the island are inconsistent. Moreover, Taiwan was identified as an area beyond the pale of Chinese civilization. Clearly the island was not linked in any important sense to China's early historical or cultural development.

In the third century AD, the Chinese government sent a 10,000-man expeditionary force to Taiwan, apparently to explore the island. But no followup missions were sent. If the purpose of the mission was to make Taiwan Chinese territory, the idea was soon forgotten. Taiwan was seldom mentioned in Chinese historical documents, which were mainly court records, for the next twelve hundred years—though there were some other official visits to the island. Later, Chinese visited the island: fishermen as a stop-off place, merchants to trade, and pirates to avoid notice. However, a thousand years ago Chinese began to migrate to Taiwan from areas on the mainland across the Taiwan Strait. China learned about Taiwan from Chinese who visited the island and from relatives of migrants, but information concerning the island and its people was kept mostly in local record books or in family histories. Few Chinese who migrated to Taiwan returned to China, since, much of the time, it was unlawful for them to leave the motherland, the punishment for doing so being death, and they usually migrated for economic reasons. Also, not many of those who returned had much contact with the government in Peking.

In the 15th century, the famous eunuch and navigator engaged by the Ming Court Cheng Ho reported to the emperor that he had "discovered" Taiwan. Since the island is visible from the mainland this was not literally true, though it is the first mention of the word "Taiwan" in Chinese history. The prohibition on migration to Taiwan remained; thus the event did not lead to colonization or a legal claim. In any case, reports about Taiwan were not complimentary, explaining in part at least why the Chinese court at this time was not interested in the island.

When the Mongols ruled China (from 1280 to 1368), a military mission brought the Pescadores under control; however, no effort was made to extend this control to Taiwan. The coastal areas of Taiwan at this time were occupied mainly by Hakka in the south and Japanese pirates in the north. The aborigines controlled the interior of the island and constituted the majority of the population.

In the 13th and 14th centuries, Chinese from various parts of China (but chiefly the Amoy area of Fukien Province) began to migrate to Taiwan in larger numbers. At this time the Fukienese became dominant among the local Chinese population. Japanese pirates at this time held control over some of the northern part of the island; Chinese pirates occupied some ports in the south. When the first Westerners arrived, Chinese, numbering 25,000 at most, were the dominant population on only a small portion of the island.

The Period of Western Colonialism

In 1517, a Portuguese ship sailing through the Taiwan Strait on the way to Japan sighted Taiwan, and in the ship's log were recorded the words *Ilha Formosa*, meaning "beautiful island." The Portuguese, however, did not lay claim to Taiwan or try to colonize it. No other Westerners were attracted to the island. In 1593, Japan, under the rule of Toyotomi Hideyoshi, made a weak and illfated attempt to colonize Taiwan.

In 1622, Dutch forces captured the Pescadores. They used their base there to control ship traffic through the Taiwan Strait and to harass Portuguese vessels traveling to and from Japan. The Dutch tried to wrest Macao, on the China mainland, from the Portuguese, but failed. Subsequently, in 1624, Dutch representatives signed a treaty with China which gave Holland posts on Taiwan and other rights in exchange for Dutch forces withdrawing from the Pescadores. The Dutch subsequently established a settlement in southern Taiwan and built three forts, including Fort Zeelandia, the most famous, near the present-day city of Tainan.

In 1626, Spanish soldiers seized the port of Keelung in northern Taiwan and established control of an area down the west coast a short distance to Tamsui. Two years later, in 1628, when the Japanese government ordered the return of Japanese traders and pirates as part of Japan's new isolationist policy, Spanish control spread. Nevertheless, in 1642, Spanish forces fell to Dutch garrisons. The Dutch subsequently suppressed a Chinese rebellion with the help of the aborigines and established jurisdiction over the entire island, though their de facto control did not extend very far inland.

The Dutch East India Company forthwith gained exclusive rights to commercial ventures in Taiwan and ruled Taiwan as a colonial enterprise. The company's officials leased land and agricultural tools to the peasants and introduced oxen to till the rice fields. They also dug new wells, conducted land surveys, introduced cash crops such as sugar, and romanized the aboriginal languages. They built large forts or castles and introduced the residents of Taiwan to opium, which the Chinese population mixed with tobacco to smoke. During the period of Dutch control, the Chinese population was estimated at 30,000; the aborigine population was estimated to be several times larger. The Dutch population was a few thousand.

At this time, the Ming Dynasty in China was threatened by the Manchus, or Manchurians, to the north. Before the Ming finally collapsed in 1644, Emperor Sze Tsung appointed Cheng Chi-lung, a Fukienese merchant-pirate of Hakka origin operating from a base in Taiwan, to train and rebuild remnant Ming naval forces to protect the dynasty. Cheng, with a fleet of 3,000 vessels, won some battles but did not succeed in his given mission. The Manchus finally captured and executed him, but were not able to wipe out his forces, and his son Cheng Ch'eng-kung, also known by the name Koxinga and whose mother was Japanese, inherited his father's fleet. The latter Cheng welcomed Chinese immigrants who fled Manchu rule and expanded his already strong navy and built a sizeable army. With 12,000 vessels and 120,000 soldiers, he battled the Manchus for more than a decade, trying to restore the Ming Dynasty. At one point he nearly captured the city of Nanking.

In 1661, after temporarily abandoning his efforts to overthrow Manchu rule in China, Cheng Ch'eng-kung decided to launch an attack on the Dutch strongholds in the southern part of Taiwan. From his bases in the north, Cheng sailed down the coast with 30,000 men to do battle with the 2,200 Dutch soldiers and 600 Dutch farmers. After a nine-month siege, the Dutch negotiated an agreement whereby they would evacuate, and in so doing abandoned Taiwan as a colony.

At nearly the same time that he defeated the Dutch, Cheng sent representatives to the Philippines to meet with the Chinese population there in hopes of rallying them to his cause of overthrowing the foreign Manchu Dynasty in China. Fearing a rebellion, Spanish officials in the Philippines ordered the suppression of Chinese political activities, killing 10,000 Chinese in the process. The Spanish then sent a message to Cheng that they had killed all Chinese residing in the Philippines. Cheng hoped for revenge, but he died two years later before retaliating against the Spanish. Cheng's demise occurred at the young age of 38; yet he had a major impact on Taiwan's history and is regarded as a national hero.

Upon Cheng's death, his son, Cheng Ching, from a power base in Fukien Province, vied with his uncle in Taiwan for the right of succession. Cheng Ching finally forced the armies of his uncle to surrender and became ruler of Taiwan's Chinese population. He subsequently led several more unsuccessful military expeditions against the Manchus, trying to fulfill his father's dream of restoring the Ming Dynasty. He died in Taiwan, like his father, at a young age.

Another, this time more destructive, struggle for succession, followed Cheng Ching's death. Cheng Ching left the throne to an illegitimate son, whom many of his subjects refused to recognize as their ruler. The Manchu government in China immediately took advantage of the situation. Peking sent a naval force to the Pescadores and destroyed the Cheng government's fleet there. In 1683, Manchu troops landed on Taiwan and without much resistance brought to a close just over two decades of Cheng family rule of Taiwan.

Taiwan under Chinese Rule

Before his premature death, Cheng Ch'eng-kung established a Ming-style government on Taiwan. He imported and nurtured Chinese culture, which he admired. He adopted the Chinese legal system and political system, recruiting the best available scholars and advisors. Cheng's court was located at Fort Zeelandia, which became a cultural and commercial center, with nearby Anping prospering as a port city. However, Cheng's political support came from Taiwan's rich land-owning families, while the social structure and economy differed from China's in important ways. In fact, Taiwan's political and social systems were feudal, similar to Japan's, unlike the bureaucratic imperial system in China.

Cheng encouraged Chinese across the Taiwan Strait to come to Taiwan, setting in motion immigration that soon brought a significant increase in the Chinese population in Taiwan. Cheng's purpose was to provide manpower for his army. Fearing that Cheng might land forces on the mainland, the Manchu government forced the evacuation of coastal areas, depriving many of their livelihood and thus forcing many more people to flee to Taiwan. Cheng Ch'eng-kung promoted foreign trade with Japan, the Philippines, Indochina, Siam, and the East Indies. Taiwan's ports became busy and its population quite cosmopolitan.

From 1683 to just before the beginning of the 20th century, Taiwan was ruled by Chinese officials sent from Peking—for the most part ineptly. Throughout most of this period, Taiwan was administratively a part of Fukien Province. It was finally granted provincial status in 1887, when Peking feared that it might be grabbed by a Western power that would use it as a base of operations for military actions against China.

While it suffered from incompetent and cruel Chinese rule during this period, agriculture did well in Taiwan—so well that parts of China became dependent on food from Taiwan. Food was shipped to Japan as well. In 1714, three Jesuits were commissioned by Peking to produce a map of Taiwan in order to plan infrastructure improvements. Also, some efforts were subsequently made to spur economic growth in Taiwan. But these were exceptions to Peking's usual policy of neglect. Officials sent to Taiwan were generally China's worst; many were sent as a form of punishment. Corruption was rampant. Harsh and inhumane punishments were meted out for even small crimes.

As a consequence of social and political unrest and opposition to official authority, Taiwan became known as a place of rebellion. In fact, in one revolt in the mid-1800s, 20,000 soldiers sent from China were killed. Peking responded with punitive vengeance, further alienating much of the population. In fact, most people on the island came to hate the government of China as a result of its oppressive rule and its use of military force to resolve problems.

Officials in Peking continued to refer to Taiwan as a "frontier area"—suggesting they did not regard it as part of China. Meanwhile, foreigners began to establish a presence in Taiwan to facilitate their trade interests. Western governments also frequently sought redress of their grievances from Peking for incidents, especially the killing of their subjects, in Taiwan. Consistently, the response was that China had no responsibility for Taiwan, thus repudiating in the minds of Westerners any claim to Taiwan. In counter-argument to the notion that Taiwan was not part of China at this time, culturally, Taiwan became more and more Chinese. Because China did not espouse the idea of nationhood as was then common in the West, but instead viewed itself as an advanced culture, this may have been more important than any official territorial claim. The Chinese government also experienced opposition to its rule elsewhere, which it dealt with in similar ways to its troubles on Taiwan.

In the 1800s, several Western powers expressed an interest in Taiwan. In fact, in the 1840s, the Chinese government spoke of suspected British plans to make Taiwan a colony. In 1854, Commodore Oliver Perry appealed to the U.S. government to establish a presence on Taiwan. Later Townsend Harris, the U.S. representative in Japan, recommended that the U.S. government try to purchase the island from China and use it as a coaling station. Washington, however, did not follow this advice.

Finally realizing the scope of the foreign threat to China, Peking sent more competent officials to rule Taiwan. Liu Ming-chuan was one. In

August 1884, he beat back a French attempt to seize the port of Keelung, which was to be a stepping stone to invade Taiwan. The next year he was appointed governor, and, upon his advice, Taiwan was made a fullfledged Chinese province. Under Liu's governorship, both economic and political conditions improved in Taiwan. But it was too late: Japan had already developed an interest in Taiwan and soon found an opportunity to acquire the island.

Under Japanese Rule

In 1894, China and Japan went to war. China lost, and in the Treaty of Shimonoseki, signed in 1895, Peking ceded Taiwan and the Pescadores to Japan. Some Japanese, especially those who envisioned a Japanese empire, had earlier shown an interest in Taiwan. This interest was encouraged by Peking's declarations of no responsibility either for the aborigine' treatment of shipwrecked sailors or for other problems on the island. In any case, the transfer was declared to be "in perpetuity" in the Treaty of Shimonoseki, and the Western powers subsequently treated Japan's colonial acquisition as a legal one.

The Chinese population of Taiwan was divided concerning the transfer of ownership to Japan. Some felt that Japanese control could not be worse than the corrupt and uncaring Chinese rule they had suffered under for more than two centuries. Many also felt that Japan might be able to deal with the problem of rival warlords. Opponents pushed for independence and managed to proclaim the Republic of Taiwan—Asia's first republic. But this turned out to be a shortlived affair. The fate of Taiwan was decided by Japanese military might, and, in the absence of any foreign power to oppose Tokyo's intentions, Japan's ownership of Taiwan became permanent.

There was scattered opposition on the island to Japanese rule for the next three years. Meanwhile, Peking, in a formal and public ceremony, turned over the reins of government to Japan, signaling to the population of Taiwan that China had no interest in Taiwan and would not help those on the island resisting Japanese rule.

Taiwan was Japan's first colonial undertaking, which meant that Tokyo had to formulate many policies with little experience in running a foreign territory. Japan's colonial policy in Taiwan may be described as highly progressive and beneficial on the one hand and as discriminatory and exploitative on the other. The Japanese first sought to establish law and order, which they did very well. The colonial government issued decrees which were, in effect, criminal laws, and they enforced these laws harshly—including using capital punishment with considerable frequency. Some felt the Japanese were cruel, but most were thankful that warlordism and crime were largely eradicated under Japanese rule, and social stability restored.

Stability laid the groundwork for economic development. The first priority for the Japanese colonial government was agriculture. Japan introduced new breeds of rice and better farming and harvesting techniques. As a result, by the 1920s, Taiwan had a higher consumption of meat, vegetables, and fruit than any place in China and higher than some parts of Japan. Surplus food was sent to Japan, especially rice and sugar.

When Japanese colonial rule began, Taiwan had 30 miles of railroads. By 1905, it had 10 times that, and work was in progress to more than double that amount. Roads and harbors were improved and new ones built. As a result, domestic and foreign commerce increased rapidly. In 1903, Taiwan was electrified, making it the first area outside Japan proper to take this step into modernity. Many diseases were eradicated, and others reduced in terms of the number of people affected, making Taiwan the most disease-free area in Asia outside Japan.

Japan also undertook progressive social reforms. Education was improved; as a result, the illiteracy rate was reduced markedly. Technical skills improved, and the public's knowledge of commerce and world events increased. Superstitions were in large part eliminated. Binding women's feet was banned. And differences between rich and poor diminished.

After World War I, Tokyo prohibited foreign enterprises on the island. Subsequently, Taiwan developed many new industries: textiles, cement and other building materials factories, a chemical industry, and more. In the 1930s, Taiwan even began to build heavy industries.

There was also a negative side to Japanese rule. Tokyo forced everyone to learn Japanese, meaning that Chinese (either Mandarin or the local dialects) was not taught in school; as a consequence, both the Chinese language and culture in Taiwan devolved. Tokyo encouraged the residents of Taiwan to study engineering, science, and medicine, but not history, law, or the social sciences. Tokyo ruled Taiwan efficiently, but not democratically. Japanese officials generally treated the local population well, but they did not consider residents of Taiwan as equal to Japanese, and they were generally condescending in their attitudes, which was reflected in their style of governance.

Japanese colonial officials found the aborigines difficult to control, though they successfully kept them from obtaining guns and stopped the practice of headhunting. The aborigines resisted Japanese rule, even into the 1940s, and maintained de facto control over much of Taiwan's mountainous areas, even to the end of World War II.

During World War II, Taiwan served as an "unsinkable aircraft carrier"—which Japan used for its expansion into Southeast Asia, including Japan's invasion of the Philippines. Taiwan's new industries helped Tokyo's war machine, and the island provided Japan with sizeable quantities of food. The Japanese army recruited soldiers in Taiwan, using some of them in units fighting in China. Some, in fact, participated in the atrocities committed against Chinese in Nanking and elsewhere.

Toward the end of the war, the United States contemplated invading Taiwan but gave up the plan when it found no good maps of Taiwan and, more important, calculated that the population would probably fight with the Japanese against U.S. forces. U.S. forces, therefore, skipped Taiwan and invaded Okinawa. Hence, with the exception of the bombing of oil storage areas and some factories, Taiwan suffered relatively little damage during the war.

In 1943, at the Cairo Conference, the United States (with the United Kingdom concurring) promised Chiang Kai-shek that Taiwan and other territories "stolen by Japan" would be returned after the war. This pledge was reiterated in the Potsdam Agreement in July 1945. Japan's loss of Taiwan was then made part of the terms of the surrender, and in the fall of 1945 the Japanese colonial government departed, along with a number of Japanese businessmen and some farmers. In all, they constituted one-eighteenth of the population. Their exit left a serious vacuum in Taiwan in the realms of political administration, business management, and more.

Taiwan's legal status was not discussed in the surrender agreement. One might assume that legal transfer was made to the Republic of China, though there were no formal documents to support this. In any case, Chiang Kai-shek forthwith sent military forces and government officials to Taiwan to replace the Japanese. The people of Taiwan generally welcomed both the end of Japanese colonial rule and the coming of Nationalist rule of Taiwan, though some discussed alternatives such as independence, a United Nations trusteeship over Taiwan, or a special relationship with the United States.

Under Chiang Kai-shek

On October 25, 1945, Nationalist Chinese officials assumed political governance over Taiwan, and it thence became part of the Republic of China. Though the population generally applauded this they soon became disappointed with Nationalist Chinese rule. Taiwan was not made a province as expected. Nor did the Nationalists give a high priority to establishing democratic government. Instead, Taiwan was placed under military rule. Chen Yi, a friend of Chiang Kai-shek's, was appointed governor and supreme commander and was granted the same kind of near-absolute power that the Japanese colonial rulers had exercised. Soldiers and administrative officials were sent to Taiwan from the mainland to fill the vacuum left by the departure of the Japanese. They could not speak the dialects of Chinese spoken in Taiwan, and many despised the Taiwanese, perceiving they had been "Japanized" and were traitors for serving in the Japanese military that the Chinese on the mainland so intensely hated. Moreover, the Nationalist government was preoccupied with a civil war on the mainland with the Communists and felt that the people of Taiwan should understand this and should be willing to sacrifice by lowering their expectations for economic improvement and democracy in Taiwan.

Taiwanese saw the economy deteriorate due to what they said was gross mismanagement. With economic deterioration, health standards declined, causing epidemics of cholera and bubonic plague. Rumors spread that these illnesses were brought by Nationalist soldiers. Public works and the education system fell into disrepair. The population began to view government officials as carpetbaggers. Many Mainland Chinese claimed property based on squatters' rights, a concept not well known in Taiwan, while others looted factories in order to send materials needed in the war effort to the mainland. All of this evoked serious resentment on the part of the local population.

"Ethnic" hostility between the local Chinese or Taiwanese and the Mainland Chinese intensified. In February 1947, when police killed a woman for selling black market cigarettes on the street, a mob formed. Police fired into the crowd. This triggered a rebellion—an event now known as *er er ba,* or 2-28, for February 28 when it started.

The hated Governor-General Chen Yi was in large measure blamed for the incident due to his inflexibility and his subordinates' corruption and callous and indifferent attitude toward local problems. He treated the rebellion as Communist-inspired, which it was not, though it had resulted in widespread beating and killing of Mainland Chinese, and called in troops to restore order. The troops used brute force against unarmed civilians, killing thousands, including many of Taiwan's best and brightest.

Chiang Kai-shek, as a result of this incident, temporarily turned his attention to problems in Taiwan. He removed Chen Yi (and later ordered him executed). He made Taiwan a province and canceled military rule. He appointed some Taiwanese to political positions. He ordered other reforms. But considerable damage had already been done.

During 1948 and 1949, Nationalist Chinese forces suffered defeats throughout China at the hands of Mao's armies. In the fall, the government and the military of the Republic of China fled to Taiwan. Taiwan became the Nationalists' base of operations, from which they hoped to regroup and counterattack Mao's forces on the mainland. In the meantime, Taiwan became home to and almost synonymous with the Republic of China (ROC); the government of the People's Republic of China (PRC) ruled the mainland.

The U.S. had temporarily abandoned Chiang Kai-shek; but when the Korean War started in June 1950, President Truman changed his position and ordered the U.S. Seventh Fleet into the Taiwan Strait to block a pending invasion of Taiwan by Mao's armies. Taiwan, thereafter, assumed a front-and-center-stage role in the Cold War, representing "free" China, which was aligned with the West against the forces of Communism. The U.S. military presence, which soon grew on the island, made Taiwan secure, allowing its government to concentrate on domestic problems. There were, in fact, serious matters to attend to: the influx of 1.5 million Mainland Chinese worsened relations between them, and the Taiwanese and the economy needed immediate attention.

The Taiwanese and their Mainland Chinese rulers both soon realized that they had to bury their differences if they were to succeed in efforts to rebuild Taiwan and launch a successful economic development program. The government was serious about fixing the economy and won praise for a highly successful land reform program launched in 1950, one that is to this day viewed as a model by scholars and officials of developing nations. With the help and advice of U.S. aid advisors, land reform laid the groundwork for increasing agricultural productivity and then for Taiwan's industrialization.

Chiang Kai-shek encouraged democracy in local government, where Nationalist officials served as mediators between local factions. But democracy in the national government had to be delayed while the people were prepared for it. This period of tutelage was earlier propounded by Sun Yat-sen. A political opposition, including new political parties that might compete with the Nationalist Party, were not allowed. Rationalizing this, ethnic problems were indeed divisive, and many felt Taiwan needed a strong government. Chiang also justified authoritarian rule with the fear of a military conflict with the People's Republic of China. In 1954, and again in 1958, fighting broke out between the two sides over the Offshore Islands. Chiang regarded Quemoy and Matsu as crucial to his dream of reconquering the mainland, though in 1959, after U.S. officials made it clear that Washington did not support actions that might involve the

United States in a war, he declared that recovering the mainland would be "seventy percent political."

Chiang subsequently sought to defeat Communism by developing Taiwan economically and making it a model. In the ensuing years, he successfully planned and engineered rapid economic growth. He was so successful, in fact, that in 1964, when the United States decided to end its foreign aid to Taiwan, Taiwan's economy took off on its own. Taiwan's economic growth was soon so rapid that Taiwan's economy became one of the fastest growing in the world. Moreover, the island experienced economic growth with equity: nearly all of the population benefited. This fostered the development of a large middle class, more contact with the outside world (since economic growth was propelled by foreign trade), and the need for democratic institutions to sustain the modernization process. Taiwan had already begun to democratize locally, but the process was slow and generally went unnoticed.

During the 1960s, support for Chiang waned with the growing realization that the People's Republic of China was not going to collapse and that Taipei had no hope of recovering the mainland without the help of the United States, which did not like the thought of going to war with Peking (having experienced that in Korea), a war which might expand into a U.S.-Soviet global war. Taipei, however, was given respite in terms of a growing feeling in the United States and elsewhere that China had to be admitted into the world community. The Great Proletarian Cultural Revolution in China paralyzed the leadership in the mid- and late-1960s. At the same time, Washington-Peking relations deteriorated as a result of the United States escalating the Vietnam War.

In 1969, the United States and the People's Republic of China altered their policies toward each other. In America's case, Richard Nixon was elected president with a mandate of getting out of the Vietnam War "with honor." To do that, he thought he needed Peking's help. Nixon also perceived a new and different (meaning better) relationship with China as desirable for other reasons, especially in light of the Soviet Union's increasing hostility and its engaging in an arms race with the United States. Peking viewed the United States differently following a border war with the Soviet Union on the Ussuri River after which Soviet military leaders clamored for military action against China to neuter it from becoming a fullfledged nuclear power—one that was intensely antagonistic toward the Soviet Union.

In the fall of 1971, Mao's government was admitted to the United Nations and Chiang's government was expelled. The next year, U.S. President Nixon traveled to Peking where he toasted Mao and other Chinese leaders and set in motion a formal process of rapprochement between Washington and Peking. The United States needed cordial relations with the People's Republic of China to offset the Soviet Union's growing military power and influence in Asia. Peking needed Washington for the same reason. Thus they built a new relationship. The new U.S.-China relationship, in fact, marked the beginning of the end of the Nationalist Chinese claim to represent China in a world polarized into Communist and democratic blocs.

In April 1975, Chiang died. His dream of deposing Mao and removing the Communists from power in China was not realized. However, he could claim success in modernizing Taiwan and making it a showcase of economic development. The population of Taiwan by this time had begun to enjoy the nation's prosperity and Chinese throughout the rest of the world began to praise and admire Taiwan's "economic miracle." Political change in the direction of democracy had also begun.

Under Chiang Ching-kuo

The death of Chiang Kai-shek marked the beginning of a new era—that of his elder son Chiang Ching-kuo. Although Yen Chia-kan became president according to the constitutional provision whereby the vice-president becomes president in the event the president dies, Chiang Ching-kuo wielded considerable power, in fact, more than Yen, from his position as premier and via his role as head of the ruling Nationalist Party. CCK, as he was fondly called, had, in fact, already assumed many of his father's responsibilities after the latter's health had begun to deteriorate in 1972. Moreover, he was widely regarded, because of his name, his experience, and support in the Nationalist Party and the military, to be, without question or opposition, Taiwan's new leader.

After Chiang Kai-shek's death, the most noticeable thing about CCK's leadership was the "man of the people" image he built by going out into the countryside on weekend visits to talk to farmers and workers and his efforts (actually begun in 1972 when he became premier) to bring more Taiwanese, who constituted 85 percent of the population, into the government and the Nationalist Party. In fact, CCK soon made the percent of Taiwanese in government and the party nearly equal to their percentage of the general population. The "younger Chiang" also promoted political reforms and began talking about the democratization of the national government. He announced stringent anticorruption policies, which, among other things, banned lavish dinners and parties. People knew he was serious when he jailed some of his close friends and relatives for corruption. Similarly, CCK made efforts to improve Taiwan's human rights record, which, while not bad by global standards, still hurt the nation's image.

In March 1978, Chiang Ching-kuo was elected president by the National Assembly. President Yen had earlier declared that he would not be a candidate; CCK was thus the only real choice. He chose Shieh Tung-min, a Taiwanese, as his vice-president. Y.S. Sun, a Mainlander and a technocrat, became premier. In May, after his inauguration, CCK picked seven new cabinet members, raising to five the number of Taiwanese in this 17-member body. The newly elected President Chiang Ching-kuo also called for an election in December that he hoped would be more open, competitive, and important than any in Taiwan's history.

But before that election came about, President Jimmy Carter, on December 15, announced that the United States would grant formal diplomatic recognition to the People's Republic of China effective January 1, 1979, and that the American embassy in Taipei would be closed. The government of the Republic of China suffered a serious blow to its pride and legitimacy as a result. CCK put the military on alert, closed the stock market, and canceled the election.

In early 1979, in order to fill the void left by President Carter's sudden decision, the U.S. Congress passed the Taiwan Relations Act (TRA). It was signed by President Carter in April. In essence, the TRA restored to Taipei its sovereignty in Washington's eyes by allowing it access to U.S. courts, according its diplomats privileges normally granted only to the representatives of sovereign nation-states, and keeping trade and investment ties on track. The TRA also guaranteed defensive weapons sales to Taiwan and pledged that U.S. military forces would remain in the area to ensure Taiwan's security. Some observers commented that the TRA's security provisions were broader than the defense treaty Washington had with Taipei that was terminated on January 1, 1980. Officials in Taiwan liked the TRA but did not want to declare so publicly because the document did not use the country's official name, the Republic of China.

The loss of U.S. diplomatic ties, which prompted a number of other nations also to derecognize Taipei, meanwhile caused opposition groups in Taiwan to make stronger demands for reform and democratization. They, not to mention many in the government (including CCK himself), perceived that Taiwan had to move faster toward adopting a democratic political system in order to fend off Beijing's (the new spelling of Peking) claims that Taiwan belonged to the People's Republic of China. Taipei perceived that the United States and the international community would probably support, especially if it democratized, Taiwan's right to choose its future—separate from or as a part of China, whichever it desired (but for the short-run certainly separation). Democratization thus meant survival and the preservation of Taiwan's sovereignty, nationhood, and much more.

But some opposition groups were quite aggressive in the pursuit of even more democracy and freer and more open politics. On December 10, 1979, Human Rights Day, demonstrators in the southern city of Kaohsiung organized a parade which turned violent. The public, which had generally supported the opposition's charges, switched to the government's side because of the violence attributed to antigovernment forces and the fear of chaos which would benefit Beijing. In the wake of the incident, the government sought out those responsible and jailed them, some on charges of sedition. Still the public wanted reform and a more democratic political system. In this context agreements were subsequently worked out between the opposition and Nationalist Party leaders. Included were a new election law and gentlemen's agreements to make the December 1980 national election a fair and meaningful one.

As it turned out, the 1980 election was a watershed event in the political modernization process in Taiwan. While there was no official opposition, independent candidates collectively known as *tang-wai* (or "outside the party"—meaning the ruling Nationalist Party) behaved like a political party; they criticized the government and the Nationalist Party in candid and harsh language. Many citizens who observed the campaign, in fact, were flabbergasted by the new political atmosphere. It was the first competitive national election in Taiwan or in any Chinese nation.

Another election in 1983 confirmed that competitive elections were now an integral part of Taiwan's political system. In 1984, CCK was reelected to another six-year term. This time he picked Lee Teng-hui as his vice president. Like Shieh Tung-min, Lee was Taiwanese; but Lee was younger and U.S. educated and was seen by many as a more serious politician and a potential president. This engendered speculation that CCK had chosen his successor, thus answering (or not) a political question which had loomed beneath the surface for some time.

In March 1986, following a Nationalist Party meeting, CCK ordered the formation of a high-level, 12-member committee to study four "sensitive questions": martial law, the ban on forming new political parties, rejuvenating the elected organs of government, and strengthening local government. Dealing with these four issues came to constitute CCK's design to make Taiwan a real democracy, which became his paramount goal during his final years.

But the opposition beat him to the draw on one of the questions: new political parties. In September, independent politicians met and announced the formation of the Democratic Progressive Party (DPP). CCK ordered government officials not to take action against them for violating the law banning new parties since it was soon to be rescinded. As a result, the DPP ran against the Nationalist Party in the December 1986 national election in what was the first two-party election in Chinese history. The DPP fared well, but the Nationalist Party or Kuomintang (KMT) did better, giving the Nationalists confidence that they could win in competitive elections against a recognized and organized opposition.

In July 1987, the government announced the termination of martial law. Since martial law had not been in effect in the sense that there was military rule, ending it had little immediate formal impact. The psychological effect, however, was important. It also had some impact on the legal system and enhanced press freedom. Most important, canceling the martial law decree gave Taiwan good press abroad: the Western media perceived Taiwan as having taken a major step on its way to democracy.

CCK died on January 13, 1988, leaving a legacy of reform, democracy, and miraculous economic growth, which his father had started. Still, some of his reforms were yet to be realized.

Under Lee Teng-hui, I

When Chiang Ching-kuo died in January 1988, Vice-President Lee Teng-hui became president according to constitutional provisions on succession. He did not, however, inherit CCK's leadership of the party. Forthwith an emergency meeting of the ruling Nationalist Party was held, and Lee was, on a temporary basis only, granted CCK's leadership of the party. In the meantime, some members of the "old guard" (including Madame Chiang Kai-shek) joined together in an effort to block Lee from gaining political power, or at least in an effort to dilute his political authority. They were troubled by the prospect of a transition of power to a Taiwanese. On the other hand, Lee was viewed as CCK's chosen successor, and he was seen to be fiercely loyal to the Nationalist Party and, therefore, had support of many party members, especially Taiwanese.

Another crisis meeting followed which resulted in Lee winning the leadership reins of the party; a motion to have a rotating party leader was voted down. Those in favor of Lee, notably James Soong, who was then deputy secretary-general of the ruling party, cited CCK's intentions and the wrong signal any effort to undercut Lee would send to the stock market, foreign countries, and Beijing.

Being Taiwanese (though of the Hakka minority) Lee's leadership in some ways weakened and in other ways accentuated "ethnic" politics. Clearly it marked the transition from a Mainland Chinese-dominated government and ruling party to Taiwanese-dominated ones. On the other hand, his rise did not dampen opposition politics. The demand for democracy was growing. Various interest groups had already learned that they could accomplish political goals through protest politics and by going to the streets. On May 20, 1988, farmers demonstrated in Taipei, leading to mass riots lasting 17 hours, resulting in widespread property damage and injury to 500 people. At this time, street demonstrations in Taiwan were taking place at a rate of 150 per month. Taiwan, in fact, had entered a new era politically, or so it seemed. President Lee had to contend with this.

At the Nationalist Party's 13th Congress, held in July, Lee was officially elected chairman of the KMT. Meanwhile, democratization had begun to permeate the party: more delegates were chosen by primaries or other democratic processes. These delegates were not so docile and demanded the power to choose a Central Committee from delegates they nominated rather than from Lee's list. They also made known their feelings about top party leaders, sometimes causing embarrassment to those who were not accustomed to criticism anywhere, much less in public. But Lee was popular and the democratization processes in large measure worked to his benefit. The new Central Standing Committee (where real decision-making power lies in the party) was chosen, and for the first time it included a majority of Taiwanese.

The KMT not only democratized itself, suggesting that it planned to be the dominant political party in Taiwan for the foreseeable future, but also made promises to further democratize the government, deal with social problems, and adopt a coherent policy toward the mainland. Visits, trade, and investment were already extensive and seemed to offset political trends that were separating Taiwan more and more from China.

Soon after the Party Congress, Lee picked a new cabinet. It too was made a Taiwanese one (meaning a majority of its members were Taiwanese). Later, Lee picked the popular Lee Huan to be premier when the less popular, but effective and loyal, Yu Kuo-hua stepped down. Lee also devoted considerable attention to improving ties with the military (where his political clout was weak) and to the problem of acquiring the sophisticated weapons needed to defend the nation.

Because of the U.S. pledge to Beijing to gradually reduce and ultimately end its arms sales to Taiwan, Taipei made plans to purchase military technology and build its own fighter plane. This plane was put on public display in December, signaling that the Republic of China planned to defend its sovereignty in the face of leaders in Beijing continuing to assert that they would resolve the "Taiwan issue" by military force if necessary. President Lee gained increased support from the military as a result.

On May 20, 1989, Taiwan officially proclaimed its support for the Democracy Movement in China. In June, after authorities in Beijing struck against demonstrators in Tiananmen Square, slaughtering students in the process, international pressure on Taipei to negotiate with the People's Republic of China diminished markedly. The KMT and the Republic of China government by comparison looked good: there was no shooting of students on the streets of Taipei; instead democratization was proceeding apace. In fact, the Tiananmen Massacre became a watershed event for Taiwan: The Republic of China was seldom after this given the appellation pariah nation; that opprobrium had been passed to Beijing.

That year, 1989, was also an important time for another reason. The opposition Democratic Progressive Party scored a major victory in the Legislative Yuan election late in the year. The DPP's election success was founded to some degree on democratic reform, which had escalated worldwide. Taiwan's separation from China, which seemed more desirable and reasonable in the context of the Tiananmen Massacre, also helped the DPP. The major opposition party had likewise learned how to campaign and win votes. Its win, in fact, was so impressive that many, especially DPP leaders, predicted that the ruling Nationalist Party might be voted out of office soon—if only the system were made democratic by expelling members of the elected bodies of government that were frozen in office after the government moved to Taiwan in 1949 or were appointed to fill vacancies in these representative organs of government.

President Lee and his ruling party accepted the challenge and subsequently backed new laws that would retire old members of the elected bodies of government and reform the elected bodies so that they no longer represented China. This was to be done in the name of democracy, though it was seen by some as burnishing a hidden two-China agenda. Other observers, however, pointed out that an independent Taiwan, which a two-China policy suggested, was not realistic since it was not in consonance with Washington's China policy (though one might argue otherwise when speaking of the Taiwan Relations Act as opposed to the Normalization Agreement made by President Carter with the People's Republic of China).

Lee meanwhile supported a new law allowing the formation of new political parties. A sizeable number of new parties thus entered the political scene. Despite the appearance of a host of new parties, none, with the exception of the DPP, performed well, leading political observers to say that Taiwan now had a two-party system.

President Lee was to some extent blamed for the Nationalist Party's "defeat" in the 1989 election. He was chided for having promoted confusing policies and was accused of not being able to fill CCK's shoes. As a result, he was challenged in the spring of 1990 when the National Assembly had to pick a new president or renew Lee's tenure. In the end President Lee dealt successfully with the situation and was elected to a new six-year term (when Lin Yang-kang and Chiang Wei-kuo dropped out of contention), with Li Yuan-tzu as his running mate.

In March 1991, Lee promised a "National Affairs Conference" to debate constitutional and other issues that related to the nation's political future. He then announced an end to the state of war with the communists, thereby de facto recognizing the legitimacy of the government of the People's Republic of China. The "Temporary Provisions" were also ended, giving citizens broader civil and political rights guaranteed in the Constitution.

Meanwhile, notwithstanding the ascendancy of hard-line leaders and a shift to the left politically in China, trade and investment ties grew to the tune of billions of dollars in each category. Reporters and scholars from China were allowed to come to Taiwan, including those with Chinese Communist Party connections. Proliferating ties with China reflected the end of the Cold War and other watershed changes going on throughout the world. Taipei clearly perceived that economic blocs were replacing political-military blocs as the basis of a new world order and that its relationship with China had to change.

In December 1991, after the Nationalist Party had made concerted efforts for some years, including making changes in the Constitution while employing various means to persuade the "elder parliamentarians" (those not elected in Taiwan) to step down, an election was held for a new or second National Assembly. The DPP, having created a divisive controversy by putting Taiwan independence in the party platform, which split the party and alienated a sizeable number of voters, did not perform well at the polls. The KMT won—giving it, according to some observes— a "democratic mandate" and public support for its policies it had never before had.

In early 1992, the National Assembly made further revisions to the Constitution, but did not resolve the issue of whether the nation should have a directly elected president or not. The Control Yuan was made a semijudicial body and other reforms were instituted, such as making the governor and mayors of Taipei and Kaohsiung elected officials. The infamous "Black List" was reduced to just a few names and the Taiwan Garrison Command was disestablished.

In mid-year Taiwan lost its formal diplomatic ties with the last important country in East Asia—South Korea. But it compensated for this to some degree with diplomatic accords with several new, albeit small, countries. More important, in the context of China acquiring new, sophisticated weapons, Taiwan was able to make purchases of top-of-the-line fighter planes abroad, including F-16s from the United States, thus maintaining some semblance of a balance of forces in the Taiwan Strait. In November, U.S. trade representative Carla Hills visited Taipei, giving the impression of improving U.S.-Taiwan relations—Hills being the first cabinet official to visit Taiwan in 13 years.

In December, Taiwan held its first nonsupplemental legislative election and, to some observers, its most important election ever. The KMT was split by the New KMT Alliance faction, led by Jaw Shao-kang advocating a firmer one-China policy than that of President Lee and the majority of members of the ruling party. Meanwhile, the DPP had regrouped after its defeat in the December 1991 election, was less divided, and was prepared to compete strongly in the election contest. Vastly improving its position in both the popular vote column and seats in the new Legislative Yuan, after the election the DPP celebrated victory and talked again of becoming the ruling party in the near future.

Under Lee Teng-hui, II

Early on in 1993, Premier Hau Pei-tsun resigned along with his cabinet, setting a precedent for cabinet dissolution after a legislative election. Hau's resignation, some said his sacking by President Lee, however, also signaled a rather deep polarization in Taiwan politics along ethnic (Taiwanese versus Mainland Chinese) lines. On January 10, before Hau stepped down 10,000 protestors called for Hau to remain in office. Three hundred thousand signed a petition to this effect. Nevertheless, Hau was replaced by the popular and experienced Lien Chan, making the premiership as well as the presidency Taiwanese. President Lee also picked a new cabinet.

Meanwhile, the new Legislative Yuan began exerting more political clout by passing laws forcing top government officials to disclose their personal finances while cutting budget requests selectively and scrutinizing government policies. This seemed to create a new era of legislative power. Legislative Yuan members, as a result, expected more authority in their respective parties and made these feelings known.

In August, leading up to the KMT convening its 14th Party Congress, several members of the New KMT Alliance, part of the Non-Mainstream faction of the Nationalist Party (a conservative wing of the party that advocated stronger allegiance to Sun Yat-sen's teachings, a one-China policy, etc.), announced their departure from the KMT and their decision to form the Chinese New Party.

Some observers said that President Lee was glad to get rid of this opposition within the party. The ruling party, however, remained split between Mainstream and Non-Mainstream factions that generally reflected ethnicity as well as policy toward China. Nevertheless, President Lee was reelected party chairman by the first secret ballot in the party's history and with 82.5 percent of the votes cast (though over 300 delegates had defaced their ballots in protest of Lee's leadership).

In March 1994, 24 tourists from Taiwan were murdered in China in a robbery incident that involved the military. Beijing first called the matter an accident and then apprehended and immediately executed three young men for the crime in what appeared to be a coverup to the public in Taiwan. Relations across the Taiwan Strait soured and Taiwan cut investments on the mainland, while public opinion polls showed the highest support ever for independence.

In the fall, the U.S. government notified the Republic of China's representative in Washington that the United States had agreed to allow a name change in Taipei's representative office there to Taipei Economic and Cultural Office and that Republic of China diplomats could visit U.S. government offices, except the Department of State and the White House, on official business. Observers saw this as an upgrading of U.S.-Taiwan relations. The Clinton Administration made these moves under pressure from Congress.

In December, Taiwan held its first election for the governor of Taiwan Province and the first for a number of years for the mayors of its two metropolitan cities: Taipei and Kaohsiung (these offices having become appointed positions in 1964 and 1976, respectively). The Nationalist Party's candidate James Soong was elected governor, with President Lee Teng-hui's help, by a sizeable margin in a campaign which saw ethnicity become an issue (Soong being Mainland Chinese) during the campaign. The KMT's Wu Den-yih won handily in Kao-hsiung, which had been a DPP stronghold. The DPP's Chen Shui-bian, however, won the mayorship of Taipei, which was an embarrassment for the KMT. The DPP and the New Party also did well in the Taipei City Council race.

In January 1995, the president of the People's Republic of China issued an eight-point proposal for the peaceful reunification of Taiwan with China. The proposal, while both tough and conciliatory, generally generated a sense of cautious or skeptical optimism in Taiwan regarding relations with the mainland. This feeling was not to last for long though.

In June, President Lee visited the United States where he spoke at his alma mater—Cornell University. The visit was reported on very favorably in the Western media, drawing attention to Taiwan's lack of official diplomatic representation and Peking's efforts to isolate Taiwan. The visit at once helped promote Lee's policy of trying to enhance Taipei's international visibility but drew criticism for being provocative to Beijing. The United States had, heretofore, been unwilling to give Lee a visa, but the Clinton Administration succumbed to Congressional pressure.

Beijing's reaction was fast and hard. Chinese Communist Party leaders bitterly criticized Lee calling him a traitor, among other harsh and uncomplimentary names. In July, the People's Liberation Army conducted military exercises at home and in the Taiwan Strait to intimidate Taiwan. Leaders in Beijing were angry because they had been lied to—told by the Department of State that Lee would not be granted a visa; they also saw the visit as mirroring a U.S. policy of containing China and playing the "Taiwan card."

Meanwhile, on February 28, President Lee apologized to victims of the *er er ba*, or February 28 (1947) Uprising at a ceremony held at Taipei New Park where a monument commemorating the tragedy was built by the government.

In December, the Republic of China held its second nonsupplemental Legislative Yuan election. The campaign was conducted under the shadow of continued People's Liberation Army missile tests that caused the Taipei stock market to fall and precipitated a run on visas to leave the country. The ruling Nationalist Party lost a significant number of seats, with the New Party making the most gains. Observers linked the election results to Beijing's actions to hurt President Lee's party. The KMT barely held onto its majority in the legislative branch of government; in fact, this election inaugurated what some called "coalition politics" that followed due to the gains of the other parties and the KMT's lack of sufficient discipline to control votes on a number of bills.

On March 23, 1996, Taiwan held the first direct election ever for its president and vice-president—a contest which was dubbed the first such election in 5,000 years of Chinese history. President Lee Teng-hui represented the ruling Nationalist Party; Peng Ming-min (the "father of Taiwan independence") was the Democratic Progressive Party's candidate; Chen Li-an, resigning from the KMT, ran as an independent with a female running mate; Lin Yang-kang, ran as an independent with New Party support and Hau Pei-tsun as his running mate. President Lee and his running mate Lien Chan won with 54 percent of the popular vote. The campaigning and the election were impacted by additional and even more threatening People's Liberation Army missile tests which included tests, with live warheads that forced the temporary closing of two of Taiwan's major ports. The United States responded by sending two aircraft carriers with nuclear weapons to the area, after which an official in Beijing mentioned the possibility of a nuclear assault on Los Angeles.

In December, a National Development Conference was held in Taipei to debate important political questions facing the nation along with constitutional issues that had been precipitated by the country's extremely rapid democratization. Major constitutional revisions were recommended, including one to eliminate or drastically reduce in size the provincial government. At the same time, promises were made to 302,000 provincial government employees that they would be hired elsewhere. Being the largest landowner, in addition to owning a number of banks and other businesses in Taiwan, provincial government assets became immediately a subject of speculation. Governor James Soong tendered his resignation, which amplified the crisis. Critics said that President Lee sought to reverse the democratic process and give more political authority to himself while promoting a two-China policy.

The return of Hong Kong to the People's Republic of China on July 1 underscored Taipei's strained relations with Beijing and along with a rise in crime and increased public concern about political corruption caused President Lee and Vice-President Lien to see their popularity ratings plummet.

In August, the KMT's 15th Party Congress met in Taipei. President Lee won an even bigger vote than at the 14th Congress to remain Party chairman. James Soong, who had meanwhile become (according to the press at least) Lee's enemy, visited the United States during the meeting but received the highest number of votes cast for membership on the Party's Central Standing Committee. Lien Chan, at this juncture, stepped down as premier (keeping his position as vice president); he was replaced by Vincent Siew.

In November 1997, the KMT suffered a serious setback in local elections for country magistrates and city mayors to the opposition Democratic Progressive Party, but did well in subsequent local elections and in the election of the Legislative Yuan, the Taipei and Kaohsiung mayorships and city councils in December 1998. In the meantime, the Taiwan Provincial Government was drastically downsized and in December 1998 the Provincial Assembly was abolished as well as the governorship.

The Taiwan Economic Miracle

Taiwan is well known—not just at home, but throughout the world—as an economic success story, evoking the appellation "the Taiwan economic miracle." Indeed the country's economic growth from the mid-1960s to the present, but especially during the first part of that period, was phenomenal as judged by the fact that few, if any, nations have ever performed so well over an extended period of time. And Taiwan did this, according to some economists, "against all odds."

When Europeans first arrived in East Asia and visited Taiwan, the aborigines were engaged in hunting, fishing, berry picking, and some farming. It was the base of operations for Chinese and Japanese pirates and there was some commerce on the island. The Dutch, who colonized the island in the 17th century, brought oxen and farm implements and created a cash economy and some trade and commerce. Under Chinese control for the next two-plus centuries, Taiwan's agriculture sector expanded markedly, and significant amounts of rice and sugar were exported to the mainland. At the end of the Chinese period, Taiwan's infrastructure was improved and the economy made more productive. Under Japanese rule for a half century prior to the end of World War II, Taiwan became a modern economy, and the island was modernized and became more prosperous than any part of East Asia, save Japan.

Nationalist Chinese rule of the island under Governor Chen Yi in 1945 saw gross mismanagement of the economy in an effort to build a socialist system and due to the fact that there was a civil war on the mainland and resources from Taiwan were appropriated for that effort. Meanwhile investment and concern for economic stability and growth were ignored. The situation became even more grim in 1949 when the Nationalists were defeated by the Communists and fled to Taiwan along with nearly two million people. Taiwan was already crowded, and its economy could not easily absorb the influx of people. In fact, because of the very unfavorable land-to-population ratio, an absence of meaningful natural resources, and a discredited government, at this juncture economists viewed the prospects for economic development as dim and even called Taiwan a "basket case" with little or no hope of economic growth and prosperity.

In 1950, when, at the onset of the Korean War, the United States decided to protect Taiwan and resumed economic aid, this changed a bit. U.S. military assistance made it possible to divert funds that were allocated for the armed forces into economic rebuilding. The huge pool of administrative talent, reform of the ruling party and the government, and the desire of the population to put the economy in a growth mode facilitated economic stability and some growth.

Land reform also made a major contribution. Rent reduction, the sale of public lands to farmers and a "land to the tiller" law, which forced landlords to sell land to the farmers who used it, made the agricultural sector more efficient and productive. Agricultural production, in fact, increased by a whopping 14 percent annually in the 1950s. This provided much of the investment capital and the labor for Taiwan's subsequent industrialization.

Taiwan's industrial sector subsequently made the economy "take off," notwithstanding the United States terminating economic assistance in 1964. During the late 1960s and 1970s factories were set up or expanded at such a rate that, by 1977, the nation's industrial index was 28 times what it had been in 1950, making the Republic of China the most industrialized nation in East Asia after Japan. Increases in labor productivity, privatization of the economy, a high savings rate coupled with large infusions of foreign investment capital, a solid infrastructure, sustained efforts to export to take advantage of the international marketplace and a global division of labor (after a short period of an import substitution policy), as well as intelligent efforts by the government and business community in guiding a market economy, account for this growth.

A number of key industries contributed to the country's industrialization and to its economic growth. Textiles was early on the most important. Sporting goods was another. Electronics, telecommunications, tools, and optical machines followed, along with chemicals, metals, and even shipbuilding. Information products also became a major part of the economy—Taiwan becoming the largest producer in the world of computer keyboards, screens, and other parts.

All of this translated into a bottom line, as measured in growth in the gross national product, of 8.2 percent average annual increases in the 1950s. In the 1960s it was 9.2 percent. In spite of the oil crisis, which hit Taiwan hard in 1973, its record for the decade of the 1970s was better than 10 percent. In the 1980s, it was 8.2 percent. Over a period of 30 years, Taiwan recorded more years of double-digit annual growth than any nation in the world. For a decade and a half Taiwan's economic expansion was double Japan's and more than triple that of the United States. Uniquely Taiwan experienced growing income equity during this time. Thus, nearly everyone benefited from Taiwan's success; in fact, income inequality became less than in the United States or Japan. Unemployment meanwhile fell from traditionally high levels to below 2 percent, and Taiwan's foreign exchange position (due to export surpluses and high savings rates) attained it the rank of number one in the world.

All of this gave Taiwan a reputation for successful economic development that other countries sought to emulate. Economists and leaders of underdeveloped countries began to examine the ingredients to Taiwan's economic success. Welcoming foreign capital (including establishing export processing zones for international companies) and engaging heavily in foreign trade were seen to be essential—thereby refuting dependency theory. Small, family-owned businesses; a high savings rate; privatization; low taxes; business community-government cooperation; astute planners who believed in a free market, guiding the economy; large investments in education, research, and development; a strong work ethic; and a government that promoted stability and kept the crime rate low were also important elements of Taiwan's success.

Taiwan was an even more attractive model of economic growth than the other Asian tigers—South Korea, Hong Kong, and Singapore—for several reasons. Hong Kong and Singapore were seen as city states and too small for their economic development experience to have relevance to most underdeveloped nations. South Korea's growth was built on very large industries. Also, while Taiwan has experienced slower growth in the 1990s (which is natural as its economy became a modern one), it was not hit hard by economic crises which have affected other countries in East Asia. In fact, some observers praised Taiwan's economic performance in the midst of so-called East Asia meltdown and offered this as further proof of the Taiwan economic miracle.

Taiwan's economic miracle has not only afforded it praise but has given it diplomatic clout far beyond what its physical size and its population would afford the government. Its foreign assistance and capital investment in other countries have facilitated its foreign policy making and have kept it in international financial institutions where Beijing has tried to exclude Taipei. Taiwan's investment in and trade with China have also played an important role in its relations with Beijing and have to some degree fostered democratization there.

Taiwan's Democratization

Not happening as early, and consequently not as well known in the rest of the world as its phenomenal economic development, Taiwan has also experienced highly praiseworthy political modernization or democratization. Few observers, either in Taiwan or elsewhere, refer to Taiwan's political system anymore—especially since the 1996 direct presidential election—as an authoritarian one. The government of the Republic of China is now seen as a democracy, though some might say it is yet-to-be-consolidated insofar as the democratization process happened so fast, and it has evoked change that requires adjustment and accommodation that are still in progress.

There are generally two views about Taiwan's democratization: One, that it occurred gradually, for a number of reasons and over an extended period of time. Two, that it happened rather quickly in the mid-1980s due to the appearance of a true opposition political party, the Democratic Progressive Party, and the end of martial law. There is also disagreement about the importance of various forces that engendered democratic change, and about who most deserves the credit. Nevertheless, Taiwan's political modernization process has been seen by the leaders of many developing countries and scholars in both the West and the Third World as a model. Clearly it occurred in the face of adversity (a state of war with the People's Republic of China), without a contributing colonial experience (unlike most other democratizing countries) and in a compacted period of time (unlike most Western democracies).

In addition to Taiwan being lauded and emulated for its democratization, the process has other implications. Taiwan's democratization contradicts the principle of one-China since the political gap between Taiwan and the People's Republic of China has become wider, and many nations of the world support Taiwan's separation based on the fact that it is a democracy and the PRC is not. In other words, it would neither be right nor supportive of democracy, which is viewed as the "wave of the future," to destroy Taiwan's accomplishments in building a democratic system and force Taiwan to merge with China. This presents a special problem for the United States, which encouraged and helped (some even say forced) Taiwan to democratize, but which espouses a one-China policy and finds the "Taiwan issue" a major obstacle in pursuing better relations with Beijing.

The factors contributing to Taiwan's democratization as well as important milestones in the process need to be cited. Both contribute to an understanding of why Taiwan became a democracy and when the important steps were taken and in what context.

Taiwan's geography, say some scholars, is a factor in its becoming a democratic nation. Taiwan is an island nation with secure frontiers, which have been common to other nations that have seen the development of democracy. It is also cut into pieces by mountains—a situation that lent itself to the growth of a feudal culture and political system in the past and which seemed to impede the implanting of the Chinese bureaucratic system on the island. In modern times feudal systems have made the transition to democracies easier than other systems.

History has also played a role. Taiwan being populated largely by immigrants, the newcomers were willing to try new ways of doing things and this mentality has been preserved over the years to a considerable extent. Taiwan also witnessed Western colonial rule (which brought some democratic ideals), self-rule, rule by China, and Japanese colonial rule. Meanwhile Taiwan experienced contacts with other peoples in East Asia through trade. All of this made Taiwan quite cosmopolitan and its population more desirous of various freedoms that are either associated with a democratic system or are essential to that kind of system.

The United States played a special role in Taiwan's becoming a democracy in 1950, and from that point on. President Truman ordered the U.S. Seventh Fleet into the Taiwan Strait to protect the island and the Nationalist government from an invasion by Mao's forces. The United States, from that juncture, became Taiwan's protector. It hardly seems a coincidence that elections were held immediately. American economic and military assistance also played a role. Both afforded U.S. advisors leverage over the government and the ruling party. One of their objectives was a "free China." Later, after economic assistance ended, Washington's pressure on Taiwan continued to work because access to the American market and arms sales were important to Taiwan. The Taiwan Relations Act written into law by the U.S. Congress in 1979 contains a provision specifically calling for improved human rights in Taiwan, implying that the United States expects further and faster democratization of the political system. In short, U.S. demands for Taiwan to democratize constituted a major reason for Taipei's decisions to reform the government, introduce a competitive political party system, end martial law, and much more.

This is not to say that Taiwan's political leaders did not otherwise have cause to democratize. They did. They brought with them from China a democratic constitution that was in large measure based on the U.S. Constitution. It contained the framework for elected institutions, civil and political rights, and more. Whereas the "Temporary Provisions" or amendments to this constitution for some time nullified many of its democratic provisions, there was never any serious attempt by any top leader or official in Taiwan to scrap the constitution and establish formally some other kind of political system. Thus the system was an aspiring democracy that was, in reality, quite authoritarian; but the framework was there for a democracy and some parts of it, in fact, worked. As other factors gradually created the infrastructure and impetus for political modernization, the constitution made the process of democratic change easier.

The Republic of China's ideology or political philosophy also had this effect. Although earlier Chinese thought, including ideas from Confucius and others, about good government and the role of political leaders played a role, most important were the teachings and writings of Sun Yat-sen. Sun advocated a U.S-style republican political system. He also propounded democracy in stages, perceiving that the Chinese people had to be prepared for democracy before it could be implemented. His blueprint, some say, prevented Taiwan from trying to implement democracy precipitously as many other developing nations unwisely did, and, therefore, explains its success. He also sought to nourish nationalism and expressed concern about the livelihood of the people. Clearly his political philosophy, which was read by nearly everyone in Taiwan in school or in some other situation, was instrumental in nurturing a democratic political culture.

Another early factor was land reform. In 1950, the government embarked on a program to restrict rents on farm land, put land into the hands of the peasants, and facilitate the growth of agriculture through market mechanisms. Taiwan's land reform program eminently succeeded and broke the bonds between the peasants and landlords and thus created the basis for local democratic politics. In this connection, some have argued that Taiwan attained democracy "from the bottom up." If this is true, then land reform must be accorded an important place in laying the groundwork for this.

Similarly the Nationalist Party or Kuomintang undertook to reform itself as soon as it and the government moved to Taiwan. Party leaders realized that they had made serious mistakes which caused them to lose the hearts and minds of the people in China and that they had to rid the party of corruption, nepotism, and other traits that would block its effective rule and impede it from winning popular support in Taiwan. The Nationalist Party was reformed. And it continued to exercise concern and vigilance lest it lose public support. Party leaders also took the view that it was their duty to implement democracy in Taiwan and that, because of factionalism and undemocratic trends in local politics, they had to take the initiative. Thus they argued for "democracy from above." And while they contradicted local leaders in their viewpoint, both, in fact, happened.

The role of Taiwan's economic miracle cannot be overestimated. It contributed to the rise of a democratic political culture and a democratic polity. Many Western scholars have argued that economic growth creates a middle class, promotes urbanization, and facilitates broad educational improvements and many more conditions necessary for democracy to work. Taiwan's very rapid growth created these conditions quickly. Growth with equity helped even more. The fact that Taiwan's transition to democracy happened at just the time when the per capita income grew to the point that Taiwan was no longer poor clearly can not be written off as an unrelated circumstance.

According to various opinion polls, the fact that, by the 1980s, most people identified themselves as middle class can be linked with growth in political participation and civic responsibility. Economic growth fostered this. The same goes for urbanization, which was probably faster in Taiwan during the 1960s and into the 1970s than in any country in the world. This engendered the need for political institutions that responded to the needs and political interests of the new city dwellers. These institutions helped make democracy function. Likewise, advances in education created a population that favored democracy and were prepared to make it work through enlightened participation.

Some also suggest that Taiwan democratized because it had a democratizer. Although Chiang Kai-shek and some other early leaders talked about democracy and laid some of the groundwork, especially economic growth, it was Chiang Ching-kuo who accomplished the most. He rooted out corruption and favoritism. He recruited Taiwanese into the government and the ruling party when they occupied few such positions. He insisted that government agencies respond to public demands and suggestions. He ordered the government to reform. Many say that he gave Taiwan democracy by edict; others contend that he did it by example and was the only person who was sufficiently respected and powerful enough to push the system away from its authoritarian character, and he did exactly that. Some also attribute such a role to Lee Teng-hui, both as Chiang Ching-kuo's successor and the leader who continued his democratization program. Lee oversaw the transition from Mainland Chinese to Taiwanese rule—an important transition if Taiwan were to truly be a democracy.

The rise of an opposition party, first in the form of *tangwai* (or non-KMT, independent politicians) and then as the Democratic Progressive Party, is also seen as a major contributing factor to Taiwan's democratization. Clearly party competition is said to be a sine qua non to competitive elections. The DPP, unlike earlier political parties, did that. It also pushed Taiwan toward a two-party system, which many say is the best form of party system for democracy. It promoted the participation in politics of many who were disenfranchised. Its members became active debaters in the parliamentary bodies of government, and the party has pushed numerous democratic reforms which were adopted. Considering its impact and the fact that Taiwan seemed to take a big step forward in the democratization process in the 1980s, it may be justified to say that it played a huge role in Taiwan's becoming a democracy.

Terminating martial law, which was done in 1987, is also seen as a watershed event. It had not only symbolized an antidemocratic government, but in many ways had institutionalized it. When it was ended, most people felt that something important had happened. Civil rights could be exercised. The Constitution provided such guarantees. The legal system subsequently changed. So did the media.

Finally, elections have played a central role in Taiwan's transition to democracy. Local elections attracted voter participation in the political system in the 1950s. National elections did so in the 1980s and after. A two-party election in 1986, "victory" (big gains in popular vote and seats) by the opposition party in 1989, nonsupplemental or plenary elections in 1991 and 1992 (to the National Assembly and the Legislative Yuan, respectively), and a direct election of the president and vice president in 1996 have been widely acclaimed as pushing Taiwan forward along the path of democratization, and by most (by at least 1996) as making Taiwan a full-fledged and genuine democracy.

THE DICTIONARY

- A -

Aborigines. Called *Shan bao* (mountain compatriot) or more recently *yuan-chu-min* (indigenous people) in Chinese, this is the general term for those people who inhabited Taiwan prior to the migration of Chinese to the island. There are nine main tribes of aborigines: the Ami, Atayal, Bunun, Paiwan, Puyuma, Rukai, Saisiyat, Tsou, and Yami. (qq.v). The Ami (q.v.) is the largest, the Saisiyat and the Yami are the smallest. There is disagreement among experts concerning the place of origin of the aborigines. One theory is that they came from Southeast Asia, probably from the Malay Peninsula area or Indonesia or, alternatively, the Philippines. The vocabulary and grammatical structure of the aboriginal languages are very close to Bahasa, the language spoken in Indonesia and Malaysia. Many cultural traits, such as tattooing, identical names for father and son, rule by the old, headhunting, spirit worship, and indoor burial, come from Southeast Asia. These cultural characteristics differ markedly from those found in other parts of Asia, including China, Japan, Korea, India, and Arabia. While many prehistoric materials found on Taiwan resemble those in China, these artifacts do not connect with what was mainstream Chinese culture; instead they are similar to things found among the early non-Chinese people in China, some of whom migrated to Southeast Asia. Thus the aborigines may have lived in what is now South China before Chinese civilization reached there. Another view is that one or more of the aborigine tribes hailed from the north, either north China or Japan. This view is based on certain myths, as well as other evidence.

The aborigines constituted a majority of the population of Taiwan until some time in the 19th century and controlled more than half of Taiwan's surface area into the 20th century. By the end of World War II, however, they constituted less than 2 percent of the population. Today they number less than 400,000, and their birthrate is below the average in Taiwan. Many aborigines have been assimilated, and most have lost their language and culture to a larger degree. Others remain out of the mainstream of society in Taiwan. Most reside in the mountainous areas of central or eastern Taiwan. Most aborigines engage in farming or fishing or make a livelihood from tourism. A large number receive government welfare or subsidies, reflecting the fact that their incomes in general are below average. Various social problems such as unemployment, and drug use are prevalent among aboriginal tribes.

In recent years, aborigines have founded organizations to enhance their political influence and to reflect concern over their problems and their minority status. Serious efforts are being made by some of these groups as well as the government to protect Aboriginal languages and cultures, though this contradicts integrating them into Chinese society. (See also Pingpu.)

Academia Historica (kuo shih kuan). Established in Nanking when the Nationalist government was on the mainland, Academia Historica was started anew on Taiwan in 1957. Organized under the Office of the President (q.v.), it is responsible for preserving documents and conducting research on modern Chinese history, especially the Republican period. It also keeps the archives and records of the Office of the President, Executive Yuan (q.v.), provincial and local governments, and some other official government organs and agencies. It has over 7.5 million publications and documents.

Academia Sinica (chung-yang yen-chiu-yuan). Considered the ROC's top research institution, Academia Sinica was established in Nanking in 1928 and moved to Taiwan (Nanking, about an hour outside of Taipei) in 1949. Its basic missions are to conduct research—done by its institutes, of which there are 22—and direct and coordinate research in various institutions and universities in Taiwan. Academia Sinica is a government organization under the Office of the President (q.v.) though in most respects it is considered an independent research organization.

The most important body of the organization is the Assembly of Members or "Academics," which is elected by Chinese scholars of reputation and distinction. The Assembly helps choose new members and plans national policy on research and education. In 1990, Academia Sinica decided to become a degree-granting institution. Li Yuan-tseh (q.v.) is the president of Academia Sinica.

Acer Group Inc. (hung chi). Taiwan's leading computer manufacturing firm and one of the nation's best known and most highly respected companies as well as its largest enterprise in terms of import and export revenues. In 1986, the company produced a 32-bit computer before IBM accomplished this feat. In 1992, it integrated a personal computer with consumer electronic technology to produce a multimedia PC called "Acer PAC." In 1997, Acer was the world's seventh-largest computer maker, turning out five million personal computers a year. The company is known in Taiwan (q.v.) for its large investments in research and development (5 percent of income) and its unique Chinese democratic-style management. Stan Shih is the founder and current chairman of Acer. Acer publishes the popular magazine *The Third Wave*.

Akashi Motojiro. Governor-general of Taiwan (q.v.) from 1918to1919. Under his rule, Taiwan became regarded as a "home territory" of Japan.

Alliance of Taiwan Aborigines (t'ai-wan yuan-chu-min lien-meng). An organization formed in 1984 to represent and enhance the political power of aborigines (q.v.). Some say it was the first civil rights or minority rights organization in Taiwan.

American Institute in Taiwan (AIT) (mei-kuo tsai t'ai hsieh-hui). A nonprofit organization incorporated in the District of Columbia in the United States in 1979, its purpose being to supplant the formal organizations, including those in the Department of State, that maintained diplomatic and other relations between the United States and the Republic of China (q.v). Headquartered in Rossyln, Virginia, it has field offices in Taipei and Kaohsiung (qq.v.). The heads of the branch offices (the main one being in Taipei) have been drawn from the Foreign Service, though they have assumed leave status when at their post. The budget for AIT is a line item in the Department of State's budget, and it receives instructions through the assistant secretary of state for Asian and Pacific affairs. U.S. employees working for AIT in Taiwan (q.v.) have "functional immunity"—meaning they cannot be arrested or tried for acts carried out in connection with their jobs. AIT, in essence, functions as a U.S. embassy and consulate. The Republic of China's counterpart of AIT in the United States was the Coordination Council for North American Affairs (q.v.) which took the name Taipei Economic and Cultural Representative Office (q.v.) in 1994.

Ami. Name of a tribe of lowland aborigines (q.v.) once inhabiting the coastal area of eastern Taiwan (q.v.), the Ami lived in large settlements, often of more than 1,000 and sometimes 2,000. The Ami had large families, generally ruled by women, with a clan frequently headed by a maternal uncle and the tribe led by the eldest man. They lived in huts constructed of bamboo, straw, reeds, and lumber. The Ami is the only tribe that has preserved pottery making. In the past, the Ami tribe was the largest aboriginal group; today the Ami constitute about one-third of the aboriginal population.

Ando Rikichi. The 19th and last Japanese governor-general of Taiwan (q.v.). Ando, an army general, served from December 1944 to the end of World War II.

Ando Sadayoshi. Governor-general of Taiwan from 1915 to 1918, who, like his predecessor, was a soldier and was not trained to run a civilian government. He did not, however, rule brutally as General Sakuma (q.v.) had.

Apollo (*wen hsing*). A reformist literary periodical published from 1957 to 1965. Li Ao (q.v.) was a contributing writer for some time.

Article 100 (hsing-fa yi-pai t'iao). A provision in the Republic of China's (q.v.) criminal code dealing with domestic criminal violence that states that "if any person behaves as if he or she intends to destroy the national polity, steal or take over national property, use illegal means to change the nation's constitution, or actually carries out these intentions, then that person has committed a crime of domestic criminal violence." This was frequently used by the Taiwan Garrison Command (q.v.) to arrest, charge, and imprison critics of the government. Even after martial law (q.v.) was terminated, this provision remained and was said to discourage political protest and free speech. In 1991, Jaw Shau-kong (q.v.) and others called for its revision, since it undermined constitutional protections of freedom of thought and speech. Many Democratic Progressive Party (q.v.) leaders said it should be abolished. In 1992, it was revised such that if there is no violence or threatening behavior there can be no punishment for causing domestic upheaval. Several dissidents were immediately released from prison after the revision was passed into law. Some said its revision created a new era of political freedom in Taiwan (q.v.).

Asia and the World Institute (ya-chou yu shih-chieh-she). A nonprofit think tank located in Taipei with interests in both domestic and global affairs. It was founded in 1976 by Han Lih-wu (q.v.).

Asian Pacific Anti-Communist League (APACL) (ya-t'ai fan-kung lien-meng). Originally founded in June 1954 in South Korea by Chiang Kai-shek (q.v.), Syngman Rhee, and Elpidio Quirino under the name the Asian People's Anti-Communist League, it constituted a response to the need for a regional alliance against the threat of Communism. Its name was changed in 1984. From eight original chapters, it has expanded to 34, including some in Middle Eastern countries. The secretariat, originally in Saigon, is now in Taipei (q.v.). The organization sponsors conferences and publications. In 1979, it established the Asia Youth Anti-Communist League—which subsequently, in 1986, changed its name to Asia Youth Freedom League.

Asia-Pacific Economic Cooperation (APEC) (ya-t'ai ching-chi ho-tso hui-yi). A regional organization, sometimes called a forum, established to promote economic ties among Asian countries. The Republic of China joined in 1991 as "Chinese Taipei" along with the People's Republic of China and Hong Kong. Other members include Australia, Brunei, Canada, Chile, Indonesia, Japan, Mexico, Malaysia, New Zealand, South Korea, Papua New Guinea, the Philippines, Singapore, and Thailand. APEC is one of the few important governmental international organizations to which Taipei (q.v.) belongs and is unique for being one where representatives of Taipei and Beijing meet.

Asia-Pacific Regional Operations Center (ya-t'ai ying-yun chung-hsin). A plan approved by the government of the Republic of China (q.v.) in January 1995 and supported by President Lee Teng-hui (q.v.) to turn Taiwan into a regional business center or hub for many large companies. At first the emphasis was on telecommunications and manufacturing. The Center reflects Taiwan's economic orientation toward the Pacific Rim region as a counterpart of and competitor with the North American Free Trade Association and the European Union. The plan envisions six subcenters: for manufacturing, telecommunications, financial services, air transportation, sea transportation, and media services. The Council for Economic Planning and Development is responsible for the planning and coordination of projects, though operations centers are handled by the Ministry of Economic Affairs, Ministry of Transportation and Communications, Ministry of Finance, Central Bank of China (q.v.), and Government Information Office (q.v.).

In March 1995, the Council for Economic Planning and Development established the Coordination and Service Office for the Asia-Pacific Regional Operations Center to attract international companies to take advantage of the opportunities provided by the Center. In fact, several large global corporations have expressed a strong interest in or have set up or expanded operations there.

Asian Development Bank (ADB) (ya-chou k'ai-fa yin-hang). Organized in 1967 with its headquarters in Manila, the Republic of China was a founding member along with a number of other Asian nations plus Belgium, United Kingdom, Italy, the Netherlands, Switzerland, United States, and West Germany. After Taipei lost its membership in the World Bank and the International Monetary Fund, the ADB became the most important international organization in which Taiwan (q.v.) participated. In 1983, the People's Republic of China (PRC) asked to join and demanded that the Republic of China (q.v.) be expelled. Taipei (q.v.), however, had a stronger position to resist Beijing's demands than other international organizations inasmuch as it was a founding member and because the organization was established after the government of the Republic of China moved to Taiwan. Also, Washington supported Taipei's remaining in the ADB. In fact, in November 1983, the U.S. Congress passed an amendment to an appropriations bill stating that it was "the sense of Congress" that Taipei should remain a member. PRC officials at the time accused the United States of trying to create two Chinas.

In May 1985, the U.S. Senate passed another resolution stating that the Republic of China should not have to change its name to stay in the ADB, but the White House did not act accordingly. ADB officials then decided that the name "Republic of China" could not be used, and instead adopted the title "Taipei, China." Officials in Taiwan complained that the change was made without their permission. In subsequent meetings, Taiwan's officials attended under that title but used the name "Republic of China" on signs and in other places. Some regarded this as evidence of Taiwan's diplomatic revival and the success of its pragmatic diplomacy. Others saw it as a precedent for dealing with the issue of two Chinas.

In early 1989, Finance Minister Shirley Kuo (q.v.) attended an ADB meeting in China, the first time a government official from Taiwan attended any high-level meeting there.

Association for Public Policy Studies (APPS) (kung-kung cheng-tse yen-chiu-hui). A political association of opposition politicians which, in the spring of 1986 under You Ching's (q.v.) leadership, began to organize branches and behave like a political party. Some saw it as a further step in a process whereby the Tangwai (q.v.) became a de facto political party. APPS's precursor organization, the Association of Tangwai Elected Officials for the Study of Public Policy, was formed in 1984 and changed its name to broaden its base of support. During 1986, some Nationalist Party (q.v.) officials and government leaders called for banning APPS, but this did not happen.

Association for Relations Across the Taiwan Strait (ARATS) (hai-hsia liang-an kuan-hsi hsieh-hui). A semiofficial organization connected to the government of the People's Republic of China. Established in December 1991, ARATS is responsible for conducting "negotiations" or talks with Taiwan (q.v.), particularly with its "counterpart" the Straits Exchange Foundation (q.v.), on a variety of non-military issues. In November 1992, the two organizations agreed that each side could construct its own view of the one-China principle. After this agreement, in 1993, the Koo-Wang (q.v.) talks were held in Singapore.

Association for Taiwan Independence (tu-li t'ai-wan hui). An organization of Taiwanese living in Japan, founded in 1967 and advocating independence. It also advocated socialism. It was founded by Shih Ming (q.v.).

Association for the Study of China's Local Self-Government (chung-kuo ti-fang tse-chih yen-chiu-hui). An organization formed in 1958 by Taiwanese politicians to reform what they charged was corrupt electoral politics in Taiwan (q.v.). The organization was not approved by the government. In 1960, a number of Taiwanese members of the organization joined Lei Chen (q.v.) to form the China Democratic Party (q.v.).

Association of Taiwanese Culture (t'ai-wan wen-hua-hui). An organization of Taiwanese political activists formed in 1921 that sought to oppose Japanese rule. The membership split with nationalists, reformists and socialists going in different directions. Some members of the Association left and founded the Party of Taiwanese People (q.v.), which emphasized social reform through lobbying rather than class conflict.

Atayal. One of the high-mountain aborigine (q.v.) groups in Taiwan (q.v.), which, until recent times, had been warlike and practiced headhunting.

Atomic Energy Council (yuan-tse-neng wei-yuan-hui). A cabinet-level agency founded in 1955 and attached to the Executive Yuan (q.v.), it is empowered to deal with safety regulations, protection from radiation, and radioactive waste disposal and to conduct research in nuclear science and probe sources of nuclear energy.

August Communiqué (pa-yi-ch'i kung-pao). An agreement between the United States and the People's Republic of China concluded on August 17, 1982, wherein the United States agreed not to maintain a "long-term policy of arms sales to Taiwan" and pledged it would "not exceed, in either qualitative or quantitative terms, the level of those (arms) supplied in recent years." The United States at this time reiterated its policy of a peaceful solution only to the Taiwan question.

Some interpreted the communiqué as both dangerous and detrimental to Taiwan (q.v.). Others said it was merely an effort on the part of the United States government to help Deng Xiaoping who was under fire from hard-line leftists who were able to make trouble over the "Taiwan question" due to the fact that Deng had done little to bring about reunification and in the course of building close relations with the United

States seemed to make "bringing Taiwan back into the fold" less likely.

Immediately after the agreement was negotiated, President Ronald Reagan said he assumed that China had made a pledge seeking a peaceful solution only of the Taiwan matter. Deng said he had not. The communiqué was not signed and Department of State officials later said that it did not have standing in international law. U.S. arms sales to Taiwan continued and even at times increased, though U.S. officials said this could happen due to inflation and did not violate the communiqué.

Notwithstanding questions about the status of the agreement and charges of the U.S. not fulfilling its provisions, U.S. officials have often cited the document as one of the three communiqués that served, together with the Taiwan Relations Act (q.v.), as the formal underpinnings of U.S. China and Taiwan policy. Beijing agreed.

The communiqué seemed to be blatantly violated and even nullified by President George Bush's decision in late 1992 to sell F-16 (q.v.) fighter aircraft to Taipei (q.v.), and the subsequent delivery of the planes and other weapons. On the other hand, neither U.S. nor Chinese officials said this invalidated the communiqué, though both at times have suggested that the large U.S. arms sales to Taipei in 1993 and after contradicted or undermined it. During 1996, when China conducted missile tests in the Taiwan Strait (q.v.), several members of Congress declared that the Taiwan Relations Act was to be regarded as having a higher status than this or any of the other communiqués and pushed for even more arms deliveries to Taipei. No serious effort, however, was made to nullify or replace the communiqué.

August 23 Battle (pa-er-san pao-chan). The battle between Nationalist and Communist forces which started the second Offshore Islands Crisis in 1958. It began with an artillery bombardment of Quemoy (q.v.) from the mainland which lasted for 44 days.

- B -

Bashi Channel (pa-shih hai-hsia). Channel separating Taiwan (q.v.) and the Philippines, about 230 miles wide at its narrowest point.

"Black List" (hei-ming-tan). A list of persons barred from leaving or entering the Republic of China (q.v.). The government contended the list was kept for national security reasons and was legal based on Article 3 of the National Security Law, which states that persons suspected of endangering national security or social stability will not be allowed to leave or enter the country. Opposition politicians claimed the list was composed chiefly of opponents of the government or the ruling party, including political dissidents, and was not useful as a security measure. They also pointed out that the U.S. Department of State's human rights reports frequently cited and condemned the black list, giving the numbers each year of people affected by it. Controversy over the black list diminished in the late 1970s and early 1980s as it was cut in size and as its use declined in importance. In July 1982, Interior Minister Wu Poh-hsiung (q.v.) said the number on the list had been reduced from 282 to 5. The black list is still used, but now it is composed of names of people living in other countries involved in criminal activities and who are considered persona non grata in the Republic of China.

Bo Yang (1920-) Pen name for Kuo Yi-tung, a journalist, who was arrested after drawing an uncomplimentary cartoon of Chiang Kai-shek (q.v.) in 1968. At his trial he was also accused of trying to obtain classified military information and persuading a friend to remain in China rather than flee to Taiwan (q.v.). He was convicted and sentenced to jail and served nine years of an 18-year sentence. In 1986 he wrote the very controversial book *The Ugly Chinese People,* which was highly critical, many said insulting, of Chinese. The book was banned in China but not in Taiwan. In 1992, Bo Yang said that the Republic of China (q.v.) was the freest society in Chinese history.

Breakfast Club (tsao-tsan-hui). A group of Nationalist Party (q.v.) legislators and other leaders who in the late 1980s offered a more progressive alternative to ruling party policies. This party "faction," as some called it, was led by legislator Jaw

Shau-kong (q.v.). It was later replaced by the New KMT Alliance (q.v.).

Broadcasting Corporation of China (BCC) (chung-kuo kuang-po kung-szu). Established in 1950, BCC grew from a few stations to 33 broadcasting networks and 177 stations by 1985. It is currently the largest broadcasting system in Taiwan (q.v.). BCC sponsored Voice of Free China and Voice of Asia programs that were broadcast in Chinese and a number of other languages in short and medium wave to China and overseas. In 1996, the Legislative Yuan (q.v.) passed the Central Broadcasting System Statute that merged BCC's Voice of Free China with the Central Broadcasting System (q.v.).

Brotherhood Association (lao-kung lien-meng). A grassroots labor organization formed in the late 1980s from nine small labor unions, mostly in the chemical and fiber industries in northern Taiwan. It was Taiwan's first labor federation not affiliated or associated with the Nationalist Party (q.v.).

Bunun. One of the high-mountain aborigine (q.v.) groups in Taiwan residing mainly in the central part of the island. Until recent times, the Bunun tribe had been warlike and practiced head-hunting. The tribe was known for its extraction of certain teeth as a sign of social identity and adulthood.

- C -

Cairo Declaration (k'ai-luo hsuan-yen). A proclamation issued following the Cairo Conference in 1943, between U.S. president Roosevelt, British prime minister Churchill, and President Chiang Kai-shek (q.v.). The Declaration stated that "territories Japan has stolen . . . such as Manchuria, Formosa (q.v.), and the Pescadores" would be returned to their rightful owners. Soviet leader Joseph Stalin accepted these provisions at the subsequent Teheran Conference, and all parties confirmed the agreement at the Potsdam Conference in July 1945. Some say the Cairo Declaration is the legal basis to the Republic of China's claim to Taiwan (q.v.) or, by extension (meaning a successor government), the People's Republic of

China's claim —though the latter interpretation is not seen as having a strong legal standing. The promise that Taiwan would be taken from Japan and returned to China was reiterated in the Potsdam Declaration (q.v.) at the end of the war.

Campaign Assistance Committee (hou yuan hui). An organization of opposition political candidates who were active in or participated in national elections in 1980, 1983, and 1986 and through which non-KMT (q.v.) candidates endorsed and assisted fellow opposition candidates. This made it possible for Tang-wai (q.v.) candidates to have some of the advantages of a political party organization. Some called this a protopolitical party. Others said it was an illegal organization, since there was a ban against forming new political parties at this time.

Cathay Life Insurance (kuo-t'ai jen-shou). Taiwan's top life insurance company, it accounts for about 40 percent of the existing policies now in force in the country. It is also Taiwan's largest financial enterprise and the country's second-largest of any enterprise measured by sales.

CC Clique (cc-pai). A powerful faction in the Nationalist Party (q.v.) active both before and after its move to Taiwan in 1949. "CC" refers to the two Chens: Chen Li-fu and Chen Kuo-fu (qq.v.).

Central Advisory Committee (CAC) (chung-yang p'ing-yi wei-yuan-hui). A group of members of the Nationalist Party (q.v.) chosen at a meting of the Party Congress every four years. This body serves to advise the party on a variety of issues, but it is often seen as a party organization for retaining elder members. In 1996, the number of members of the CAC was increased to 286.

Central Bank of China (CBC) (chung-yang yin-hang). An organ of the central government attached to the Executive Yuan (q.v.) which is responsible for regulating banking operations and maintaining monetary stability. It also sets money supply and interest rates. In 1992, it set up its first overseas office in New York, mainly to acquire financial information. In 1994, CBC approved most foreign exchange derivative products. In late 1995 and early 1996, CBC took measures to protect the NT dollar and wedded it to the U.S. dollar at a rate of 27.5 to one, though during the subsequent "Asian meltdown" it allowed the NT dollar to float downward some.

Central Broadcasting System (CBS) (chung-yang kuang-po tian-t'ai). A large radio broadcasting organization with short- and medium-wave transmitters, which broadcasts to both Taiwan and China about political, economic, social, educational, and other issues. CBS broadcasts mainly in Mandarin, but also in several Chinese dialects. In 1996, CBS merged with the Voice of Free China, which was part of the Broadcasting Corporation of China (q.v.).

Central Committee (chung-yang wei-yuan-hui). A 232-member body of the Nationalist Party (q.v.) which makes decisions when the National Party Congress (q.v.) is not in session. It is chosen through secret ballot by delegates to the National Party Congress at meetings held every four years. Its functions include the execution of National Party Congress resolutions, administering party affairs, appointing and training party cadres, and enforcing party discipline. In reality, it is considered more powerful than the NPC, but, since it usually meets only once a year in plenary session, it is not considered the center of power in the ruling party. It, however, elects a Central Standing Committee (q.v.), which is widely regarded to be the center of authority and is made up of Taiwan's most powerful political leaders. The Democratic Progressive Party (q.v.) is organized in a similar way to the Nationalist Party and also has a central committee.

Central Daily News **(chung-yang jih-pao).** A major newspaper in Taiwan (q.v.) owned and operated by the Nationalist Party (q.v.). It claims a circulation of around one-half million. Many consider it the official party newspaper.

Central Election Commission (CEC) (chung-yang hsüan-chu wei-yuan-hui). Formed in 1980, the CEC is an organ of the central government, attached to the Executive Yuan (q.v.), and is given responsibility for supervising national and local elections, screening candidates, determining qualifications for office, recalling elected officials, and drafting or amending election laws. Its functions are set by the Public Officials Election and Recall Law (q.v.). The CEC is headed by a chairman and consists of members called commissioners who are nominated by the premier, approved by the president, and serve for a six-year term. The CEC's activities and rulings during election campaigns have often been controversial and have frequently been criticized by various candidates; however, the CEC generally has a good reputation for overseeing fair and orderly campaigns and elections.

Central News Agency (CNA) (chung-yang t'ung-hsün-she). CNA is Taiwan's oldest and largest news agency and its only nationwide news service. Prior to 1973, when it became a private corporation, it was both owned and operated by the Nationalist Party (q.v.). In 1996, CNA was reorganized and became a state-run corporation. It operates 24 hours a day and maintains 30 overseas offices and a number of overseas correspondents. CNA began computerized Chinese-language transmissions in 1983 and English transmissions in 1984. CNA provides audiovisual news services to local radio and cable television stations. It also provides 200,000 words over the Internet to Chinese and English-language newspapers daily. In the absence of diplomatic ties with many nations of the world, it functions as a quasi-official link between the Republic of China and other countries.

Central Reform Committee (CRC) (chung-yang kai-tsao wei-yuan-hui). Formed in July 1950 to overhaul the basic structure of the Nationalist Party (q.v.) in the wake of the Nationalist defeat by the Communists, its main goals were to get rid of factionalism in the Party, restore control over the Legislative Yuan and the Control Yuan (qq.v.), and improve party discipline. The CRC was composed of 16 young, well-educated, and able Nationalist Party members who were loyal to Chiang Kai-shek (q.v.). Their work on party reform was generally successful.

Central Standing Committee (CSC) (chung-yang ch'ang-wu wei-yuan-hui). A 33-member top decision-making organ of the Nationalist Party (q.v.), which many regard as including the most powerful and influential leaders in Taiwan; thus it is seen as the nation's most important locus of political decision making power and authority. The Central Standing Committee (earlier called the Central Executive Committee) functions for the Central Committee (q.v.) when it is not in session, though it is not controlled to any great extent by the latter, which meets only once yearly. The CSC meets weekly. Sixteen of its members are picked by the chairman of the Nationalist Party; 17 are chosen by members of the Central Committee.

In recent years, however, some analysts have said that the CSC has lost power to or has been "captured" by party-state economic bureaucrats and technocrats, as evidenced by the fact that it has had little to do recently with the formulation of commercial policies, regulation of the economy, and some other important policies that require a high degree of specialized or technical knowledge. Those who challenge this view say that it has promoted democratization both in the party and in the government, and its members are highly qualified and do not reflect entrenched interests now that it is elected every year.

The 1988 Central Standing Committee was for the first time composed of a majority of Taiwanese; some saw this as significant and reflecting the transfer of political power from Mainland Chinese to Taiwanese (qq.v.). The 1993 and 1997 Central Standing Committees gained an even larger proportion of Taiwanese.

Chang, Carson (1887-1969). Considered the primary author of the Constitution (q.v.) of the Republic of China (q.v.), he was influenced by the American founders' political thoughts and the organization of the Weimer republic and, of course, Sun Yat-sen's (q.v.) teachings and writings.

Chang Chun-hung (1938-). Chosen secretary-general of the Democratic Progressive Party (q.v.) in 1988, Chang was a well-known opposition political figure and editor of the magazines *The Intellectual* and *Taiwan Political Review* (qq.v.). He was jailed from 1979 to 1987 for his involvement in the Kao-hsiung Incident (q.v.).

Chang Hsiao-Yen (1941-). Also known as John Chang, he is currently secretary-general of the Nationalist Party (q.v.). Chang has served as vice foreign minister, director of the cultural division of the Nationalist Party, foreign minister, and vice-premier. Chang is the illegitimate son of Chiang Ching-kuo (q.v.).

Chang King-Yu (1937-). Chairman of the Mainland Affairs Council (q.v.) from February 1996 to the present, he has served as president of National Chengchi University (q.v.), director-general of the Institute of International Relations (q.v.) at that university, and director general of the Government Information Office (q.v.).

Chang Tsan-hung (1936-). Founder of the U.S.-based World United Formosans for Independence (q.v.). He was sentenced to prison in 1976 for masterminding a letter-bomb attack which blew off the hand of Shieh Tung-min (q.v.), then Taiwan provincial governor. He is currently the mayor of Tainan and, during the Legislative Yuan (q.v.) and metropolitan mayor and city council elections in 1998, had a referendum put on the ballot in Tainan regarding Taiwan's independence, causing considerable controversy and upsetting leaders in the People's Republic of China.

Chang Yung-fa (1927-). Chairman of Evergreen Group (q.v.), his personal wealth is valued at over U.S.$1 billion.

Chao Yao-tung (1916-). National policy advisor for the president, Chao was minister of economic affairs from 1981 to 1984 and concurrently chairman of the Council for Economic Planning and Development (q.v.) and minister of state from 1984 to 1988. He had considerable influence on Taiwan's economic policies.

Chen Cheng (1907-1965). A general in the Nationalist Chinese military and Chiang Kai-shek (q.v.) loyalist, Chen was sent to Taiwan (q.v.) in 1948 to fortify the island in preparation for the Nationalist retreat. In December 1948, he was appointed the third governor of Taiwan under the rule of the government of the Republic of China (q.v.). He served as premier from 1950 to 1954 and 1958 to 1963. In 1954, he was elected vice president of the Republic of China, the first elected in Taiwan. Chen was considered the most powerful official in Taiwan in the 1950s and 1960s after Chiang Kai-shek. He is also credited with Taiwan's successful land reform (q.v.) and the country's early economic modernization. He is the father of Chen Li-an (q.v.).

Chen Chung-ho. A sugar trader in Kaohsiung (q.v.) before Japan controlled Taiwan (q.v.), he dominated that trade thereafter. He founded the Hohsing Sugar Company and later the Taiwan Sugar Company and the Hsinhsiung Sugar Company. Chen supported Japan during the Sino-Japanese War and during the Russo-Japanese War.

Chen Kuo-fu (1891-1951). A high-ranking official in the Nationalist Party (q.v.) and very close associate of Chiang Kai-shek (q.v.) for many years, Chen opposed many reforms proposed by members of the Nationalist Party before it moved to Taiwan (q.v.) and after. See also CC Clique.

Chen Li-an (1937-). Son of Chen Cheng (q.v.) and long regarded as one of Taiwan's young and promising politicians, Chen served as president of the Control Yuan (q.v.) from 1993 to 1995, having been minister of national defense from 1990 to 1993, minister of economic affairs from 1988 to 1990, chairman of the National Science Council (q.v.) from 1984 to 1988, and deputy secretary-general of the Central Committee of the Nationalist Party (qq.v.) from 1980 to 1984. In 1996, he left the Nationalist Party and ran for president as an independent against Lee Teng-hui (q.v.) and two other presidential candidates, but especially against Lee. He ran on a platform of clean government. He was also known as a devout Buddhist and won sympathy or support from many people for that reason. His vice presidential running mate was Wang Ching-feng (q.v.), the first female to run for such a high office. Chen won 9.97 percent of the popular vote—fourth among the four presidential candidates.

Chen Li-fu (1900-). A close associate of Chiang Kai-shek (q.v.), he held a number of top positions in the Nationalist Party (q.v.) and the government prior to 1949. He served as minister of state from 1948 to 1950. See also CC Clique.

Chen Shui-bian (1951-). Elected mayor of Taipei (q.v.) in 1994 as the candidate of the Democratic Progressive Party (DPP) (q.v.), his victory gave control of the capital city for the first time to a member of an opposition party. Chen had long been a DPP activist, but campaigned for mayor more on his qualifications. Chen had been a member of the Taipei City Council from 1981 to 1985 and was a member of the Legislative Yuan (q.v.) from 1989 to 1994. He strongly supported democratic reform in Taiwan and early on opposed Article 100 (q.v.). He has avoided formal ties with the two main factions of the DPP, but has been closer to the Formosa faction (q.v.). In 1991 he founded the Justice Alliance "group" in the DPP, which has been called another faction, though its members have also tried to avoid factionalism and, in fact, have made efforts to patch up factional differences in the party. Chen has been praised for his job as mayor and has been touted as a likely candidate for the presidency in 2000. However, he lost a reelection bid for the Taipei mayorship in 1998.

Chen Yi (1833-1950). A Nationalist military general who became the first governor of Taiwan (q.v.) after it became part of the Republic of China (q.v.) following World War II. He had gained Chiang Kai-shek's (q.v.) friendship after joining him in 1927 during the Northern Expedition. He was the leading executive authority in Taiwan before and during the February 28, 1947, or *er er ba* (q.v) uprising and the massacre that followed in March and is widely blamed for that incident. After the incident, Chiang Kai-shek recalled him to the mainland and gave him a nominal post. He was subsequently made governor of Chekiang Province. Later, however, because of his alleged connivance with the Communists and being convinced of his responsibility for the February 28 incident, Chiang had him arrested, and, on June 18, 1950, brought before a firing squad in Taiwan and executed. Chen is regarded by most historians and the majority of Taiwanese (q.v.) as a grossly incompetent leader who caused Taiwan's economic, social, and political situation to deteriorate after World War II and who, due to his poor performance in office, precipitated the *er er ba* incident. Some historians, however, say that his failings resulted from his hiring corrupt subordinates and not understanding the fact that Taiwan's population had absorbed Japanese culture during a 50-year period as a colony of Japan, while thinking that he could sinicize the island quickly. In addition, he mistakenly tried to institute socialist policies in Taiwan and was more concerned about what was happening on the Chinese mainland than events in Taiwan during his tenure as governor.

Cheng Ch'eng-kung (1624-1662). Also commonly known as Koxinga, Cheng was born in Japan of a Japanese mother and Cheng Chi-lung, a Chinese pirate operating from a base in Taiwan who was later appointed by the Chinese Emperor Sze Tsung to command remnant Ming Dynasty naval forces in a last-ditch effort to prevent the Manchus from conquering China. Cheng Ch'eng-kung inherited his father's forces and recruited more until he had an army of 100,000 and an armada

The Dictionary / 55

of 3,000 vessels. From 1648 (four years after the Ming Dynasty fell) to 1658, he fought the Manchus in the hope of restoring the Ming Dynasty. He nearly captured the city of Nanking at one point. Abandoning this effort, in 1661, he attacked the Dutch stronghold of Zeelandia (q.v.). After nearly two years of fighting, the Dutch conceded defeat and concluded an agreement to leave—ending 38 years of Dutch colonial rule of Taiwan.

Cheng Ch'eng-kung then established a Ming-style government on Taiwan (q.v.), including a Chinese legal system, a court, and the recruitment of scholars as advisors. He also promoted Chinese culture. His political system, however, was more a feudal system than a Chinese bureaucratic system. Cheng encouraged Chinese migration to Taiwan, thus increasing the Chinese population. He promoted trade with Japan, the Philippines, and other areas of Asia.

Still clinging to the goal of ridding China of Manchu rule and in an effort to accomplish this, Cheng tried to enlist support from Chinese living in the Philippines. This angered the Spanish, who killed 10,000 Chinese residents there. They then informed Cheng they had killed all Chinese in the Philippines, causing, according to some accounts, Cheng to have a heart attack and die. In any event, Cheng passed away at a young age—38. Had he lived he may have accomplished much more. Nevertheless, he had a greater impact on Taiwan's history than perhaps any other single person, and for that reason he is acclaimed as a hero in Taiwan. His son, Cheng Ching (q.v.), assumed power after he died.

Cheng Ching (1642-1681). Cheng Ch'eng-kung's (q.v.) son, who from a power base in Fukien Province vied with his uncle on Taiwan for succession after his father's death. He won, and continued his father's reign in Taiwan and his father's mission of ridding China of the Manchus. Like his father, he failed in that effort, and like his father, he died at a young age. Upon his death and in large part because of trying to install an illegitimate son as heir, the Cheng family rule of Taiwan (q.v.) disintegrated, and Manchu troops conquered the island in 1683.

Chi Cheng (1944-). A former secretary-general of the Republic of China's Track and Field Association and former member of the Legislative Yuan (q.v.), she broke or set a number of world records in women's track events in the 1970s.

Chia Shan Project (chia-shan chi-hua). A secret air force base built in the mountains in eastern Taiwan near Hualien. Begun in the mid-1980s it was partially completed in 1990 when information about the base, which could hide jet fighter planes and would presumably be a command headquarters in the event of war with the People's Republic of China, was made public.

Chianan Irrigation Association (chia-nan ta-chuan hsieh-hui). The largest of 15 irrigation associations in Taiwan (q.v.), it supplies water for the municipality of Tainan and the county of Chiayi. Like some other irrigation associations it is considered an interest group of some importance. See also Chianan Irrigation System.

Chianan Irrigation System (chia-nan ta-chuan). A large irrigation project started by the Japanese in 1920 and finished in 1930, it directed water from the Tsengwen River into an artificial Coral Reservoir that was formed by a major dam. The system converted 68,000 acres of poor land on the west coast of Taiwan into fertile farmland that could grow rice and sugar cane. It had a marked positive impact on Taiwan's agriculture. See also Chianan Irrigation Association.

Chiang Ching-kuo (1909-1988). Best known as Chiang Kai-shek's (q.v.) eldest son and the nation's third president, serving from 1978 until his death in January 1988. He is also regarded as Taiwan's foremost political reformer.

Fondly known as CCK, he was sent by his father to the Soviet Union at the age of 16 where he studied at the Sun Yat-sen University in Moscow. Subsequently, when relations between the elder Chiang and Stalin soured he became a virtual hostage. As a consequence he suffered considerable hardship for a number of years in the Soviet Union. In 1937, he was allowed to return to China, with his Russian wife, and was given various political and leadership positions by his father to determine his leadership abilities.

After the government moved to Taiwan in 1949, he became director of the political department of the Nationalist

Party (q.v.) and subsequently served in various other positions, including deputy general-secretary of the National Security Council (q.v.), minister of state, deputy minister of national defense, deputy premier, and head of the China Youth Corps (q.v.).

In 1972, he became premier and from that office launched various kinds of reform measures, including an anticorruption campaign and an "affirmative action" program to recruit more Taiwanese into government and the ruling Nationalist Party. He subsequently appointed a Taiwanese provincial governor and vice president. He also issued guidelines for democratization of the political system. He assumed more authority as his father's health deteriorated, particularly after his father's death in 1975. From 1975 to 1978, he was considered the Republic of China's top leader, even though he was not the nation's president, by virtue of his being head of the ruling party and premier. He was elected president in 1978 and again in 1984. In 1986, CCK organized a task force to recommend political reforms that included lifting the ban on forming new political parties, ending martial law (q.v.), and reorganizing the government's parliamentary bodies. The Democratic Progressive Party (q.v.) formed shortly after this announcement. Martial law was terminated the next year. Meanwhile he established a system of rotating military officers to limit their influence in politics. In 1984, he chose Lee Teng-hui (q.v.) as his vice president and made him his de facto successor.

Chiang Ching-kuo was considered a quiet, austere, no-nonsense, man-of-the-people person, in many ways quite unlike his father. He is widely regarded as the force behind Taiwan's economic miracle and even more so behind its political modernization and democratization.

Chiang Ching-kuo Foundation (chiang ching-kuo chi-chin-hui). A foundation, whose full name is the Chiang Ching-kuo Foundation for International Scholarly Exchange, which is headquartered in Taipei (q.v.) with a regional office in McLean, Virginia, in the United States. It was established in 1989 in memory of the late President Chiang Ching-kuo (q.v.) to promote the study of Chinese culture and society. Operating funds come from interest on an endowment provided by both private and public sources. The Foundation provides grants to universities, institutes, museums, and individuals.

Chiang Kai-shek (1887-1975). Best known as the president of the Republic of China (q.v.) when the Nationalist Party (q.v) ruled China before 1949 and Taiwan (q.v.) after that until 1975. Chiang was born in Chekiang Province and was named Juiyuan by his grandfather and Chung-cheng by his mother. He later took the name Chieh-shih, which is written "Kai-shek" in Cantonese. Chiang Kai-shek's father died when he was nine and he was raised by his mother. Chiang was married twice. His eldest son, Chiang Ching-kuo, was from his first marriage. He later married Soong Mayling (q.v.). They, however, had no children. He allegedly fathered another son, Chiang Wei-kuo (q.v.), by a Japanese woman, though this son stated just before his own death that Chiang was not his father.

Chiang received a local education, but went to Japan at the age of 19 to study. In 1908, while in Japan, he joined the Tung Meng Hui—a revolutionary organization led by Sun Yat-sen (q.v.) that overthrew the Manchu Dynasty in 1911. That event prompted Chiang to return to China, whereupon he assumed command of a military unit and quickly built a reputation as a military leader. He also cemented a very close relationship with Sun Yat-sen and his followers and gained political power and a leadership position in the Nationalist Party (q.v.).

After Sun Yat-sen's death in 1925, Chiang struggled briefly to become his successor. He succeeded, after which, in 1926, he launched the Northern Expedition from South China to expel the warlord government in Peking and unify the country—a task he accomplished in 1928. Chiang at that point became the head of the Nationalist government and the ruler of China. During the 1930s and 1940s, Chiang fought the Japanese and the Chinese Communists while trying to prevent China's disintegration. He managed to tie down a large number of Japanese troops during World War II, for which the United States was very grateful, though Japan was ultimately defeated at sea and as a result of bombing the home islands by the United States. For that reason Chiang attained little glory from the war, which had caused his regime and China hardship and very serious problems. Partly as a result, but due also to corruption among his followers and mistaken policies, he was defeated by the Communists and resigned from the presidency of the Republic of China in 1949.

He and many of his supporters in the Nationalist government, the Nationalist Party, and the military subsequently fled to Taiwan. In March 1950, Chiang returned to power, once again assuming the presidency of the Republic of China, which no longer governed China but only Taiwan, the Pescadores, and the Offshore Islands (qq.v.). It was Chiang's dream to recover China, or the mainland, from the Communists. The dream, however, faded with time because of the strength of Mao's military in the newly formed People's Republic of China, the viability of Mao's government, and lack of support from the United States. Also this goal never had much support in Taiwan from locally born Chinese or Taiwanese (q.v.). Chiang himself seemed to revise, or perhaps give up, this hope, when, in the late 1950s, he referred to the goal as "seventy percent political" and focused more of his attention on economic development.

Meanwhile, Chiang remained adamant about retaining the Offshore Islands, notwithstanding attempts by Mao to seize the islands leading to global crises in 1954-55 and 1958. Chiang saw them as stepping stones to return to China and as important symbols. Throughout his life, but varying through time, Chiang had considerable support in the United States in the form of the China Lobby (q.v.); but there were also many who criticized him. His support abroad, especially his claim to be the legitimate ruler of all of China, began to wane in the 1960s, but it was given respite by the Cultural Revolution in China and the Vietnam War. He was criticized at home when the Republic of China lost the China seat in the United Nations in 1971.

Chiang remained president of the Republic of China and head of the Nationalist Party until his death in April 1975. Though criticized for his misrule of China during the 1940s, his defeat in China at the hands of the Communists, and, later, his authoritarian-style rule in Taiwan, Chiang is credited with launching and building Taiwan's economic miracle and for starting, though belatedly according to some critics, its political development.

Chiang groomed his son, Chiang Ching-kuo (q.v.), to be head of the Nationalist Party and the nation's leader after his death and to carry on his policies, even though Yen Chia-kan (q.v.), who was vice president at the time, succeeded him as president.

Chiang Kai-shek International Airport (chung-cheng kuo-chi fei-chi-ch'ang). Located at Taoyuan, it is the larger of Taiwan's two international airports. It serves Taipei (q.v.) and northern Taiwan (q.v.). It was one of six major transportation projects completed in the 1980s.

Chiang Kai-shek, Madame. See Soong Mayling.

Chiang Kai-shek's Birthday (chiang-kung yen-chang chi-nien-jih). October 31, an official holiday in Taiwan.

Chiang Peng-chien (1940-). One of the founders and first chairman of the Democratic Progressive Party (q.v.), he held the post from 1986 to 1987. Chiang also served in the Legislative Yuan (q.v.) from 1984 to 1987 and was the founding president of the Taiwan Human Rights Association (q.v.). Chiang is currently a member of the Control Yuan (q.v.).

Chiang Pin-kun (1932-). Currently chairman of Council for Economic Planning and Development and minister of State, Chiang, also known as P.K. Chiang, was former minister of economic affairs from 1993 to 1996. He is considered one of the country's top leaders in economic affairs and a person with a good political future.

Chiang Wei-kuo (1915-1997). Also known as Wego Chiang, he was long regarded as Chiang Kai-shek's (q.v.) second son (by a Japanese women to whom Chiang Kai-shek was not married) and half brother of Chiang Ching-kuo (q.v.). He was a general in the Army of the Republic of China and in 1986 became secretary-general of the National Security Council (q.v.). In 1990, together with Lin Yang-kang (q.v.), he (as a possible vice presidential candidate) presented a challenge to President Lee Teng-hui (q.v.). However, he and Lin subsequently withdrew their candidacies and the National Assembly (q.v.) voted for the reelection of Lee as president. In 1997, shortly before his death, he declared publicly that he was not Chiang Kai-shek's son but rather the son of a close friend of Chiang's.

Chiayi. One of Taiwan's five largest cities administered by Taiwan Province, located in south-central Taiwan (q.v.).

Chieh Yen Fa. Literally a command or warning of strictness. It is usually translated as an emergency decree in Taiwan (q.v.) but martial law (q.v.) elsewhere.

Chien Fu (1935-). Also known as Frederick Chien, he is currently president of the Control Yuan (q.v.), having served as speaker of the National Assembly (q.v.) from 1996 to 1998 and minister of foreign affairs from 1990 until 1996. He had previously been secretary-general of the Council for Economic Planning and Development (q.v.) from 1988 and prior to that was the Republic of China's "unofficial ambassador" to the United States. He is best known for his role in the conduct of the nation's diplomacy for a period of more than two decades. He is also the author of several books and numerous articles and speeches on international and foreign affairs.

China Airlines (CAL) (chung-hua hang-kung kung-szu). A government-owned domestic and international airline in Taiwan (q.v.) that was long the only official flag carrier of the Republic of China (q.v.).

China Democratic Party (chung-kuo min-chu-tang). A political party founded in 1960 by Lei Chen (q.v.), which was the first serious attempt to organize an opposition to the Nationalist Party (q.v.). The formation of a new party being illegal at the time, the party was immediately disbanded.

China Democratic Socialist Party (chung-kuo min-chu she-hui-tang). See Democratic Socialist Party.

China Development Corporation (CDC) (chung-kuo k'ai fa kung-szu). A holding company run by the ruling Nationalist Party (q.v.) that has been involved in investing, construction, and other commercial enterprises. In 1997, it won a contract to build the Taipei International Financial Center in Taipei (q.v.), which will include building Taiwan's tallest building. It is also said to be the venture-capital arm of the Nationalist Party that invests in other countries and has been responsible for Taiwan's sizeable capitalization of projects and loans in Southeast Asia. Liu Tai-ying (q.v.) is the chairman of CDC.

China External Trade Development Council (CETDC) (chung-hua-min-kuo tui-wai mao-yi fa-chan hsieh-hui). The principal organization in Taiwan (q.v.) established to facilitate cooperation between business and government, it also maintains trade offices abroad and promotes bilateral economic relations. It is a semiofficial organization. CETDC gathers trade information, conducts market research, and promotes Taiwan-made products. It helps foreign nations and local governmental organizations in other countries (including state governments in the United States) establish offices in the World Trade Center (see Taipei International Convention Center) in Taipei (q.v.) and improve trade relations with Taiwan.

China Lobby (chung-kuo yu-shuo t'uan). Formed in the summer of 1940 by T.V. Soong, Madame Chiang Kai-shek's (q.v.) brother, in an effort to get U.S. support for the Republic of China (q.v.) in the war against Japan. It later became known as a group of influential people in the United States, especially Republicans, who supported the Nationalist Chinese against the Communist Chinese, both before and after they fled to Taiwan (q.v.). In the 1970s, it lost much of its influence, many say because its supporters in the United States had lost their political clout. Others said it was no longer needed in view of the fact that Taiwan had become popular in the United States due to its democratization.

China News **(yin-wen chung-kuo jih-pao).** One of Taiwan's two major English-language newspapers.

China Post **(chung-kuo yu-pao).** One of Taiwan's two major English-language newspapers.

China Shipbuilding Corporation (chung-kuo tsao-ch'uan ku-fen yu-hsien-kung-szu). Taiwan's largest shipbuilding company and formerly one of Taiwan's largest state-owned companies, it produces both civilian and naval craft.

China Steel Corporation (chung-kuo kang-t'ieh kung-szu). Taiwan's largest steel producer, formerly a state-owned company.

China Television Company (CTV) (chung-kuo tian-shih ku-fen yu-hsien kung-szu). The second television network established in

Taiwan (q.v.), Broadcasting Corporation of China (q.v.) was its major shareholder. It had, and retains, close ties with the Nationalist Party (q.v.), which some critics charge controls its programs and its political views. It is now one of four major television broadcasters.

China Tide (ch'iao-liu). A reformist literary and political magazine that began publishing in the early 1970s, including articles on Taiwan's history, society, economic development, and international relations. It propagated what became known as the "native soil movement," which called for the restoration of a dying agrarian society and romanticized the lives of farmers, fishermen, and workers. Some of the contributors later joined the Democratic Progressive Party (q.v.). The magazine also called for the reunification of Taiwan (q.v.) with China and showed sympathy toward the People's Republic of China. Some of its staff and supporters joined the labor movement in the mid-1980s and helped form the Labor Party (q.v.).

China Times (chung-kuo shih-pao). One of the two largest Chinese-language newspapers in Taiwan (q.v.). The China Times organization also publishes the *China Times Weekly*, the *China Times Express,* and a number of other publications. In September 1995 the company went digital with the China Times Website. In 1996, *China Times* reported a circulation of over 1.2 million. The *China Times* is considered moderate but politically slightly to the left of its main rival, the *United Daily News* (q.v.). Its publisher, Yu Chi-chung, is also politically influential through holding a high position in the Nationalist Party (q.v.).

China Trust (chung-kuo hsin-t'uo). Taiwan's largest private bank, operated by Jeffrey Koo, nephew of Koo Chen-fu (q.v.).

China Youth Corps (CYC) (chung-kuo ch'ing-nien fan-kung chiu-kuo-t'uan). A non-governmental, but quite politically oriented organization, formed in Taiwan in 1952 by Chiang Kai-shek (q.v.) in response to the failures of the Nationalist government to attract and maintain the support of the youth in China during the war against the Communists. Chiang Ching-kuo (q.v.) served as director-general until 1973, after which CYC was headed by Lee Huan (q.v.) and then Sung Shih-hsuan. Its main functions during the early years were to administer reserve officer training programs on college and university campuses and in high schools and manage young peoples' organizations. After 1957, it began to focus more on youth work and emphasized culture, sports, and recreational activities. In 1967, it expanded its functions to factories and towns and built youth activity centers. Since 1992, CYC has organized cultural and educational exchanges with China.

CYC operates a wire service and a broadcasting station and publishes journals. It runs 23 youth activity centers or retreats. It has close ties to the Nationalist Party (q.v.), and its leaders have been both politically active and influential. In many of its projects and endeavors it works with the ministries of defense, education, and interior as well as the Overseas Chinese Affairs Commission (q.v.). It is regarded as both an anti-Communist mass organization and a civic organization similar to the Boy Scouts of America.

China Youth Party (CYP) (chung-kuo ch'ing-nien-tang). A political party that formed in China in 1923 and moved to Taiwan in 1949 after the Nationalist defeat. It was formally called an opposition party, though many felt it served as only token opposition to the Nationalist Party (q.v.). Before the formation of the Democratic Progressive Party (q.v.) it was the larger of two opposition parties in Taiwan. In 1960, two of its members were involved in forming the China Democratic Party (q.v.). In 1982, Taiwanese (q.v.) members tried to wrest control of the party from Mainland Chinese (q.v.) party leaders, but failed. In 1987, it held seven nonelective seats in the Legislative Yuan (q.v.) and 45 in the National Assembly (q.v.), but as a result of the 1989 election it lost most of its Legislative Yuan seats. It has had an estimated membership of 10,000. In recent years the CYP has declined dramatically in visibility and importance and has become generally inactive.

Chinese Association for Human Rights (chung-hua jen-ch'uan hsieh-hui). A national human rights organization, founded in Taiwan in 1979 by the efforts of Han Lih-wu (q.v.), it is concerned with human rights problems in both Taiwan and China. A provincial section was established in 1985 in Taichung, and another branch was established in Kaohsiung (q.v.) in 1988. The organization sponsors seminars, legal consultations, and various publications. See also Taiwan Human Rights Association.

Chinese Federation of Labor (CFL) (chung-kuo lao-kung tsung-hui). A labor organization founded in 1950 and restructured in 1975, it controls a number of local labor organizations nominally affiliated with the Federation. This includes several national and local unions in Taiwan's export processing zones (q.v.). The Federation is closely linked to the Nationalist Party (q.v.), and its president has served in the Legislative Yuan (q.v.) representing both the Nationalist Party and labor. Critics say that the CFL, because of ties with the ruling party and the government and the fact that it receives subsidies from the government, in addition to its representatives being from occupational unions with many owning businesses, it is weak in fighting for labor rights.

Chinese National Federation of Industries (kung-shang-yeh tsung-hui). Established in 1948 it is one of the oldest, largest, and most influential interest groups in Taiwan (q.v.), according to a law representing all industrial organizations in Taiwan.

Chinese New Year (ch'un-chieh). Also called Lunar New Year, this is the most important holiday of the year in Taiwan (q.v.). It is the first day of the lunar year, usually falling in January or February using the solar calendar. Most people return home and eat and talk with relatives.

Chinese Petroleum Corporation (CPC) (chung-kuo shih-yu hua-hsueh kung-yeh kai-fa ku-fen yu-hsien kung-szu). A state-owned corporation founded in Shanghai in 1946 which moved to Taiwan (q.v.), it is responsible for petroleum and natural gas exploration, importing, and marketing. It is the largest non-U.S. firm in the world without publicly traded stock. It is also Taiwan's largest company measured by sales. In 1997, sales exceeded U.S.$12 billion. CPC is owned by the Ministry of Economic Affairs, but will be privatized in 2001.

Chinese Social Democratic Party (CSDP) (chung-hua she-hui min-chu tang). A political party formed in 1990 by Ju Gao-jeng (q.v.). The CSDP was the third-largest party in terms of the number of candidates it nominated for the 1991 National Assembly (q.v.) election, and was one of four parties to receive time allotted for television advertising during that campaign. However, receiving just over 2 percent of the popular vote, it failed to win enough seats to qualify for party-allocated national representatives. A left-of-center party advocating many of the tenets of European social democratic parties, the CSDP declined in subsequent years and disappeared from Taiwan's political scene. Its founder later joined the New Party (q.v.).

Chinese Taipei Olympic Committee (CTOC) (chung-hua ao-lin-p'i-k'e wei-yuan-hui). An organization in Taiwan (q.v.) responsible for international amateur sports activities and liaison with the International Olympic Committee. It has exclusive powers to organize participation in the Olympic Games, the Asian Games, and other sports activities. It has 58 members, most of whom are presidents of national sports associations. CTOC has been involved in a number of feuds and controversies over the Republic of China's status in international sports competition, especially the Olympic Games, because the People's Republic of China insists that the Republic of China (q.v.) cannot use its official name or claim national status in international sports contests.

Chinese Television System (CTS) (chung-hua tian-shih ku-fen yu-hsien kung-szu). Established in 1970 from a public education television network set up by the Ministry of Education in 1962, it was co-owned by the Ministry of Education and the Ministry of Defense but gradually became privatized. It now broadcasts both educational programs and regular entertainment. It is the only station to broadcast in both VHS and UHF, the latter being used for educational programs.

Ching Chuan Kang Air Base (ching-ch'uan-kang k'ung-chün chi-ti). A large air base in central Taiwan (q.v.) near Taichung, used in part by U.S. forces until their departure in the late 1970s. At the peak of U.S. involvement in Vietnam, there were 10,000 U.S. personnel on the base. In 1965, it was enlarged to accommodate large planes. While B-52s did not use the base, as some said Taipei (q.v.) had hoped, it was used by C-130s and other planes that were part of the U.S.-Vietnam War effort. The base is now used by the Republic of China's Air Force.

Ching-kuo. See Indigenous Defense Fighter.

Chiou I-jen (1950-). Currently the secretary general of the Democratic Progressive Party (DPP) (q.v.), he was a leader of the "new generation" faction of Tangwai (q.v.) and later became a founding member and then deputy general director of the DPP. He helped organize a protest demonstration against Formosa Plastics (q.v.) in 1986 and a farmers' protest on May 20, 1988, that became known as the largest public political demonstration up to that time. He is also currently the leader of the DPP's more radical New Tide faction (q.v). Chiou has been a strong proponent of the view that Taiwan (q.v.) must become independent before it can democratize successfully.

Chiu Chuang-huan (1925-). Currently a senior advisor to the president, Chiu served as minister of interior from 1978 to 1981, vice-premier from 1981 to 1984, and governor of Taiwan (q.v.) from 1984 to 1990. He was regarded for many years as one of Taiwan's top political elite.

Chung Sha. See Macclesfield Bank.

Chunghua Telecom (CHT) (chung-hua tien-hsin). One of Taiwan's three largest state-owned enterprises founded in 1966 in a spin-off from the Directorate General of Telecommunications, it operates telephone services throughout the country, owning 100 percent of the fixed telephone services and a huge portion of the cellular telephone and pager services. It is owned by the Ministry of Transportation and Communications, but it is to be privatized by 2001.

Chungli Incident (chung-li shih-chien). A mass protest that led to violence in the city of Chungli in 1977, precipitated by reports of irregularities or cheating in vote counting, in particular involving the candidacy of Hsu Hsin-liang (q.v.). An angry crowd overturned and burned cars and set fire to a police station. One person was killed and several others were injured. The protest was anti-KMT (q.v.) and was the largest in scale since February 1947. Some observers have seen the incident as the beginning of a unified opposition movement in Taiwan (q.v.). See also Tangwai.

Chungshan Institute of Science and Technology (chung-shan h'o-hsueh yen-chiu-yuan). One of the nation's foremost research institutes and one devoted to the development of advanced military equipment and weapons. Its scientists have engineered and built the Hsiung-feng I and II surface-to-air missiles, the Tien-kung surface-to-air missile, the Tien-chien air-to-air missile, and a number of other sophisticated weapons. The Institute has over 6,000 scientists and a large facility at Lungtan in Taoyuan County. The government is in the process of integrating military and other research and development and this will probably result in a bigger role for the Institute along with more private sector involvement.

Chunghsing New Town (chung-hsing hsin-ts'un). The administrative center of the Taiwan provincial government, located near Taichung (q.v.).

Civic Organizations Law (kung-min szu-chih-fa). Titled in full the Civic Organizations Law During the Period of National Mobilization for the Suppression of Communist Rebellion, this legislation was revised in 1989 to allow new political parties to form in a follow-up to President Chiang Ching-kuo's (q.v.) request of June 1986 that the ban on political parties be lifted. Although the Democratic Progressive Party (q.v.) was already founded in 1986 and participated in the national election that year, and furthermore was widely recognized as a political party, it and other new political parties did not become legal until 1989. At that time a host of other new political parties also formed.

Coastal Patrol General Headquarters (hai-hsun tsung-pu). Created in 1992 to control smuggling, illegal entry and exit, and infiltration, it is administratively under the Corps Area Command. It was established at the time of dissolution of the Garrison Command (q.v.) and assumed some of its functions.

Coastal Removal Policy (hai-chin). Policy of the Manchu government of China established in 1660 to force the coastal residents of China to move 30 to 50 *li* (one-third of a mile) in-land in order to prevent them from making contact with and supporting Cheng Ch'eng-kung (q.v.). As a result of this policy many people were forced to abandon their homes and their rice crops and yet were still taxed. The economic dislocation and hardship in the long run caused more migration of China's coastal population living near the Taiwan Strait to Taiwan (q.v.).

Committee on Overseas Economic Cooperation (hai-wai ching-chi ho-tso wei-yuan-hui). An organization established by the Ministry of Economic Affairs to assist developing nations, mainly in Central and South America and Southeast Asia, and, in the process, to use Taiwan's economic clout to pursue foreign policy goals, including establishing informal ties or even diplomatic recognition with other countries.

Committee on the Discipline of Public Functionaries (kung-wu yuan ch'eng-chieh wei-yuan-hui). A committee of the Judicial Yuan (q.v.) that serves as a check on decisions made by the Control Yuan (q.v.) involving impeachment and dismissal of public civilian officials.

Constitution Day (hsing-hsien chi-nien-jih). December 25, an official holiday in the Republic of China. This day was chosen in some part to give foreigners working in Taiwan a vacation day to celebrate Christmas.

Constitution of the Republic of China (chung-hua-min-kuo hsien-fa). Written in 1946 and promulgated on January 1, 1947 when the government of the Republic of China ruled the mainland as well as Taiwan, it was modeled in large part after the U.S. Constitution particularly inasmuch as it sets forth provisions for a republican form of government, though the government designed by this constitution is a mixture of a presidential and cabinet system. Also, instead of three branches of government, the Constitution provides for five, adding branches that performed major government functions in ancient China. (See Control Yuan and Examination Yuan.) It contains provision for many of the civil and political liberties found in the U.S. Constitution's Bill of Rights and incorporates the political philosophy of Sun Yat-sen (q.v.), especially his teachings found in *The Three Principles of the People* (q.v.). However, some of its important provisions, especially guarantees of civil and political rights, were for some time nullified or held in abeyance by the "Temporary Provisions" (q.v.) and by the declaration of martial law (q.v.).

Critics who said the government of the Republic of China was not democratic did not usually attack the Constitution or advocate writing a new constitution, but rather called for its full and complete implementation. Thus, abolishing the Temporary Provisions and ending martial law were their targets. Ending both, in fact, made the Constitution a democratic one and the civil and political liberties provided in it meaningful. In recent years, amending the Constitution has also made the political system more democratic and has had a major impact on the organization and working of the political system, though there remain additional changes to be made.

Consumer Protection Commission (ching-fei-che pao-hu wei-yuan-hui). A commission established in the Executive Yuan (q.v.) in 1994 to study and review policies on consumer protection.

Consumers Foundation of the Republic of China (chung-hua-min-kuo ching-chi-hui). An independent organization founded in 1980 in response to consumer anger toward what they considered irresponsible actions by manufacturers, and to some, the business community in general. In May 1981, the foundation began publication of the magazine *Consumer Reports*. The foundation has since evolved into a powerful interest group.

Control Yuan (chien-cha-yuan). One of the five branches of the central government and formerly one of three parliamentary or elected bodies of government, it was called the supervisory or oversight branch of government. It functioned something like the Censorate in the ancient Chinese system, which was designed to check on officials and bureaucrats and guard against corruption. In the Constitution (q.v.), it was given the powers of impeachment, censure, audit, and consent (of presidential appointments). Members were elected indirectly for six-year terms by provincial and special city councils, and Mongolian, Tibetan, and Overseas Chinese (q.v.) groups.

Early on, critics charged that Control Yuan appointments were controlled by the Nationalist Party (q.v.) and that it lacked Taiwanese (q.v.) members. Beginning in the late 1960s, however, Taiwan-elected members caused numerous allegations of corruption and increased the public's distrust of the body. Because of this, some, especially the Wisdom Coalition (q.v.), said that its functions could be better handled by the more democratic Legislative Yuan (q.v.). Constitutional amendments passed by the National Assembly (q.v.) in 1991, 1992, and 1993 changed the Control Yuan from a parliamentary branch of government into a quasi-judicial organization. Its members are no longer elected, but are, rather, appointed by the president with the approval of the National Assembly. Its original membership was 223. That number was reduced to 51 in 1991. In 1993, it became 29 strong. The Control Yuan also no longer approves presidential nominations of presidents and vice presidents of the Judicial and Examination Yuans (qq.v), leaving it with only the powers of impeachment, censure, and audit. Its impeachment power, however, applies to all levels of government, including the president. Its monitoring authority comes from the Law on Discipline of Public Functionaries.

The December 1996 National Development Conference concluded that the Legislative Yuan should have the powers of audit, investigation of government agencies and impeachment.

There has been, for this and other reasons, speculation that the Control Yuan is being marginalized and that it may, in fact, be abolished.

Cooperative System (ho-tso shih-yeh). Based on the Constitution's (q.v.) provision that "cooperative enterprises shall receive encouragement and assistance from the state," the government assists, generally through the social affairs department of the Ministry of Interior, both single-purpose and multipurpose cooperatives. The former are mostly to respond to economic issues: agriculture, industry, marketing, labor, transportation, public utilities, insurance, and so forth. The latter are community or regional cooperative schemes. Agriculture and the handicraft industries have especially benefited from cooperative arrangements. As of 1996, there were more than 5,000 cooperative associations with a membership of seven million with capital of around U.S.$200 million.

Coordination Council for North American Affairs (CCNAA) (pei-mei shih-wu hsieh-ti'ao-hui). An unofficial organization that represented the Republic of China (q.v.) in the United States in lieu of an embassy and consulates after the United States broke formal diplomatic relations in January 1979. CCNAA was headquartered in Taiwan, but its real operation was in Washington, D.C. (where it functioned as an embassy), and in other cities in the United States (where it functioned as consulates), including New York City, Chicago, Atlanta, Houston, Seattle, San Francisco, Los Angeles, Honolulu, Boston, and Miami.

CCNAA was divided into 10 divisions: Secretariat, which handled political and governmental matters; Service Division, which took visa and passport applications; Administrative

Division, which handled housekeeping; Public Affairs Division, which did congressional liaison work; Telecommunications Division, which managed communications with the home office in Taipei (q.v.); Cultural Division, which did the equivalent work of a cultural attaché; Information and Communications Division, which was responsible for press and public relations; Science Division, which promoted scientific and technological cooperation with the United States; Economic Division, which mainly dealt with U.S.-Taiwan trade and economic issues; Service Coordination Division, which took care of military matters. There was also an Investment and Trade Office (located in New York City) and a Procurement Service Mission in Washington, D.C. The former provided information and services to U.S. investors; the latter was responsible for purchasing weapons in the United States. CCNAA's counterpart organization in Taiwan (q.v.) was the American Institute in Taiwan (AIT) (q.v.).

In 1994, following a Clinton Administration reassessment of U.S. Taiwan policy, CCNAA was renamed the Taipei Economic and Cultural Representative Office (q.v.), which assumed all of the functions of CCNAA. This was considered an upgrading of Washington-Taipei relations inasmuch as the latter title signifies what nation the organization represents; CCNAA did not. AIT remained the counterpart organization in Taipei.

Council for Cultural Planning and Development (wen-hua chien-she wei-yuan-hui). Established in 1981 under the jurisdiction of the Executive Yuan (q.v.), the Council is responsible for developing Chinese culture and culture in general.

Council for Economic Planning and Development (CEPD) (ching-chi chien-she wei-yuan-hui). Created in 1977 to replace the Economic Planning Council (q.v.) it is considered Taiwan's top economic planning organization. It approves projects that have government involvement, coordinates the nation's financial and economic activities and studies the local and global economic trends and problems. It has eight departments: Overall Planning, Sectoral Planning, Economic Research, Housing and Urban Development, Financial Analysis, Manpower Planning, Performance Evaluation, and General Affairs.

Council for International Cooperation and Development (kuo-chi ho-tso fa-chan wei-yuan-hui). Created in 1963 to adjust to the coming termination of U.S. economic assistance, its purpose was to attract foreign investment and loans and to help launch Taiwan's first export processing zone at Kaohsiung (qq.v.). It was reorganized by Chiang Ching-kuo (q.v.) in 1969 and lost some of its most important functions. In 1972, it was replaced by the Economic Planning Council (q.v.).

Council for U.S. Aid (mei-kuo yuan-chu wei-yuan-hui). An organization established in 1948 to implement U.S. economic assistance programs, it was restructured in 1958 to design tax, finance, and investment plans and to regulate exchange rates. The Council was replaced by the Council for International Cooperation and Development (q.v.) in 1963.

Council of Grand Justices (ta-fa-kuan hui-yi). Established in 1948 and made up of 15 grand justices appointed by the president with the approval of the Control Yuan (q.v.), its members were the top officials of the Judicial Yuan (q.v.). Its major functions were interpreting the Constitution (q.v.) and unifying the interpretation of laws and ordinances. In 1958, when the Law of the Council of Grand Justices was promulgated, the Council of Grand Justices began making rulings on constitutional interpretations made by individuals. In the late 1980s the council made some important rulings on tax laws, nullifying some provisions of the tax code.

A very important and controversial decision was made by the Council of Grand Justices in June 1990: an interpretation of the Constitution to the effect that senior parliamentarians (q.v.)—those members of the National Assembly and the Legislative Yuan (qq.v.) not elected by Taiwan's electorate—would have their tenure terminated by the end of 1991. The Nationalist Party (q.v.) and the Democratic Progressive Party (q.v.) had both tried to get them to retire, and a law had been passed earlier to force them to step down, but these efforts had proven unsuccessful. While there was strong opposition to the Council of Grand Justices' decision by the senior parliamentarians and by those who saw their retirement as undermining the nation's one-China (q.v.) policy, it was carried out and had a momentous impact on the nation's political system and its democratization.

The Council of Grand Justices currently has 16 members who serve nine-year terms. The body meets twice or three times a week and may call extraordinary meetings. An interpretation of the Constitution requires a three-fourths vote of members present; other decisions are made by a single majority. Its opinions, interpretations, and dissenting views are published by the Judicial Yuan (q.v.).

Council of Labor Affairs (CLA) (lao-kung wei-yuan-hui). An organ of the Executive Yuan (q.v.) created in August 1987 to administer labor laws, regulations, and policies. The CLC also serves as an advocate for labor, protects workers' rights, supervises labor-management relations, and promotes better working environments. It comprises several subcabinet agencies and bureaus. One of the major functions of the Council of Labor Affairs in recent years has been the responsibility for retraining Taiwan's displaced and elderly farmers. Another has been oversight of Taiwan's foreign laborers.

Council of Presbyterian Churches (chang-lao chiao-hui). The most active religious organization in Taiwan (q.v.), it has long advocated Taiwan independence and for that reason has often been at odds with the ruling Nationalist Party (q.v.) and the government. See also Taiwan Independence Movement.

Culture Society (wen-hua hui). An organization of Taiwanese (q.v.) formed during the Japanese colonial period. Its purpose was to strengthen Formosan-Chinese identity. Being apolitical, it survived the demise of its parent organization, the Home Rule Association (q.v.).

- D -

Dai Wan. Literally "big bay" in Japanese. Japanese traders used this term for Taiwan (q.v.) in the 14th century. It is also a native word for aborigines (q.v.). Some say that this is the origin of the term "Taiwan."

Democracy Foundation (min-chu chi-chin-hui). A Nationalist Party (q.v.) think tank formed in November 1990 by then party election strategist John Kuan after a split with President Lee Teng-hui (q.v.). The foundation, which had considerable financial backing from a number of Taiwan's businesses, represented a faction in the party that opposes Taiwan's independence. It has been less active in recent years.

Democratic Progressive Party (DPP) (min-chu chin-pu tang). Considered Taiwan's major opposition party, the DPP was formed on September 28, 1986, mostly of Tangwai (q.v.) politicians, many of whom had been political prisoners and/or well-known dissidents. It was the first new political party successfully formed in Taiwan under the government of the Republic of China (q.v.). Soon after it was organized, the DPP became regarded as Taiwan's major and only serious opposition party. It was founded illegally, since forming new political parties was banned by the Temporary Provisions (q.v.), but, inasmuch as President Chiang Ching-kuo (q.v.) had stated a few months earlier that new political parties would soon be allowed, the government did not take action against DPP leaders. The DPP competed against the Nationalist Party in the December 1986 election, winning over 20 percent of the votes for National Assembly and Legislative Yuan (qq.v.) seats. Some observers said this was evidence that Taiwan had evolved into a two-party system; others, however, doubted that.

At its first party congress in November 1986, the DPP elected Chiang Peng-chien (q.v.) party chairman. Also elected was a Central Committee and a 10-member Central Standing Committee (qq.v.). While the chairman was to serve for but one year and the DPP leadership was supposed to be a collective one, the organizational structure of the party was Leninist. Some considered this quite ironic since its members had long been highly critical of this aspect of the Nationalist Party (q.v.).

The party immediately advocated reduced defense spending; political reform, such as ending the Nationalist Party's hold on political power; the retirement of senior parliamentarians (q.v.) (members of the National Assembly and the Legislative Yuan elected before the government moved to Taiwan) so as to make the political system truly democratic; a free press; the end of martial law; and more. Its platform supported the rights of women, senior citizens, children, workers, aborigines (q.v.), farmers, and other disadvantaged people. The DPP advocated expanded social programs that some say indicated it wanted a welfare state, though it argued that it could expand welfare benefits by simply increasing government efficiency and would not have to raise taxes. It railed against corruption, which it blamed on the Kuomintang (q.v.), though it had its own problems in this realm. It affirmed the country's anti-Communist policy, but also called for self-determination for Taiwan so its residents could decide their political future. The DPP party platform called for a "flexible foreign policy" and Taiwan's readmission to the United Nations, but party leaders offered few serious suggestions as to how this might be accomplished.

During the early years, the DPP engaged in "street politics" by organizing demonstrations, protests, and other forms of political expression. It also employed disruptive tactics and sometimes violence in Legislative Yuan sessions to draw press attention to its issues and/or demands or to block opposed legislation. Some regarded the party's activities and success as proof of democracy evolving in Taiwan; opponents saw the DPP as demeaning the democratic processes. In any event, experiencing considerable success over a period of time in electing its members to various offices in the local as well as national government, the DPP has moderated its policies.

Almost from the onset of its founding, the DPP experienced factional problems and intra-party strife resulting from personal power struggles and differing views on some critical issues, especially the issue of Taiwan's independence. The DPP has also seen its leaders at odds over the party's relations with the KMT. Some observers have seen these problems as nothing unusual for a new opposition party; others have viewed them as casting doubt on the party's future.

In 1989, the DPP performed well in the Legislative Yuan election, prompting some pundits to predict that it would be in office soon, or when the senior parliamentarians were retired. It performed poorly, however, in the first nonsupplemental election in 1991 after the nonelected senior parliamentarians (q.v.) stepped down, due to putting the issue of Taiwan's independence in its platform. Yet it did very well in the first nonsupplemental Legislative Yuan election in 1992. The DPP also performed quite well in elections in the mid-1990s, although it did not do well in the Republic of China's (q.v.) first direct presidential election in 1996. It performed very well in local elections in November 1997, prompting observers to predict that the DPP may win the presidential election in 2000, especially if the KMT continues to experience factional and other problems. It did less well in the Legislative Yuan election in December 1998 and lost the Taipei (q.v.) mayorship, which it had won in 1994.

During 1997, the DPP worked with the ruling KMT in various lawmaking efforts and in passing amendments to the Constitution (q.v.), even though the party had said the Constitution is archaic and should be replaced. This DPP-KMT cooperation, in fact, prompted some observers to see their mutual efforts as marking the beginning of coalition politics in Taiwan. Others say that this is only a temporary strategy on the part of the DPP and is something that will not last.

DPP leaders, especially those in office, have angered the People's Republic of China with their independence stance, and have been assailed frequently by Beijing for trying to split China even though the DPP's stance on independence has gradually moderated. The United States has also warned DPP leaders about pushing Taiwan independence, especially those advocating a more radical position including a referendum to determine Taiwan's future.

Unlike the Nationalist Party (which is mixed in membership) the DPP's membership of about 80,000 is almost exclusively Taiwanese (q.v.). Also unlike the KMT its leaders are almost all lawyers, political activists, and elected government officials. The DPP is considered Taiwan's only mass mobilization political party and the only party capable of competing seriously with the Nationalist Party.

Democratic Socialist Party (DSP) (min-chu chin-pu tang). A political party, which formed in Shanghai in 1946 and moved to Taiwan in 1949, it is the smaller of two legal opposition parties that functioned before the formation of the Democratic Progressive Party (q.v), the other being the China Youth Party (q.v.). DSP ideology resembled European democratic socialism. Members of the DSP for some time held a number of nonelected seats in the Legislative Yuan and National Assembly (qq.v.). The DSP has also elected a number of city mayors. Its membership is approximately 6,000. In recent years, especially since Democratic Progressive Party (q.v.) successes in major national elections, the DSP has lost support and has not been very active.

Den Kojiro. The eighth governor-general of Taiwan (q.v.) under Japanese rule and the first civilian governor-general.

Dependency theory. The view that underdeveloped nations are hampered in their developmental efforts by investment and trade ties with Western capitalist countries. Most economists in Taiwan (q.v.) as well as Western economists who have studied Taiwan's economic development believe that Taiwan's economic development experience repudiates dependency theory.

Dialects. In addition to Mandarin (q.v.) Chinese, the national language in both the People's Republic of China and the Republic of China (q.v.), and which derives from the Peking dialect, Taiwanese and Hakka (qq.v.), and a number of other Chinese dialects and Aboriginal languages also are spoken in Taiwan (q.v.). Taiwanese comes from Southern Fukienese or the Amoy Dialect, and is spoken widely throughout Taiwan. Hakka is prevalent in Hsinchu, Miaoli, Taoyuan, Pingtung, and some other parts of the island. Both are spoken with different accents depending on the area of Taiwan. Teaching in public schools in Taiwan is in Mandarin. Television and radio programs are mainly in Mandarin and Taiwanese, though since 1989 Hakka is heard more frequently on radio and television. The president's national addresses are given in Mandarin and dubbed in Taiwanese and Hakka. Although all Chinese dialects are written in the same script, they are generally unintelligible in the spoken form to Chinese who have not been brought up with them or have not learned them. Most residents of Taiwan, however, are bilingual, or more, if the different dialects are considered separate languages. In other words, most speak a dialect in addition to Mandarin Chinese.

Diaoyu Islands. See Tiao Yu Tai.

Dollar diplomacy (chin-yuan wai-ch'iao). The term used to describe the Republic of China's policy of granting economic assistance to some small Third World countries to ensure keeping formal diplomatic ties with that country, or establishing such relations with a Third World country. The term has been used by the People's Republic of China and by Taipei's critics in Taiwan and elsewhere. The government denies that it "buys" diplomatic ties. See also International Cooperation and Development Fund.

Double Ten Day (hsuang-shih-chieh). Meaning the 10th day of the 10th month, or October 10, this is the Republic of China's National Day. It commemorates the Wuchang Uprising staged by Sun Yat-sen's (q.v.) followers in 1911, which ignited a nationwide revolt against the Manchus, or Ch'ing Dynasty, government then ruling the mainland part of China. The establishment of the Republic of China followed the next year. Parades and other festivities are held on this holiday, and the president gives a formal public address on this day.

Dutch East India Company. The de facto colonial government of Taiwan for nearly four decades prior to 1662, it ruled the island from its Asian headquarters established in Jakarta. By 1650, the Company controlled almost 300 Chinese villages. It ruled the island by dividing it into districts which were formally ruled by an aborigine chieftain. Though the company maintained political control by force of arms, it also used proselytizing and economic leverage. The company brought new crops and farming techniques to Taiwan (q.v.) and exported large amounts of venison, deer skins, and sugar from Taiwan to both China and Japan. For some years, Taiwan was the company's second-most-profitable venture, drawing a handsome revenue from both taxes and trade. It also brought progress to Taiwan by building roads and irrigation works, conducting surveys, and romanizing aboriginal languages.

- E -

East Asia Association (tung-ya hsieh-hui). Taiwan's quasi- embassy and consulate in Tokyo, set up after Japan and the Republic of China (q.v.) broke diplomatic relations in 1972.

Economic Cooperation Administration (ching-chi ho-tso hui-yi). A
U.S. government organization established to provide
economic assistance to the Nationalist government after it
moved to Taiwan in 1949.

**Economic Planning Council (EPC) (ching-chi chi-hua fa-chan hui-
yi).** Established in 1973, the EPC became the successor to the
Council for International Cooperation and Development (q.v.).
It was a smaller and less powerful body but like its
predecessor organization it was responsible for planning
economic growth.

Economic Stabilization Board (ching-chi an-chuan wei-yuan-hui).
Established in 1953 as a successor to the Taiwan Production
Board (q.v.), the Economic Stabilization Board was
responsible for ensuring currency stability and promoting
economic development, especially by helping Taiwan's
fledgling industries.

Eight-Point Proposal (chiang ba tian). Points made in a speech given
by Jiang Zemin in January 1995 entitled "Continuing to
Promote the Reunification of the Motherland." The speech did
not contain new policies but rather was a reiteration of
Beijing's policy (by Jiang Zemin as Deng Xiaoping's heir
apparent) toward Taiwan that would make it a special
administrative region of the People's Republic of China
(PRC). The proposal was apparently made because of concern
about a shift in U.S. Taiwan policy (see Taiwan policy
review), the maturing of democracy in Taiwan, and a
succession problem in the PRC (Deng Xiaoping being old and
ill at this time). The proposal seemed generous and
conciliatory, stating that China did not intend to "swallow up"
Taiwan and would allow it a "high degree of autonomy." Jiang
blamed "foreign forces" that were trying to "split" Taiwan
from China and independence advocates in Taiwan and
viewed the two as connected. He declared that China would
use military force to stop this, though he also said that
"Chinese should not fight Chinese." To Taiwan's political
leaders and its population, since the proposal denied the
sovereignty of the Republic of China, it was not considered
acceptable. President Lee Teng-hui (q.v.) responded with a
"Six Point Proposal" (q.v.)—the first time Taipei (q.v.) ever
responded directly to any PRC proposal.

Eighties **(pa-shih nien-tai).** A monthly magazine founded and operated by Kang Ning-hsiang (q.v.) in the late 1970s which advocated democracy and supported opposition causes. It was considered more moderate than *Formosa* (q.v.).

Elder parliamentarians. See Senior parliamentarians.

Emergency decree. See Martial law.

Enlightenment Society (ch'i-meng she-hui). An organization formed in Japan in 1918 by Taiwanese who sought a voice in the Japanese National Diet. The organization had some influence in Japan, but Governor-General Akashi (q.v.) did not allow it to establish branches or publish in Taiwan.

Environmental Protection Administration (EPA) (huan-ching pao-hu-shu). Elevated to cabinet-level status in August 1987 and renamed in 1988, the EPA has sought to respond to and correct the increasingly dangerous environmental situation in Taiwan (q.v.) caused by the nation's rapid industrialization. Protection of the environment was handled by the Bureau of Environmental Sanitation in the Department of Health and later the Bureau of Environmental Protection, before the creation of the EPA. Jaw Shau-kong (q.v.) became the EPA's director in 1991 and very aggressively pushed for stricter environmental standards. The EPA has been responsible for passing a host of new environmentally friendly laws and for providing Taiwan with cleaner air and water. See also Taiwan Environmental Protection Agency.

Er Er Ba. Meaning 2-2-8 in Chinese and referring to February 28 of 1947, the term recalls a period of bloody repression in Taiwan (q.v.) by the Nationalist government that had taken control of the island two years earlier. On that date Taiwanese (q.v.) spontaneously took to the streets to protest, or rebel (the use of the terms varies), following an incident in which the police detained a woman who was selling black market cigarettes on the street and subsequently fired into a crowd of people that threatened them. At this time tensions had been building between Taiwanese and the Nationalist government because of months of misrule of Taiwan under the leadership of Governor Chen Yi (q.v.), during which time the economy collapsed and social order disintegrated while soldiers looted and stole private property. The Nationalist government, thus, after being initially welcomed by Taiwanese after World War II, became seen as a vile, incompetent, carpetbagger government.

On February 28, thousands of Taiwanese who were provoked into action by the incident took this opportunity to vent their anger against the government and assault Mainland Chinese (q.v.). Many Mainland Chinese, or frequently, simply anyone who could not speak Taiwanese, were beaten and killed. Military forces were brought in from the mainland and the "rebellion" was suppressed with a vengeance resulting in widespread killing. Many Taiwanese leaders were among those who died, and many more were imprisoned or executed after order was restored—causing some to say that a generation of the "best and brightest" Taiwanese was lost. Most Taiwanese subsequently recalled the incident with strong ill-feeling. However, for many years it was taboo to discuss the incident and little was said or written about it. With democratization, however, details of the event have been discussed and made public.

In February 1992, the government issued a detailed report of the incident based on formerly classified documents and put the number killed at between 18,000 and 28,000. In February 1995, President Lee Teng-hui (q.v.) made a public apology on behalf of the government for the incident, and the Legislative Yuan (q.v.) passed a bill to pay compensation to victims' families. A monument was also established. In 1997, February 28 was made a national holiday. Opposition politicians, however, still evoke memories of the event as a means of provoking public opinion against the Nationalist Party (q.v.) and the government.

Evergreen Group (chang-yung chi-t'uan). One of Taiwan's largest corporate groups, it controls Evergreen Marine, the largest container shipping company in the world. In July 1991, it founded EVA Airlines, Taiwan's first private international airline. Chang Yung-fa (q.v.) is the chairman and major owner.

Examination Yuan (kao-shih-yuan). One of five branches of the central government of the Republic of China (q.v.), and the branch given responsibility for writing and administering civil-service examinations used to recruit government officials; the employment and management of civil service personnel; and setting criteria for evaluating, promoting, and compensating government employees. By making it a separate branch of government the framers of the Constitution (q.v.) wanted it to remain free of partisan political influence. Its high status is also attributable to the importance of civil service testing and recruitment in Chinese political culture and to the fact that it has a counterpart in the ancient Chinese system. Its 17 members are appointed by the president with the approval of the National Assembly (q.v.) for six-year terms. The Examination Yuan is made up of a council, a secretariat, the Ministry of Examination, the Ministry of Civil Service, and the Civil Service Protection and Training Commission.

Executive Yuan (hsing-cheng-yuan). One of the five branches of the central government of the Republic of China. The Executive Yuan is considered the highest administrative organ of government and the most powerful organ of the government. It is made up of policymaking organs, executive organs (the cabinet), and subordinate organizations such as its Secretariat, the Government Information Office (q.v.), Directorate-General of the Budget, Accounting and Statistics, the Council for Economic Planning and Development (q.v.), and the Research, Development, and Evaluation Commission (q.v). The most important organs of the Executive Yuan are the eight ministries: interior, foreign affairs, national defense, justice, finance, economic affairs, communications and education.

The Executive Yuan is constitutionally responsible to the Legislative Yuan (q.v.), but in many respects it acts quite independently. The head of the Executive Yuan is the premier, who is appointed by the president. Second in command is the vice premier. The premier performs the duties of the president in the event the president and vice president cannot (for a period up to three months), presents administration policy to the Legislative Yuan, countersigns laws and decrees, and requests the Legislative Yuan to reconsider resolutions. When Chiang Kai-shek (q.v.) died, his son Chiang Ching-kuo (q.v.) ran the government from the position of premier. After Lee Teng-hui (q.v.) became president there developed some controversy about the role and powers of the premier, especially vis-à-vis the president. With Lee appointing new premiers and with constitutional changes dealing with this issue, the president has emerged clearly the stronger.

Executive Yuan Council (hsing-cheng-yuan hui-yi). Made up of the premier (who is chairman), vice premier, heads of ministries and commissions, and ministers of state, it meets every Thursday morning to discuss the finalization of bills, declarations, and treaties to be submitted to the Legislative Yuan (q.v.) for approval, in addition to matters of concern to one or more ministries or commissions. It is considered an important locus of power in the government of the Republic of China (q.v.). See also Executive Yuan.

Export Processing Zone (EPZ) (chia-kung ch'u-kou-ch'u). First established in Kaohsiung (q.v.) in the mid-1960s, with two more zones added three years later at Taichung and Nantze, their purposes were to attract foreign investment through minimizing red tape and by offering tax incentives and, of course, to export Taiwan-made products. They combined an industrial complex with a free port. Foreign companies were not allowed to sell their products in the domestic market; however, this policy was later softened. They were so successful that, by the late 1970s, they accounted for nearly 10 percent of Taiwan's exports. They increased exports, reduced unemployment, and upgraded the country's labor skills. Taiwan's export processing zones have since been phased out but have been copied by other countries, including China.

- F -

F-5E. The designation given to an aircraft manufactured by Northrop Corporation of the United States together with several companies in Taiwan (q.v.). It was for many years the backbone of the Republic of China's (ROC) (q.v.) Air Force. Taipei (q.v.) for some time asked the United States to sell it a more advanced plane, but the United States refused (see FX). The ROC then decided to build its own fighter plane (see Indigenous Defense Fighter). In 1993, the United States decided to sell F-16 (q.v.) fighter planes to Taiwan, and France sold Taiwan the Mirage 2000-5 (q.v.). Since then the F-5Es have been withdrawn from service or used for training.

F-5G. An aircraft built by Northrop Corporation of the United States that Taiwan considered buying to replace the F-5E (q.v.) but decided against in favor of the FX (q.v.).

F-16. A high-performance fighter aircraft manufactured by General Dynamics of the United States, 150 of which were sold to Taiwan (q.v.) by the United States in 1992 for the stated purpose of maintaining a force balance in the Taiwan Strait (q.v.), following the purchase of a number of high performance MiG aircraft from Russia by the People's Republic of China. Though some said the sale was made by President George Bush to help him win votes in Texas where the plane was built, others noted the sale helped maintain a balance of forces in the Taiwan Strait and thus helped prevent conflict. Taipei wanted to purchase the more sophisticated F-16C/D model, but was allowed to buy only the F-16 A/B, though this plane was modified to meet Taiwan's defense needs and armed with AIM-7 Sparrow air-to-air missiles, AIM-9 Sidewinder missiles, Maverick missiles, cluster bombs, and other advanced weapons. Delivery of the planes began in 1997. The F-16s will be based in Chiayi and Hualien and, in combination with the Indigenous Defense Fighter and Mirage 2000-5 (qq.v.) aircraft, will give Taiwan formidable air defense capabilities.

F-20. A fighter plane, also called the Tigershark, which Northrop Corporation of the United States planned and built in prototype, and intended to sell as an air defense plane. Taiwan (q.v.) seriously considered buying this plane. However, Northrop did not get sufficient orders elsewhere, with most nations favoring the F-16 (q.v.), and, therefore, did not produce the F-20.

Fair Trade Commission (kung-p'ing mao-yi wei-yuan-hui). Established in 1992 and made part of the Executive Yuan (q.v.), this commission seeks to promote a fair trade system.

Family planning program (chia-t'ing chi-hua). A nationwide campaign launched in 1964 to curb the Republic of China's (q.v.) very high birthrate at the time. It reflected an awareness of Taiwan's very dense population and the economic cost of population growth. The program was so successful that the birthrate dropped precipitously. By 1990 the government became concerned about a "population gap" and began to encourage an increase in the birthrate. Family planning meanwhile had begun to emphasize promoting genetic health and screening for chronic diseases.

February 28 Uprising (er-er-ba shih-pian). See Er Er Ba.

Fei Hsi-ping (1911-). A guerrilla leader who fought against Japan during World War II and later became a high Nationalist Party (q.v.) official and member of the Legislative Yuan (q.v.) representing Manchuria. In the 1970s, he quit his post and resigned his party membership because of disenchantment with party and government policies. In the early 1980s, Fei advocated expanding basic freedoms and democracy. He subsequently became a founding member and leader of the Democratic Progressive Party (DPP) (q.v.). In 1988, however, he left the DPP because of its support for Taiwan's independence and in protest of the DPP's stance on the retirement of senior parliamentarians (q.v.). Fei was one of the few Mainland Chinese (q.v.) DPP leaders.

Five-power system (wu-chuan chih-tu). The term used to describe the Republic of China's (q.v.) political system that has five main branches. Three are similar to those in Western democracies: Executive Yuan, Legislative Yuan, and Judicial Yuan (qq.v.). Two others, the Control Yuan and the Examination Yuan (qq.v.), come from the traditional Chinese system. Sun Yat-sen (q.v.) devised this system of government.

Five Principles (wu-ta yuan-tse). Cited by President Chiang Ching-kuo (q.v.) on December 28, 1978, to be the basis of future relations between Taiwan and the United States in the absence of formal diplomatic relations. The principles were: continuity, reality, security, legality, and governmentality.

Flexible diplomacy (t'an-hsing wai-ch'iao). The term used for Taipei's shift in foreign policy stance in the late 1980s regarding dealing with nations and international institutions that had formal ties with the People's Republic of China (PRC). According to the precepts of flexible diplomacy, the Republic of China (ROC) (q.v.) should deal with such nations and institutions and not demand formal recognition or even the use of the term "Republic of China."

Some said it was a policy that originated from Taipei's diplomatic setbacks in the 1970s and 1980s. Others said it related to confidence on the part of government leaders in Taipei (q.v.) due to Taiwan's successful and widely lauded democratization. Still others said it reflected the reality of two Chinas. Many associate flexible diplomacy with President Lee Teng-hui (q.v.), though it seems to have originated with President Chiang Ching-kuo (q.v.) and what was earlier called "practical diplomacy."

In any event, in 1988, the ROC resumed participation in the Asian Development Bank (q.v.) as "Taipei, China." In November 1988, when Saudi Arabia announced initial steps toward establishing formal diplomatic relations with the People's Republic of China, Taipei declared that it would no longer insist on being recognized as the sole legitimate government of China. At this same time a spokesman for the Ministry of Foreign Affairs said that Taipei "did not flatly reject" offers to establish relations with nations which recognize the PRC. In 1989, Taipei welcomed ties with Grenada and Liberia despite their formal diplomatic ties with Beijing. In 1990, the Republic of China applied to the General Agreement on Tariffs and Trade as the "Customs Territory of Taiwan, Penghu, Kinmen and Matsu." In 1991, the ROC joined the Asia-Pacific Economic Cooperation (q.v.) forum as "Chinese, Taipei." See also Dollar diplomacy; Pragmatic diplomacy; Substantive Foreign Relations; Vacation diplomacy.

Formosa. The Portuguese word "beautiful." Portuguese sailors, being the first Westerners to see Taiwan (q.v.), gave it the name Ilha Formosa (q.v.), "Beautiful Island." It was for a long time, and to some extent still is, the Western term for Taiwan or the Republic of China (q.v.). Although it is a term associated with the period of Western colonial rule over Taiwan it is often used by the advocates of independence to suggest that Taiwan should not be regarded as historically (or now legally) part of China, as the term "Taiwan" might suggest. See Taiwan; Republic of China.

Formosa **(Mei-li-tao li-k'an).** A magazine launched in February 1979 by the "Formosa group" (q.v.)—the most radical, anti-government political opposition in Taiwan at the time. *Formosa* followed the themes of an earlier magazine called

Taiwan Political Review (q.v.) in calling for reform and democracy while criticizing the Nationalist Party's (q.v.) "monopoly" political rule and economic growth with high social costs. It was also highly critical of what it considered the slow process of democratization in view of the country's lack of credibility internationally after U.S. derecognition of the Republic of China (q.v.). It was banned after a short time but had considerable influence for several months at a watershed time in Taiwan's recent history.

Formosa faction (mei-li-tao hsi). The larger of two major factions of the Democratic Progressive Party (DPP) (q.v.), generally regarded as the moderate wing or faction, especially when compared to the New Tide faction (q.v.). Though it was once a radical faction, it changed in the late 1980s when many of its members were elected to political office or saw hopes of gaining political position. The Formosa faction advocates self determination (demanding that the National government reflect the fact that it rules only Taiwan and some other small islands and not the mainland of China) rather than independence. It also generally advocates negotiations rather than street action as a tactic to gain political power domestically, in contrast to the New Tide faction. In recent years it has advocated more extensive trade and other commercial relations with the People's Republic of China, and negotiations that set aside the issue of sovereignty and focus on economic, social, and technical issues. It also differs from the New Tide faction in pressing the view that the DPP should appeal to the middle class and the business community, rather than underprivileged groups, and that the DPP abandon its socialist views. At the October 1988 DPP's third congress, Huang Hsin-chieh (q.v.), then head of the Formosa faction, was elected chairman of the party. The Formosa faction is currently headed by Hsu Hsin-liang (q.v.). See also Formosa group.

"Formosa group" (mei-li-tao cheng-t'uan). A group, sometimes called a "political action" body, organized by Yao Chia- wen, Chang Chun-hung, Huang Hsin-chieh (q.v.), Hsu Hsin- liang (q.v.), and Lin Yi-hsiung (q.v.) in 1979 to publish the *Formosa* (q.v.) magazine, advocate democracy and Taiwan's independence, and criticize the Nationalist Party (q.v.) for its authoritarianism and failed foreign policy among other things. Members of this group organized an antigovernment protest demonstration and parade in Kaohsiung (q.v.) in December 1979 that led to violence, after which a number were convicted of sedition and sentenced to prison. See also Formosa faction.

Formosa Plastics Group (t'ai-wan suo-ch'iao kung-yeh yu-hsien kung-szu). Taiwan's largest corporate group, made up of Formosa Plastics Corporation, Nan Ya Plastics, and some other companies, it is also regarded as one of its most financially sound enterprises. It is headed by Y.C. Wang (q.v.).

Formosa Resolution (t'ai-wan chueh-yi-an). A resolution adopted by the U.S. Congress one month after the United States-Republic of China Defense Treaty (q.v.) was negotiated and ratified, it authorized the U.S. president to "employ the Armed Forces of the United States as he deems necessary for the specific purpose of securing and protecting Formosa and the Pescadores against armed attack . . . to include related positions . . . ." This extended the authority of the president to take action to help Taipei defend against an attack by the People's Republic of China on the Offshore Islands (q.v.) of Quemoy and Matsu (qq.v.).

Formosa Strait. See Taiwan Strait.

Formosa Television Corporation (FTV) (min-shih). Taiwan's first fully private over-the-air television, which was approved by the government in 1996 and began broadcasting in June 1997. FTV is the fourth television provider that can be received island-wide but is the first that is not "state run." FTV stocks are owned by a large number of shareholders, reportedly more than 10,000. Its sister station, Formosa News, broadcasts over cable. Although FTV officials say the station is unbiased and will not yield to any business or political interests, its board of directors is made up mainly of Democratic Progressive Party (q.v.) members or supporters.

Formosan Association for Public Affairs (FAPA) (t'ai-wan-jen kung-kung shih-wu-hui). An organization formed in 1982 by Taiwanese (q.v.) including Peng Ming-min (q.v.) in the United States, its purpose being to influence the U.S. government and world public opinion to support democracy, selfdetermination, and human rights in Taiwan (q.v.). Located in Washington,

D.C., it became known as a lobbying group. However, FAPA also established chapters around the United States and in major cities in some other countries. In 1986, FAPA succeeded in getting Representatives Stephen Solarz and Jim Leach to sponsor a resolution calling for freedom of expression and association in Taiwan and the establishment of a fully representative government. However, the resolution failed to pass. Some say the debate initiated by FAPA prompted Tangwai (q.v.) leaders in Taiwan to subsequently form the Democratic Progressive Party (DPP) (q.v.). FAPA is associated with the Formosa faction (q.v.) of the DPP. See also World United Formosans for Independence.

Formosan Christians for Self-Determination (t'ai-wan chi-tu-t'u tze-chueh hsieh-hui). A group of Christians formed of former World United Formosans for Independence (q.v.) members who rejected armed struggle and the use of violence but instead supported human rights declarations regarding Taiwan (q.v.).

Formosans for Free Formosa (t'ai-wan-jen-ti szu-yu t'ai-wan). A pro-independence group formed in 1955 by students in the Philadelphia area. It supported Liao Wen-yi (q.v.) in Japan. In 1960, it became the World United Formosans for Independence (q.v.).

Fourteen Projects (shih-szu-hsiang chien-she). A group of large and very important infrastructure development projects started in 1985 as a sequel to the Ten Projects and the Twelve Projects (qq.v.). Most were scheduled to be completed in the early 1990s. Total cost was projected to be about U.S.$33 billion. Projects included: Expansion of China Steel Corporation (q.v.), Power Projects (Taiwan's fourth nuclear power plant plus hydroelectric and thermal plants), Oil and Natural Gas Project, Modernization of Telecommunications, Railway Expansion, Highway Expansion, Underground Railroad in Taipei, Taipei Mass Transit System, Flood Control and Drainage Improvement, Development of Water Resources, Ecological Protection and Domestic Tourism, Municipal Solid Waste Disposal Project, Medical Care Program, and Community Development Projects.

***Free China Fortnightly* (szu-you chung-kuo).** A literary journal established in 1949 in China with Ministry of Education funding and which shortly thereafter moved to Taiwan (q.v.). "Free China," a group associated with this publication, advocated constitutional democracy and ending one-party rule in Taiwan. The journal was managed by the well-known intellectual Lei Chen (q.v.). Free China followers advocated Anglo-American liberalism, which Hu Shih (q.v.) tried to promote. Hu was supportive of the group at first, but withdrew that support when the leaders of Free China became involved with the China Democratic Party (q.v.). The journal ceased publication in September 1960. Those involved with this publication were predominantly Mainland Chinese (q.v.), and are regarded by some to have established the first real opposition movement in Taiwan.

Free China Journal (**szu-yu chung-kuo ch'i-k'an**). A biweekly English publication of the Government Information Office (q.v.) in Taipei (q.v.), published before 1964 under the name *Free China Weekly.*

Free China Review (**szu-yu chung-kuo yue-k'an**). A monthly magazine published by the Government Information Office (q.v.) in Taipei (q.v.).

FX. Designation of two jet fighter planes—the F-16/J79 and the F-5G (q.v.)—which the United States considered selling to Taiwan (q.v.) in the 1970s. In December 1981, however, the Reagan administration decided against the sale because the planes were considered "offensive" weapons. Beijing had strongly opposed the sale.

- G -

Garrison Command (or Taiwan Garrison General Headquarters) (**t'ai-wan-ch'u ching-pei tsung-pu**). Created in 1950 to administer martial law (q.v.), the Garrison Command was one of the main commands under the Ministry of Defense. It was also considered the most powerful security organization in Taiwan (q.v.) for a long time because of its authority over arrests and prosecutions for sedition, its responsibility for checking mail, its carrying out censorship, and its monitoring overseas travel. Its powers were diminished by the termination of martial law and it was disbanded in 1992. A new Coastal Patrol General Headquarters (q.v.) was created to handle its role in controlling smuggling.

General Chamber of Commerce of the Republic of China (chung-hua-min-kuo hsiang-yeh tsung-pu). Founded in 1946, the chamber is the longest-existing interest group in Taiwan and is one of its largest business organizations. It has three district organizations, in Taiwan Province, Taipei City, and Kaohsiung City, plus various other suborganizations. The chamber has two foreign liaison offices located in San Francisco and Toronto.

German formula (the-kuo mo-shih). Said, in retrospect, to be a policy objective of the United States in the late 1960s and early 1970s in negotiating with the People's Republic of China (PRC): establish diplomatic relations with Peking and keep official diplomatic relations with Taipei (q.v.). This policy, if it was U.S. policy, was never realized. In essence, the German formula meant two Chinas, or at least two governments, and for that reason it found many opponents on both sides of the Taiwan Strait.

The German solution more recently has been cited as a formula whereby the PRC and the Republic of China (ROC) (q.v.) might mend their differences and unification be realized: by allowing the ROC to participate in international organizations and a legitimate place in the international arena, after which Taipei might be willing to talk about some kind of federation. The rationale is that PRC efforts to isolate Taiwan diplomatically make Taipei more recalcitrant and unwilling to negotiate unification. The German formula, in fact (though the term is not used often), is the policy of many government leaders in Taipei and may be said to be similar or identical to the idea of one country, two areas; one country, two entities (q.v); or one country, two governments (q.v.).

In 1993, Taipei (q.v.) announced a goal of joining the United Nations General Assembly under the divided nationsformula that allowed the two Germanies and the two Koreas to join. Some at this time said that the Republic of China had formally accepted the German formula. See also Singapore Solution.

Go South policy (nan-hsiang cheng-tse). A government guided initiative or informal policy announced in 1993 and promoted by President Lee Teng-hui (q.v.) that encourages Taiwan business people to invest in Southeast Asian countries rather than the People's Republic of China (PRC) due to a fear that Taiwan was putting too much investment capital in the mainland and that Beijing would gain too much leverage over the Republic of China as a result. President Lee advocated this policy even more strongly in 1995 and 1996 in response to the missile tests Beijing conducted in the Taiwan Strait (q.v.) to intimidate Taiwan during a Legislative Yuan (q.v.) election and Taiwan's first direct presidential election. As of mid-1998 it was reported that Taiwan had invested US$37 billion in Southeast Asian countries. This policy has led to political contacts between Taiwan's top leaders and high officials in some Southeast Asian countries and has therefore been condemned by the PRC. See also Go West policy; No haste policy.

Go West policy (hsi-hsiang cheng-tse). A policy enunciated by some leaders in Taiwan saying that investment should be encouraged in the People's Republic of China, rather than discouraged according to the Go South policy (q.v.). This view has generally been opposed by the Democratic Progressive Party (DPP) (q.v.), though it has been advanced by former DPP chairman Hsu Hsin-liang (q.v.).

Goto Shimpei. The first civil administrator of Taiwan (q.v.), in office from March 1898 to November 1906. He helped bring reform to Taiwan under Japanese rule.

Government Information Office (GIO) (hsin-wen chu). A government agency attached to the Executive Yuan (q.v.) that explains government policies to the press and disseminates information about the Republic of China (q.v.) abroad through its numerous overseas offices. In the past it censored the press; today it has the job of overseeing the media and serving as the government's voice in making its policies known and in doing public relations work. Various of its directors have been quite influential while in a very visible job.

Grand Hotel (yuan-shan ta-fan-tian). A large hotel built in traditional Chinese architectural style located on the Keelung River in the outskirts of Taipei and owned by the Taiwan Friendship

Society. Madam Chiang Kai-shek (q.v.) was an initiator of building the hotel in the 1950s and was part owner. It has been the site of many important diplomatic meetings and conferences over the years. U.S. president Eisenhower stayed there during his visit to Taiwan (q.v.) in the 1950s. In recent years the hotel has not done so well due to the large number of competing top-notch hotels in Taipei. The current chairman of the board is Koo Chen-fu (q.v.).

Greater China (ta chung-kuo). The idea or proposal that Hong Kong (before July 1, 1997), Macao, Taiwan (q.v.), and possibly Singapore and the Overseas Chinese (q.v.) all constitute Chinese nations or political entities and should form some kind of union, such as a federation, commonwealth, or regional organization. The vast economic links among them formed after Deng Xiaoping came to power in 1978 and pushed capitalist reform and encouraged foreign trade and investment in the People's Republic of China. The end of the Cold War and proliferating contacts among these groups have also given rise to this notion, which is offered as a solution to the one-China (q.v.) versus two-Chinas question as well as the national identity question in Taiwan (q.v.).

Green Island (lü tao). An island off the east coast of southern Taiwan (q.v.) about 25 miles from Taitung that is the location of a prison where a number of political prisoners were kept in the past, especially during the years of martial law (q.v.). The prison remains, though the government has recently been trying to make the island a tourist attraction by encouraging the building of international-class hotels. Few places in Taiwan can compete with Green Island for unspoiled beauty. The island is called Green Island for its green mountains which contrast with the turquoise ocean around it. The island is quite small, about 6 square miles, and has a population of around 3,000, most of whom engage in fishing.

Guidelines for National Reunification. See National Unification Guidelines.

- H -

Hakka (k'e chia). The term designating one of the two major groups of Chinese who migrated to Taiwan before the end of World War II. The Hakkas were probably the earliest Chinese to move to Taiwan in any numbers, migrating there beginning as early as a thousand years ago, from South China, mainly Kuangtung. The Hakkas had been earlier displaced from their homes in North China and for that reason became known as "guest people"—the literal meaning of *Hakka*. They also suffered from various kinds of discrimination, including being barred from taking the civil service examination for many years. Not long after they arrived in Taiwan (q.v.) they were forced from the best coastal farming areas by Fukien Taiwanese. Today, Hakkas compose 10 to 15 percent of the population of Taiwan. The Hakka are culturally, linguistically, and in many other ways different from the Fukien Taiwanese and have a history of conflict with them, particularly before the arrival of the Nationalists. Hakkas constitute a majority of the population in some areas of Taiwan, including Taoyuan, Miaoli, Taichung, and Pingtung counties. Most Hakka speak their own language, in addition to Taiwanese and Mandarin (q.v.). Many are active politically, holding jobs in the police systems, railroads, and other government agencies. President Lee Teng-hui (q.v.) is Hakka.

Han Lih-wu (1975-1991). Minister of education from 1949-1950, advisor to the president from 1950-1956, he subsequently served as ambassador to a number of countries. Han, however, is best known for his efforts in bringing many antiques and other national treasures from the mainland in 1949 and for being the last person on China's "most wanted list" among Nationalist Chinese officials. Nevertheless, in Taiwan, and even in China, he has been regarded as a hero for his actions, since many of these invaluable artifacts would have been destroyed by Red Guards during the Cultural Revolution in China. The treasures he brought make up a large portion of those things on display in the National Palace Museum (q.v.).

Hasegawa, Kiyoshi. The governor-general of Taiwan (q.v.) from 1940 to 1944. Hasegawa was an admiral in the Japanese navy.

Hau Pei-tsun (1919-). An army general who had a long and distinguished military career, including serving as chief of the general staff. Hau was also a top official in the Nationalist Party (q.v.) and served as minister of defense from 1989 to 1990 and premier from 1990 to 1993. His appointment to the premiership was opposed by the Democratic Progressive Party (q.v.) and others who felt a military person should not serve in this office, though he soon gained public respect due to his success in cracking down on crime and social disorder. During his tenure as premier, Hau on many occasions disagreed with President Lee Teng-hui (q.v.), this being characterized as a personal feud and a struggle for power between Mainland Chinese and Taiwanese (qq.v.) by the media. His resignation in 1993 signified a subsequent Taiwanese-dominated government and a strengthening of presidential authority. In late 1995, Hau resigned his membership in the KMT. In 1996, Hau was a candidate for vice president on a ticket with Lin Yang-kang (q.v.). The two ran as independents, but had support from the New Party (q.v.).

Heaven and Earth Society (t'ien-ti-hui). One of the largest and most famous of China's secret societies, it was similar to the sworn brotherhoods (q.v.) but had much stricter rules of secrecy: participants could not divulge information about their membership to anyone, including their family. The Heaven and Earth Society was responsible for organizing and leading many of the great rebellions during Ch'ing rule; in fact, to "oppose the Ch'ing and restore the Ming" was one of its avowed political goals. It had a following in Taiwan (q.v.) for some time.

Home Rule Association (szu-chih hsieh-hui). An organization that was founded and grew in Taiwan (q.v.) in the early 1920s during the period of Japanese colonial rule. Its members were active in both Taiwan and Japan. Its main tenet was the advocacy of home rule for Taiwan rather than assimilation. Lin Hsien-t'ang (q.v.) was an active member and led the organization for a number of years. The organization also worked for better treatment of Taiwan by the Japanese government and equal rights for Taiwanese (q.v.). For a while it enjoyed considerable influence in Tokyo. In 1936, after the Japanese colonial government cracked down on the organization's activities in Taiwan and arrested some of its members, many left and joined Chiang Kai-shek (q.v.) or Mao

Zedong in China. Some other members formed the Taiwan Proletarian Youth League, which had ties with the Japan Communist Party. The association had six associated or subordinate organizations, of which one—the Culture Society (q.v.)—survived.

House of Lin (lin chia). A family "dynasty" founded by Lin P'ing-hou, who gained wealth and government position in the Ch'ing Dynasty in China, and who migrated to Taiwan (q.v.) from Fukien Province in 1778. His son, Lin Kuo-hau, relocated the family to Pan-ch'iao in Taiwan, and subsequently became Taiwan's largest landholder. Kuo-hau had several successful sons, one of whom helped Liu Ming-ch'uan (q.v.) in his modernization efforts. The family was later co-opted by the Japanese, but remained rich and powerful for some time. The Lins founded a sugar company in 1909 and the Hua Nan Bank in 1919. Today, the Lin home and garden, recently donated to the county of Taipei, are tourist attractions.

Hsi Sha. See Paracel Islands.

Hsiao Liu-ch'iu. Literally meaning "Small Liu-ch'iu" or Small Ryukyus, the term was used in China, even as late as the 16th century, to refer to Taiwan. See also Pakkan Tao.

Hsiaokang International Airport. Located near Kaohsiung (q.v.), it is Taiwan's second international airport.

Hsieh Chang-t'ing (1946-). Also known as Frank Hsieh, he became in the 1980s a leader in the Democratic Progressive Party (DPP) (q.v.) and a member of the Legislative Yuan (q.v.). He founded the Taiwan Welfare State Alliance, a DPP faction or support group, and ran as the party's candidate for vice president with Peng Ming-min (q.v.) in 1996. In 1998, he ran for the position of mayor of Kaohsiung and won.

Hsinchu. One of Taiwan's five large cities administered by Taiwan Province, it is located on the west coast of the northern part of the island near the Hsinchu Science-Based Industrial Park (q.v.).

Hsinchu Science-Based Industrial Park (hsin-chu k'e-hsueh kung-ye yuan-ch'u). A 5,200-acre industrial park established in 1980 near the city of Hsinchu (about an hour from Taipei [q.v.]) patterned after California's Silicon Valley. By 1989, 99 high-tech companies were operating there generating revenues of over U.S.$2 billion. By 1996 revenues had reached U.S.$11.34 billion. U.S. investment in the Park was said to be around U.S.$1.38 billion and trade between the Park's industries and the United States, U.S.$4.6 billion. The Park is projected to have an annual production value of US$36 billion by 2003, representing 12 percent of Taiwan's manufacturing output. A number of companies in the Park have offices in Silicon Valley in the United States and companies from there have offices in the Park.

Hsu Hsu-tung (1942-). Also known as Douglas Hsu, he is chairman of the Far Eastern Textile Group and is one of Taiwan's richest individuals. The family also owns Asia Cement and the Far Eastern Department Stores.

Hsu Hsin-liang (1941-). The chairman of the Democratic Progressive Party (DPP) (q.v.) from early 1996 to 1998, Hsu was formerly a Nationalist Party (q.v.) official but ran for magistrate of Taoyuan County in 1977 as an independent when he failed to get the party's endorsement. He won the election after rumors spread of ballot box tampering, which sparked public violence. (See Chungli Incident.) He fled to the United States in 1979 after continuous feuding with the government and the KMT. He remained "in exile" in the United States until 1988 during which time he established the Taiwan Revolutionary Party (q.v.) and wrote articles advocating urban guerrilla warfare in Taiwan (q.v.) to overthrow the government. In 1986, Hsu established the Taiwan Democratic Party in San Francisco and offered to make his party an overseas branch of the Democratic Progressive Party (q.v.) when it was established in September of that year.

In November 1986 Hsu tried to return to Taiwan but was refused entry. Supporters who had gone to the airport to meet him engaged in stone throwing to which the police responded with water hoses and tear gas—creating a widely debated incident. Hsu returned to Taiwan after martial law (q.v.) was lifted in 1987 and joined the DPP. He subsequently became a popular and influential opposition politician and DPP leader but also mellowed, changing in particular his formerly radical views about political reform in Taiwan. In June 1990, Hsu attended the National Affairs Conference (q.v.) and met with

President Lee Teng-hui and Premier Hau Pei-tsun (qq.v.). Hsu currently heads the more moderate Formosa faction (q.v.) of the DPP.

Hu Chih-chiang (1948-). Also known as Jason Hu, he is currently Minister of Foreign Affairs, having served as head of Taipei Economic and Cultural Representative Office (q.v.) in the United States from 1996 to 1997 and head of the Government Information Office (q.v.) from 1991 to 1996.

Hu Shih (1891-1962). A professor of philosophy at Beijing University, who in 1917 launched a movement to promote a written vernacular Chinese. Hu engaged in a "war of pens" with leftist and pro-Communist writers in the years that followed. Hu was active in the May the Fourth Movement (q.v.), which marked the beginning of Chinese nationalism. He was subsequently the Republic of China's (q.v.) ambassador to the United States. Hu went to Taiwan with the Nationalist government (q.v.) and there became a leader in advocating democratic reform.

Huang Hsin-chieh (1917-). The chairman of the Democratic Progressive Party (DPP) (q.v.) for three terms from 1988 to 1991, his rise in politics was through elections, beginning with city councilor and ending with election to the Legislative Yuan (q.v.). He was one of the Formosa group (q.v.) leaders who was arrested after the Kaohsiung Incident (q.v.) and sentenced to jail. In total he served more than seven years in prison. After his release he became a major figure in the establishment of the Democratic Progressive Party; some say he was its "spiritual founder." He subsequently became a leader of the more moderate Formosa faction (q.v.) before becoming party chairman. In the summer of 1997, Huang accepted President Lee Teng-hui's (q.v.) offer to serve as vice chairman of the National Unification Council (q.v.), which critics in the DPP said contradicted the party's stance on independence and for which Huang's membership in the DPP should be suspended. Huang argued that his position on unification had not changed and that in accepting this job he was working for the good of the nation. Huang is now seen as a DPP elder statesman.

- I -

Ilha Formosa. Meaning "beautiful island" in Portuguese, the term was used by Portuguese explorers, the first Westerners to see Taiwan in 1590, to refer to the island. See also Formosa.

Indigenous Defense Fighter (IDF) (ching-kuo-hao chan-chi). Also called the Ching-kuo, the IDF is Taiwan's home-built high-performance jet fighter plane. Its construction began after the Reagan Administration's decision not to sell Taiwan the FX (q.v.) aircraft. In March 1986, it was revealed that General Dynamics Corporation had been licensed as a consultant to help in the effort, though this was not a "full service" role—meaning that the consultants could not design the plane but could point out flaws in design and advise Taiwan's engineers and scientists. Beijing viewed this as reneging on the August 1982 Communiqué (q.v.), but the United States argued that it was a private arrangement and did not violate the agreement.

Taipei announced the completion of the aircraft in 1988. The first demonstration flights were conducted in October 1989. The first squadron of IDFs was commissioned in 1994, and a second in 1995. In April 1997, the 427th Wing, composed of 70 IDFs, went into service. Another wing of 60 IDFs was formed in 1999. The plane was intended to help Taiwan maintain its defenses against an attack by the People's Republic of China by denying the PRC air superiority over Taiwan and the Taiwan Strait (q.v.). It was also built so Taipei would have to rely less on the United States for arms purchases. In fact, some have said that the IDF resolved the thorny issue between Washington and Beijing concerning U.S. arms sales to Taiwan and also that it marked the beginning of Taiwan getting into the business of manufacturing arms. The plane, however, was built at a very high cost—one that will probably never be recouped. Its future was, moreover, brought into question in 1992 when the United States changed its policy and agreed to sell Taiwan F-16 (q.v.) fighter planes, after which France decided to sell Mirage 2000-5 (q.v.) fighters; Taiwan contracted to buy 150 of the former and 60 of the latter. Recently Taipei decided to build only 130 IDF planes after originally planning to build 250. IDFs are based in Taichung and Tainan.

Industrial Technology Research Institute (ITRI) (kung-yeh k'e-chih yen-chiu-yuan). Established in 1973 to develop technology in Taiwan (q.v.), ITRI is a nonprofit organization that transfers research to local companies, in some cases under contract. It is located in Hsinchu. Its projects are largely generic and are done under government supervision. They are categorized by industry, including eight at present: electronics, information, mechanical engineering, material science and technology, energy and mining, electrooptics, pollution abatement, and measurement technology. ITRI has made a number of technological contributions to Taiwan's technological modernization and can take credit for some research breakthroughs, including work on microchips and successful experiments with superconductivity. ITRI has about 5,000 employees, mostly engineers.

Institute for National Policy Research (kuo-chia cheng-tse yen-chiu-yuan). Founded in 1988 by Chang Yung-fa (q.v.), it is the nation's first and foremost private think tank involved in public policy research. The institute is considered pro-Democratic Progressive Party (q.v.).

Institute for Taiwan Studies (t'ai-wan yen-chiu-suo). Policy research organization in the Chinese Academy of Social Sciences in Beijing. In recent years it has held meetings and talks with a sizeable number of individuals and groups from Taiwan (q.v.). A number of universities also have organizations with the same name, the most famous being at Xiamen (Amoy) University in Fujian Province.

Institute of International Relations (cheng-ta kuo-kuan chung-hsin). Affiliated with National Chengchi University (q.v.), it is considered Taiwan's foremost think tank on communist nations and international politics. It holds frequent conferences, publishes books and journals and has considerable input into the foreign policy making process.

Intellectual, The. A reformist magazine that began publication in 1968 and advocated major social and economic reform, political pluralism, and the realization of Sun Yat-sen's (q.v.) Three Principles of the People (q.v.). It was started and operated by a group of university professors, students, and younger Nationalist Party (q.v.) officials, many of the latter associated with Lee Huan (q.v.). The tone of the articles carried in the magazine contrasted, according to some analysts, with Lei Chen's (q.v.) intellectualist elitism.

International Cooperation and Development Fund (kuo-chi ho-tso fa-chan yin-hang). Established in March 1988 as the International Economic Cooperation and Development Fund with N.T. $30 billion (just over U.S.$1 billion) it was designed to assist the economic development plans of friendly developing nations. Since then its funding has been increased. Creating this aid-giving organization reflected Taiwan's new prosperity and its large foreign exchange holdings. According to some, however, its purpose was to "buy" diplomatic relations, which it clearly managed to do, or at least influence, in some cases. See also Dollar diplomacy.

International Technological Cooperation Program (kuo-chi k'o-chi ho-tso chi-hua). A technical aid program established in 1961 to assist the technological development of several African countries and to help keep or expand diplomatic relations with African and other Third World countries. It has since enlarged to include 24 nations. Through this organization, Taiwan (q.v.) has also offered technical courses for participants from 70 different countries.

Investigation Bureau (fa-wu-pu tiao-cha-chu). An arm of the Ministry of Justice sometimes called "Taiwan's FBI," the Investigation Bureau is responsible for domestic law enforcement and counterintelligence work. In the past, it was under the jurisdiction of the National Security Council (q.v.).

Issues and Studies (wen-ti yu yen-chiu). A monthly journal published by the Institute of International Relations (q.v.) that deals with global affairs and Communism.

- J -

Japan Interchange Association (jih-pen ch'iao-liu hsieh-hui). Japan's quasi-embassy in Taipei (q.v.), similar to the American Institute in Taiwan (q.v.).

Japan-Taiwan Parliamentarians' League. A low-keyed and loosely organized group of approximately 300 members of the Diet in Japan that includes members of various parties but mostly the Liberal Democratic Party. Though it does not meet formally, or at least with regularity, and little is known about its workings, it has had considerable influence on Japan's relations with Taiwan (q.v.), but also the People's Republic of China. It is reputed to have influenced Japan's policy a number of times, including its recent decision to reject Beijing's Three Nos Policy (q.v.) on Taiwan.

Jaw Shau-kong (1950-). The popular former head of the Environmental Protection Administration (EPA) (q.v.) and one of the activist leaders of the Nationalist Party's Breakfast Club (qq.v.) and the New KMT Alliance (q.v.). Jaw was, for some time, called the "golden boy" of Taiwan (q.v.) politics. In 1992 he resigned from the EPA to run for a seat in the Legislative Yuan (q.v.) in its first ever nonsupplemental election. He did not have the endorsement of the party and in so doing created difficulties for the KMT (q.v.). But he won a large number of votes—more than any other KMT candidate. Thus he was not punished by the party. However, in 1993, after continued feuds with the Mainstream Faction (q.v.) of the KMT, he left the ruling party to help form the New Party (q.v.). In 1994, Jaw was a candidate for the position of mayor of Taipei (q.v.) representing the New Party. He beat the KMT's candidate, but came in second to Chen Shui-bian (q.v.), the DPP's standard- bearer. Some charged at the time that KMT leaders had, knowing their candidate would lose, diverted votes to the DPP candidate so that Jaw would not win. In 1996, Jaw nominally withdrew from politics to pursue a business career, which included taking the position of chairmanship of UFO Broadcasting Corporation. However, he has maintained an influential role in the New Party and in 1998 served as the party's campaign manager.

Joint Commission on Rural Reconstruction (JCRR) (chung-kuo nung-tsun fu-hsing lien-ho wei-yuan-hui). Originally composed of two U.S. and three Chinese commissioners, it planned, and to a large extent effectuated, Taiwan's successful land reform (q.v.) program in the 1950s. It continued to operate after land reform was completed, creating farmers' associations and government programs to improve agriculture. Many of the commission's reports have been studied by economists and officials in other countries. President Lee Teng-hui (q.v.) worked for JCRR for several years early in his career.

Ju Gao-jeng (1954-). A former leader of the Democratic Progressive Party (q.v.) and parliamentarian who became known as "Rambo" because of his ostentatious and sometimes very aggressive and disruptive tactics used in sessions of the Legislative Yuan (q.v.). He left the DPP in 1990 after failing to get the party's nomination to run for a seat in the Legislative Yuan in 1989. He ran as an independent and was elected. Subsequently he formed the Chinese Social Democratic Party (q.v.). In 1994, Ju ran as the New Party's (NP) (q.v.) candidate for Taiwan provincial governor but was not elected. In 1995, he was again elected to the Legislative Yuan and became the New Party's whip, but was expelled from the NP after internal disagreements in 1997. In 1998, he ran again for the Legislative Yuan as an independent but was not elected.

Judicial Yuan (sz fa yuan). One of five branches of the national government of the Republic of China (q.v.), it is similar in its organization and functions to judicial branches in Western political systems. It comprises a Council of Grand Justices (q.v.), three levels of ordinary courts, administrative courts, and a Committee on the Discipline of Public Functionaries (q.v.).

- K -

Kabayama Sukenori. Taiwan's first Japanese governor-general, serving from 1895 to 1896. He consolidated military control over the island and built an effective police force. He also launched civilian rule in Taiwan (q.v.).

Kang Ning-hsiang (1938-). A Taiwanese politician who served on the Taipei City Council in the 1960s and won a seat in the Legislative Yuan (q.v.) as an independent in 1972. Together with Huang Hsin-chieh (q.v.) and others, Kang organized the Tangwai (q.v.). Kang also founded a number of publications, including the *Taiwan Political Review* and *The Eighties* (qq.v.) and wrote a number of books. Early in his career Kang was viewed as a radical but subsequently became a leader of the moderate opposition. He led the mainstream faction of the Democratic Progressive Party (DPP) (q.v.) in the late 1970s and after the Kaohsiung Incident (q.v.) became, in the eyes of many observers, the DPP's most prominent leader. In a few years, however, Kang lost his influence in the DPP and in 1988 his mainstream faction was absorbed by the Formosa faction and the New Tide faction (qq.v.). In 1998, he joined the Koo-Wang (q.v.) delegation that visited the People's Republic of China (q.v.), but he was snubbed while he was there.

Kao Chun-ming (Reverend) (1929-). The general secretary of the Presbyterian Church in Taiwan (q.v.) in the 1970s, in 1979, he was arrested for giving sanctuary to Shih Ming-teh (q.v.), who was said to have masterminded the Kaohsiung Incident (q.v.).

Kaohsiung. Taiwan's second-largest city and its largest port, handling nearly two-thirds of its exports and imports. Kaohsiung also has had the distinction of being one of the world's largest container ports. Kaohsiung is located in southwest Taiwan (q.v.) and was the cite of Taiwan's first export processing zone (q.v.).

Kaohsiung City Government (kao-hsiung shih-cheng-fu). Similar to the Taipei City Government (q.v.). it gained the status of a special municipality in 1979, the reason given being that it was Taiwan's biggest and most important port and its second-largest city.

Kaohsiung Eight (tsan-yu kao-hsiung shih-chien chih pa jen). Eight defendants convicted in a widely publicized and controversial trial in March 1980 and given sentences ranging from 12 years to life for their roles in the Kaohsiung Incident (q.v.). They were Chang Chun-hung (q.v.), Chen Chu, Huang Hsin-chieh (q.v.), Lin Hung-hsuan, Lin Yi-hsiung (q.v.), Lu Hsiu-lien, Shih Ming-teh (q.v), and Yao Chia-wen (q.v.).

Kaohsiung Incident (kao-hsiung shih-chien). A violent affair that occurred in the city of Kaohsiung (q.v.) in December 1979 following an antigovernment protest demonstration parade that was organized by the Formosa group (q.v.). It happened on, and the parade was intended to commemorate, Human

Rights Day—December 10. The demonstration led to an outbreak of chaos and violence, during which 183 police were reported injured, though only a few seriously. Whether the demonstrators planned to attack the police or whether they panicked when the police tried to surround them is uncertain. Also, whether the attacks were precipitated by gang members using the occasion as an opportunity to get revenge against the police, were planned by the Formosa group, or were simply spontaneous is not known. In any event, the demonstration followed the loss of diplomatic relations with the United States early that year, which caused the government to lose credibility, and opposition activists thus to try to promote the rapid democratization of the political system, saying that only through democracy could Taiwan (q.v.) justify asking for support from the international community for keeping its sovereignty. They had considerable public support for promoting democratization.

However, after the violence occurred the public changed its view and sympathized more with the government. In fact, there was little public outcry when those accused of causing the violence, including a number of well-known political figures, were convicted and sentenced to prison (see Kaohsiung Eight). Subsequent to the Kaohsiung Incident there were compromises made between the government and the opposition and "gentlemens' agreements" about democratization. A tangible product was a new election law written for the December 1980 election, which became a watershed event in Taiwan's political development.

Katsura Taro. Taiwan's second Japanese governor-general, who served in office only three months in 1896.

Keelung. A seaport on Taiwan's northern coast, often referred to as Taipei's (q.v.) harbor city.

Ketagalan. A tribe of aborigines (q.v.) regarded by some scholars as the oldest inhabitants of Taiwan. The Ketagalan were Pingpu (q.v.) or plains dwelling people of the island who resided on its west coast before the arrival of Chinese settlers. Like other Pingpu tribes they were assimilated by the Chinese or driven into the mountains where they were absorbed by other aborigines. The Ketagalan are close to extinction now. The name "Ketagalan" also refers to the street in Taipei (q.v.) where the Presidential Palace is located.

Kinmen. See Quemoy.

KMT. See Nationalist Party.

Kobayashi Seizo. The governor-general of Taiwan (q.v.) appointed in the fall of 1936. He was a retired naval admiral and his appointment, after 17 years of civilian rule, signaled Japan's militarization and the coming war with China. Kobayashi renovated the education system in Taiwan during his four-year rule and made other improvements.

Kodama Gentaro. The governor-general of Taiwan (q.v.) from February 1898 to April 1906. General Kodama also served as Japanese minister of war after 1900, leaving Goto Shimpei (q.v.) in de facto charge of the colonial government in Taiwan. See also Kodama Report.

Kodama Report (er-yü pao-kao-shu). A report allegedly written by General Kodama, governor-general of Taiwan (q.v.), in 1901. The report contained a detailed plan of a Japanese attack on French possessions in Southeast Asia, using Taiwan as a base of operations. It was reprinted in a French publication engendering controversy in France while causing Japanese and French relations to be strained. The Japanese government subsequently called it a fabrication. The report resurfaced in 1941, when U.S. intelligence officials noted that nearly all of the projects cited in it had been completed and said that Taiwan was to be used as a stepping-stone for Japan to expand southward.

Kominka. The policy of assimilation practiced off and on by Japan vis-à-vis Taiwan. It was advocated by the political left in Japan as opposed to a policy of separate rule.

Koo Chen-fu (1917-). A senior advisor to the president, patriarch of the China Trust Group, chairman of the Taiwan Cement Corporation and the Chinese National Association of Industry, Koo has wielded considerable political and economic influence in Taiwan for a number of years though he has never held any official government position. Koo, also known as C.F., is also the founding chairman of the Taiwan Stock

Exchange. Koo has garnered considerable press attention and public acclaim through several semiofficial positions, the most important being his chairmanship of the Straits Exchange Foundation (q.v.), which has engaged in negotiating various issues with Beijing. He is the son of Koo Hsien-yung (q.v.). His family fortune is valued at several U.S.$ billion. See also Koo-Wang talks.

Koo Hsien-yung (1866-1937). Born in Lukang, a port city on Taiwan's west coast, he assisted the Japanese army to enter Taipei (q.v.) (then a walled city) shortly after the signing of the Treaty of Shimonoseki (q.v.) in 1895 and during a time of intense debate concerning whether to fight the Japanese or allow them to take control of the island. Later, Japanese authorities gave him a position in the government's security apparatus and a monopoly over the salt trade, plus land in central Taiwan (q.v.). Koo also got into sugar, manufacturing, retail trade and land development and served as the director of a number of companies when Taiwan was a Japanese colony. Koo was very active politically, becoming the first Taiwanese to sit in the Japanese House of Peers. He also served on the GovernorGeneral's Advisory Council. He helped set up the Public Interest Society in 1923 and later became its president. He established the progressive *Taiwan Magazine*, the Public Interest Society, and the Taiwan Youth Association (q.v.) (in Tokyo). He was opposed by members of the Home Rule Association (q.v.). Koo Chen-fu (q.v.) is his son.

Koo-Wang Talks (ku-wang hui-tan). Unofficial but important negotiations held in Singapore in April 1993 that were considered to have marked a breakthrough in relations between Taipei (q.v.) and Beijing. The meeting was unprecedented in many respects. The talks were led on the two sides by Koo Chen-fu (q.v.), head of the Straits Exchange Foundation (q.v.), representing Taipei, and Wang Daohan, head of the Association for Relations Across the Taiwan Strait (q.v.), representing Beijing. Four agreements were signed. The talks were to be followed by more meetings, but were not due to anger on the part of the leaders of the People's Republic of China at President Lee Teng-hui's (q.v.) visit to the United States in 1995. Another meeting, however, took place in October 1998 that again resulted in some minor agreements but more importantly signaled better relations between Taipei and Beijing. Many observers said the United States had helped promote this meeting.

Koxinga. See Cheng Ch'eng-kung.

Ku Cheng-kang (1902-1993). A senior advisor to the president in the 1980s, he is also known as the founder of the World Anti-Communist League, which he headed for a number of years. He was also head of the Asian Pacific Anti-Communist League (q.v.) for a number of years.

Kuan Chung (1940-). Also known as John Kuan, he served as deputy secretary-general of the Central Committee (q.v.) of the Nationalist Party (q.v.) from 1989 to 1990. After a disagreement with Secretary-General Soong Chu-yu (q.v.) he caused a split in the party, he subsequently established the Democracy Foundation (q.v.) that has played an important role in KMT politics. He is also known as the genius behind Nationalist Party election victories and has been blamed at other times when the party did not perform well.

Kung Teh-cheng (1920-). A senior advisor to the president, he is also a 77th-generation lineal descendant of Confucius and is the only person in Taiwan who holds a hereditary title: Duke of Yen Sheng.

Kuningtou. Located on the island of Quemoy (q.v.) a bloody battle was fought here between Nationalist and Communist forces in October 1949. Following a fierce artillery barrage, the Communist People's Liberation Army launched an assault using 300 small craft (carrying 17,000 troops) against Quemoy. During a two-day siege, Nationalist forces killed 8,000 Communist troops and captured more than 6,000. Communist military units then gave up capturing the island and it remained in Nationalist hands.

Kuo, Shirley W.Y. (1930-). Currently an advisor to the president, she is an economist who published several books on Taiwan's economic miracle and who later became a prominent Nationalist Party (q.v.) and government official. In July 1988, she was the first woman to become a member of the Central Standing Committee (q.v.) of the Nationalist Party and almost at the same time was appointed minister of finance. The next year she attended the Asian Development Bank (q.v.) meeting in the People's Republic of China (PRC), the first time a high government official visited the PRC on official business. In 1990, she was appointed head of the Council for Economic Planning and Development (q.v.). After 1993, she served for several years as a minister of state.

Kuo Yu-hsin (1908-1985). An opposition leader who, following defeat in the 1975 national election, went to the United States. He later announced that he sought to run for the presidency against Chiang Ching-kuo (q.v.), but did not attain sufficient support to become a serious candidate.

Kuomintang (KMT) (kuo-min-tang). Literally "Nation-Citizen Party." See Nationalist Party.

- L -

Labor Disputes Law (lao-tse cheng-yi ch'u-li-fa). A Republic of China law regulating labor-management problems. It was amended in June 1988 to extend the right to strike to any group of 10 or more workers involved in a dispute, or two-thirds of the work force of enterprises with fewer than 10 employees, regardless of whether the dispute is in the public or private sector.

Labor Standards Law (lao-tung chi-chun-fa). Passed in 1984 by the Legislative Yuan (q.v.), this law, known as Taiwan's "key labor law," defined the role of workers, employers, wages, and contracts while extending labor standards to many workers not previously covered. It also provided guarantees of maximum wages, hours, vacation time, pensions, severance pay, pay equity, maternity leave, and occupational safety and health. Initially, the law covered about 40 percent of the nation's more than eight million workers. In May 1997, the law was extended to cover workers in financial organizations and some other occupations. In December 1996, the law was revised and extended to many workers not covered by the law. By early 1998, the Labor Standards Law covered over 57 percent of Taiwan's workforce. Although the law had a major impact in improving labor conditions, critics complain that it punishes violators with fines only and does not treat infractions as criminal offenses.

Labor Union Law (kung-hui-fa). A Republic of China law which regulates union organizing and limits unionization to firms with 30 employees or more. The Labor Union Law allows strikes only after a majority vote of affected workers support it and if mandatory mediation fails. Critics say the law should be expanded and strengthened and note that it allows only one workers' union to establish at the national level. See Chinese Federation of Labor.

Land reform (t'u-ti kai-k'e). Refers to three separate policies carried out during the period 1949 to 1953. The first was rent reduction, which set the rent limit on cultivated land at 37.5 percent of the annual standard yield of chief crops no matter what the actual harvest. (Landlords had previously collected about half of the crop in rent.) The government also included provisions for rent relief in the event of crop failure or calamity. The second part mandated the sale of public farmland to farmers, mostly land previously owned by Japanese and confiscated by the Nationalist Chinese government after World War II. This land, amounting to 20 to 25 percent of Taiwan's arable land, was sold to cultivator farmers during the period of 1948 to 1958. The third measure was the land-to-the-tiller program passed into law in 1953 which forced landlords to sell to the government any farmland in excess of 2.9 hectares of medium- grade paddy for a price equal to two and one-half times the annual yield. The government then sold it to tenant farmers. Around 22 percent of the private farmland in Taiwan (q.v.) changed hands as a result of this law.

Land reform in Taiwan set the stage for rapid growth in the agricultural sector. More efficient farming released laborers to work in Taiwan's new factories, thus spurring industrial growth. Land reform also contributed to the end of feudalism in rural Taiwan, rapid urbanization, and the popularity of the Nationalist Party (q.v.) in the countryside. On the negative side, it caused instability in the countryside for a while and is said to have cheated the landlords, who received payment in low-interest bonds.

Taiwan's land reform program is widely regarded as one of the most successful, if not the most successful, in the world. Western scholars and Third World leaders still study Taiwan's experience in land reform. See also Joint Commission on Rural Reconstruction.

Law on Civic Organizations (kung-min szu-chih-fa). A law passed by the Legislative Yuan (q.v.) in 1989 to regulate trade associations, social organizations, and political parties. The law's most important provision was to make forming new political parties legal. It also put various civic organizations under the jurisdiction of the ministry of interior. The number of civic organizations, including political parties, proliferated after the passage of this law.

League for the Re-emancipation of Formosa (t'ai-wan tsai-chieh-fang lien-meng). An organization founded in Hong Kong by Liao Wen-yi and Ms. Hsieh Hsueh-hong after the February 28 uprising or rebellion (see er er ba). The former advocated a United Nations plebiscite that would allow for self-determination and eventual independence; the latter advocated Communism. Liao later moved his faction to Japan. Hsieh went to the People's Republic of China.

Lee Huan (1917-). A close associate of Chiang Ching-kuo (q.v.) for many years, he served as minister of education from 1984 to 1987, secretary-general of the Nationalist Party (q.v.) from 1987 to 1989 and premier from 1989 to 1990. He lost power following disagreement with to President Lee Teng-hui (q.v.) in early 1990.

Lee Teng-hui (1923-). The eighth president of the Republic of China and chairman of the Nationalist Party (q.v.), Lee attended Kyoto University in Japan during World War II but returned to Taiwan (q.v.) to receive his B.S. degree from National Taiwan University (q.v.) in 1948. In 1953, he got an M.A. at Iowa State University, and in 1968, a Ph.D. in agricultural economics from Cornell University. His first political job in Taiwan was with the Joint Commission on Rural Reconstruction (q.v.) in 1957. He subsequently served in several positions before being appointed mayor of Taipei (q.v.), serving in that position from 1978 to 1981, and governor of Taiwan Province from 1981 to 1984.

Lee then became vice president under Chiang Ching-kuo (q.v.) from 1984 to January 1988, whereupon he became president following Chiang Ching-kuo's death. He was, in fact, picked by Chiang to be his successor. He also became acting chairman of the Nationalist Party upon Chiang Ching-kuo's death, though he was briefly challenged by some top officials in the party, including Madam Chiang Kai-shek (q.v.). He was elected party chairman in July 1988 at the Nationalist Party's National Party Congress (q.v.). He was reelected president by the National Assembly in May 1990 after a brief challenge by Lin Yang-kang and Chiang Wei-kuo (qq.v.) and reelected party chairman in 1993. In 1996, Lee was elected president for another term in the nation's first direct presidential election, winning over 54 percent of the vote in a four-way race. This election became a widely reported event throughout the world because of missile tests conducted by Beijing to intimidate Taiwan and send a signal that the PRC would not tolerate Taiwan independence. In 1997, Lee was again reelected chairman of the Nationalist Party.

Being the first Taiwanese (q.v.) president, Lee represented a transition from Mainland Chinese (q.v.) to Taiwanese rule as well as an end of the "Chiang Dynasty," though Lee has also been known for his loyalty to CCK and his determination to continue Chiang Ching-kuo's reforms and in many ways has remained loyal to his mentor. He has been criticized, however, for breaking from the Nationalist Party's one-China (q.v.) policy, for causing the KMT to split—one faction forming the New Party (q.v.)—and the decline of the party in terms of public opinion polls and election defeats. He has not only been assailed by the right-wing of the Nationalist Party for abandoning Sun Yat-sen's (q.v.) principles and for his alleged stance in favor of Taiwan independence, but also by the Democratic Progressive Party (q.v.) and Beijing—the former because of its advocating a one-China policy, the latter because it does not. This seems in large part the product of Taiwan democratizing so quickly and the result of inevitable differences arising in Taiwan's domestic politics as a result of Taipei's shaky relationship with the PRC. Lee's critics also cite his authoritarian style of leadership and blame him for money politics and the rise of crime in Taiwan.

Lee will likely be most remembered for furthering the democratization of Taiwan started by Chiang Ching-kuo, launching Taiwan's pragmatic diplomacy, changes made in the Constitution (q.v.), the Republic of China's first direct presidential election, his Taiwanization of the nation's political system and its politics, and differences with Beijing concerning unification.

Lee Yuan-tseh (1936-). President of Academia Sinica (q.v.) and national policy advisor to the president, Lee won the Nobel Prize in chemistry in 1986 and is regarded as one of Taiwan's foremost scholars. He has also been mentioned as a possible candidate for high political office (though he has often denied any interest in such) and is often consulted and interviewed by the media about policy issues, especially in the realms of education and science.

Legislative Yuan (li-fa-yuan). One of the five branches of the central government and considered the highest legislative or lawmaking organ of government in the Republic of China. It hears reports from the Executive Yuan (q.v.) and makes policy both on its own and on recommendations from the Executive Yuan. Its functions may be summarized as passing laws, confirming emergency orders of the president, hearing reports on government policy, examining budget bills, consenting to nominations of the premier and other high officials, proposing constitutional amendments (to the National Assembly [q.v.]) and settling disputes among other organs of government.

Many of its members for some time were holdovers from elections on the mainland. Thus, in the past the Legislative Yuan was criticized as undemocratic since most of its members did not represent the territory under control of the nation. In the 1980s, however, with new members elected in supplemental elections, Taiwan-elected members began to have more influence in Legislative Yuan sessions. In fact, they did more than their numbers suggested because of their vitality and their closer contacts with the populace. By the end of that decade, locally elected members, because senior parliamentarians (q.v.) often missed sessions or were not energetic, often dominated debates on important issues. After the Democratic Progressive Party (q.v.) did well in the 1989 election its leaders charged that the DPP could not become the ruling party even if it won an election because of the senior parliamentarians. Pressure thus increased on the elder parliamentarians to resign. In 1991, those not elected in elections held in Taiwan (q.v.) agreed to step down in preparation for the election of a new Legislative Yuan in December 1992. Since that time the Legislative Yuan has been much stronger and has played a larger role in Taiwan politics. The opposition has likewise had a much bigger voice in the Legislative Yuan and this has enhanced its political influence.

According to the amended Constitution (q.v.), two members are elected from each province or special municipality but where the population exceeds 200,000 one member is added for each 100,000 and where the population exceeds one million, another member will be added for each 200,000 people. Three members represent lowland and highland aborigines (q.v.) and six represent Chinese citizens abroad. Those representing aborigines or Chinese abroad are elected by party-list proportional representation. Thus, 176 of the total of 225 seats are filled through direct ballot; the remaining seats are allocated by political party. Elections use single and secret ballots and transpire three months before a legislative session.

The Legislative Yuan holds two sessions each year: from February to the end of May and September to the end of December. Members cannot be held responsible for opinions expressed or votes cast or arrested, except in the case of very serious crimes. No member may hold concurrently another government post.

The Legislative Yuan has been the site of protests, antics, and violence since the 1980s, but this has decreased in recent years. The Legislative Yuan has also been at odds with the Executive Yuan and the National Assembly (qq.v.) on various matters, most serious being the powers assumed by each and their relationships in terms of political authority. Notwithstanding frequent contention, bad publicity because of disruptions in conducting business, and frequent stalemates in passing laws, the Yuan has increased in importance and generally in prestige as a result of democratization.

Lei Chen (1897-1979). Mainland Chinese intellectual, writer, and high-ranking Nationalist Party (q.v.) official, who, before the Nationalist government moved to Taiwan, was an assistant secretary general to the People's Political Council. He was also minister without portfolio in the Executive Yuan (q.v.)

and advisor to the president on national strategy. In Taiwan, Lei founded the journal *Free China Fortnightly* (q.v.) and wrote for and managed the journal for 11 years. He was associated with Hu Shih (q.v.) and other intellectuals as well as the Republic of China's (ROC) (q.v.) top political leadership. Lei, however, opposed the KMT's dominance in Taiwan's politics and its extraconstitutional powers, and the ROC's authoritarian political system. For this he became controversial and made enemies. In 1960, shortly after founding the China Democratic Party (q.v.) (at a time when establishing new political parties was illegal) he was accused of harboring a Communist agent on his staff and was sentenced to 10 years in prison for sedition. Critics of the government and many outside observers called the charges false. In 1988, opposition politicians protested when the army allegedly burned his prison memoirs.

"Letter to Taiwan Compatriots" (chih t'ai-wan tung-pao shu). Public letter sent by the Standing Committee of the National People's Congress of the People's Republic of China (PRC) to officials in Taiwan (q.v.), proposing the establishment of trade, travel, and communications links while promising to "respect Taiwan's status quo, adopt reasonable and rational policies and methods, and refrain from causing Taiwan people to suffer." This letter was "sent" on January 1, 1979, the date that official diplomatic relations were established between the United States and the People's Republic of China. It was the first of many efforts by the PRC, after the normalization of relations with the United States, to persuade Taipei (q.v.) to agree to talks aimed at reunification. It reflected what officials in Beijing thought was an opportunity, because of the severe blow to Taipei and a desperate situation for the government and the ruling Nationalist Party (q.v.) caused by U.S. derecognition, to negotiate unification of Taiwan on Beijing's terms.

Li Ao (1935-) Taiwan's most famous dissident writers, Li has published more than one hundred books, including two autobiographies. He was a contributor to *Apollo* (q.v.), a reformist literary periodical, for some time. Li's writings were very provocative and many were banned, and he served a number of years in jail or prison. Li is considered an iconoclast and a political critic. With democratization Li became popular. He might have had more influence had he written in English. Since 1995 he has hosted a popular television show.

Li Kwoh-ting (1910-). Senior advisor to the president and honorary board chairman of the Chiang Ching-kuo Foundation (q.v.). Li was considered for some time, and still is so viewed, the brains behind Taiwan's economic miracle. Also known as K. T. Li, he served as minister of economic affairs from 1965 to 1969 and minister of finance from 1969 to 1976. Li is also the author of a number of books on economics and business.

Li Tchong-koei (1938-). Director of the China Youth Corps (q.v.), she has also served as deputy secretary general of the Central Committee of the Nationalist Party (q.v.). She has been a member of the Central Standing Committee of the Nationalist Party and is considered one of Taiwan's most politically prominent women. She was previously president of the Pacific Cultural Foundation.

Li Tsung-jen (1891-1969). Leader of the Kwangsi faction of the Nationalist Party (q.v.) in the mid-1940s, he was elected vice president of the Republic of China in the spring of 1947. When it became clear that the Nationalists would lose the civil war to the Communists, Chiang Kai-shek (q.v.) resigned, leaving Li president. He was president when Nationalist forces fled to Taiwan (q.v.) and after, up until December 1949, when he had to abandon his temporary seat of government in Chengtu. The next day, Taipei (q.v.) was proclaimed the new temporary capital of the Republic of China. Li, however, went to the United States for medical help and remained there. His supporters fled to Hong Kong. Li met President Harry Truman in March 1950 to obtain support for a so-called Third Force (meaning neither the Nationalists nor the Communists). At the same time he wrote to Chiang Kai-shek, protesting Chiang's resumption of the presidency, saying that without an election of the National Assembly (q.v.) he had no legal grounds for this. Li subsequently hoped to return to Taiwan where he might play a potential role or influence America's China policy, but failed at both.

Li Yuan-zu (1923-). Former vice president and currently a vice-chairman of the Nationalist Party, Li was close to both Chiang Ching-kuo and, subsequently, Lee Teng-hui (qq.v.). He served as minister of education from 1977 to 1978 and minister of justice from 1979 to 1984. He was secretary-general to the president before he became vice president in 1990. His nomination for the vice presidency by Lee Teng-hui, however, caused controversy, as Li was not so well known and had not been considered a strong contender for that office. He was replaced by Lien Chan (q.v.) in 1996.

Liao Wen-yi (also known as Thomas Liao) (1910-1976). One of the founders of the League for the Reemancipation of Formosa (q.v.) that was formed in 1947 in Hong Kong and later moved to Japan. Liao also established a "provisional government of the Republic of Formosa" and was one of Taiwan's leading advocates of independence for some time, perhaps its most well known advocate. By the late 1950s, however, most younger activists had abandoned him.

Lien Chan (1936-). Elected vice president in 1996, Lien was premier from 1993 to 1997, governor of Taiwan province from 1990 to 1993, minister of foreign affairs from 1988 to 1990, vice-premier from 1987 to 1988, and minister of transportation and communications from 1981 to 1987. He has also been vice-chairman of the Nationalist Party (q.v.) from 1993 to the present. He was, at 45, the youngest minister ever in the government and the youngest member ever of the KMT Central Standing Committee. Lien is considered one of Taiwan's most experienced and most promising politicians. He is also widely regarded as Lee Teng-hui's (q.v.) chosen successor and many thus predict that he will be nominated by the KMT and elected president in 2000.

As premier for four and a half years from 1993 to 1997, Lien presided over considerable change in Taiwan (q.v.): the final steps in democratization, increased social pluralism (with advances in minority rights), and an economic recovery, with budget deficits brought under control—though this was costly in terms of government investment. He introduced a universal health insurance program in 1995, which, though popular, was also very expensive. During the latter years as premier, and in the absence of a significant Nationalist Party majority, Lien had to deal with a hostile Legislative Yuan (q.v.) that often opposed his programs. Thus it was very difficult for him to deal with the Legislative Yuan on many issues and, in many cases, get legislation passed. After Lien was elected vice president, in the nation's first direct election of the president and vice president, he remained premier; members of the legislature protested this and even on occasion blocked his entry into the Legislative Yuan, saying that he should not hold the two offices concurrently.

Though Lien has been considered by most as very successful in office, he has not fared very well in public opinion polls, especially recently—perhaps because he has shunned the public spotlight in order to avoid an appearance of competing with his mentor Lee Teng-hui; alternatively it is because he is seen by many as rich and elitist and lacks the charisma of some other top political figures.

Lien is considered Taiwanese (because his father is Taiwanese), and some thus say he can bridge the gap between Taiwanese and Mainland Chinese (qq.v.) and between Taiwan and China. He was born in Sian in Central China; his mother hails from Manchuria. He is rumored to have been involved in the Taiwan Independence Movement (q.v.) when he was young, though he married a Mainland Chinese, a former Miss China. Lien's grandfather, Lien Heng, who wrote *A History of Taiwan,* which was widely read by students and others in the past, said he was loyal to both Taiwan and China.

Lin Hsien-t'ang (1881-1956). A member of the Lin family of Wu-feng in central Taiwan, near Taichung, that supported and aided Liu Ming-ch'uan (q.v.) when the latter was governor of Taiwan. The family became very wealthy in business, especially through trade with China and retailing. Lin later founded the Taito Trust Company under Japanese rule and was very influential politically. For some time he opposed General Sakuma's (q.v.) harsh rule of Taiwan and supported a policy of assimilation. He was a spokesman for the Home Rule movement (see Home Rule Association) and advocated a democratic Taiwan under Japanese rule.

Lin Yang-kang (1927-). Long considered one of the nation's most charismatic and experienced Taiwanese politicians and one of its best campaigners, Lin was commissioner of the Taiwan Provincial Department of Reconstruction from 1972 to 1976, Taipei (q.v.) mayor from 1976 to 1978, governor of Taiwan from 1978 to 1981, and, subsequently, minister of interior. He served as vice premier from 1984 to 1987, and president of the Judicial Yuan (q.v.) from 1987. Lin, together with Chiang

Wei-kuo (q.v.), briefly challenged Lee Teng-hui (q.v.) for the presidency in 1990, causing the Nationalist Party (q.v.) to suffer an internal split. He subsequently dropped his challenge and the National Assembly (q.v.) elected Lee. In 1996, after resigning his membership in the Nationalist Party, Lin again ran for the presidency, with Hau Pei-tsun (q.v.) on the ticket as his vice presidential candidate, as an independent, though he had support from the New Party (q.v.). During the campaign Lin criticized Lee's authoritarian style and actions, which he said caused a crisis in retaliation with the People's Republic of China. The Lin-Hau ticket received 14.9 percent of the popular vote and was third among four teams of candidates running for the presidency and the vice presidency.

Lin Yi-hsiung (1941-). Eighth chairman of the Democratic Progressive Party (DPP) (q.v.) chosen in 1998 for a two-year term, Lin was elected to the Taiwan Provincial Assembly in 1977. In 1979, he was arrested after the Kaohsiung Incident (q.v.) and was sentenced to 12 years in prison. Lin's mother and two daughters were murdered in 1980, a crime that has still not been solved and for which accusations have been pointed at the Nationalist Party (q.v.) and security agencies of the government. Lin served over four years of his prison term, after which he spent time in the United States, the United Kingdom and Japan. He returned to Taiwan in 1989 at which time he presented a draft of a basic law for an independent "Republic of Taiwan" (q.v.). In 1996, Lin unsuccessfully sought the DPP's nomination to run for president. As DPP chairman, Lin is considered a stronger advocate of Taiwan's independence than his two predecessors.

Lin Yu-tang (1895-1766). Born in China, Lin became one of China's and, later, Taiwan's most well known writers and philogists. He supported the Nationalist revolution and served in an official position, but gave that up to write in the late 1920s. He studied in the United States and Europe and wrote in English. His two most famous books were *My Country and My People* and *The Importance of Living.* Both were non-fiction and depicted the nature of Chinese thought and the character of the Chinese people to the West. He founded and edited several journals. He also devised a system for romanizing Chinese and wrote a widely used Chinese-English dictionary. In all he wrote 36 books

Lite-On Group (tian-teng tu'an-t'i). One of Taiwan's leading manufacturing groups with 50 plants worldwide, it produces five products that are ranked among the top 10 worldwide products, including notebook computers, lighting products, and network systems.

Liu, Henry (1932-1984). Businessman and writer of Chiang Ching-kuo's (q.v.) biography, who was murdered at his home outside of San Francisco in October 1984. Members of the local Bamboo Gang who were arrested for the murder implicated a high official in the government in Taiwan, Wang Hsi-ling, who headed military intelligence. The incident had an adverse effect on U.S.-Taiwan relations, even causing a congressional committee to hold hearings and attempt to tie arms sales to Taiwan's untoward activities in the U.S. Subsequently it was learned that Liu had been a triple agent: for the United States, China, and Taiwan (q.v.), and that Wang was angry at him for disclosing the names of agents working in China, allegedly resulting in some being captured and executed. Also it came out during the trial that Wang had acted on his own, and the killing was not ordered or approved by a higher authority in Taiwan.

Liu Ming-ch'uan (1837-1896). Sent by the Chinese government to rule Taiwan (q.v.) in 1884, Liu promoted needed and widely heralded innovation. He introduced a railroad and postal system, developed mines and harbors, and encouraged trade. He established Taipei (q.v.) as the capital of the island. He also established foreign-language schools and encouraged trade and other contacts with other areas of Asia and with the West. Taiwan experienced progressive change and boomed economically under his leadership. In 1891, however, he returned to China before many of his plans were fulfilled, discouraged because of the Chinese bureaucracy's opposition to his reforms. Still, Liu is considered one of Taiwan's foremost reformers and is regarded as a national hero.

Liu Tai-ying (1936-). Chairman and CEO of the China Development Corporation (q.v.) and chairman of the ruling Nationalist Party's (q.v.) Business Management Committee, Liu is considered to be the person responsible for the KMT's finances and its investment policies, and therefore is seen as having considerable political power. He has been cited in the press for making contributions to political causes and political parties abroad, and was mentioned in connection with the U.S. Democratic Party's fundraising scandal in 1996, though Liu denied giving any money and no such charge was proven. Liu was supportive of, and some say planned, President Lee Teng-hui's (q.v.) trip to the United States in June 1995 that caused strained relations with Beijing.

Lunar New Year. See Chinese New Year.

- M -

Ma Ying-jeou (1950-). Long considered one of Taiwan's young political stars, Ma early on served as an interpreter for President Chiang Ching-kuo (q.v.), following which he held a number of important positions in government and the Nationalist Party (q.v), including head of the Research, Development, and Evaluation Commission from 1988 to 1991, and vice-chairman of the Mainland Affairs Council (q.v.). He was concurrently minister of justice and minister of state from 1993 to 1996, and subsequently minister without portfolio. He gained a reputation for honesty and promoting clean politics when he headed the Ministry of Justice as a result of his arresting and indicting a large number of politicians for vote buying and other kinds of corruption. In May 1997, he resigned from government service in protest over continued corruption and crime. In early 1998, however, he entered the race for Taipei (q.v.) mayor as the Nationalist Party's candidate and won that race against the popular and competent DPP mayor Chen Shui-bian (q.v.).

Macclesfield Bank (chung-sha chun-tao). Group of islands, called Chung Sha in Chinese, in the South China Sea claimed as territory of the Republic of China. See also Paracel Islands; Pratas Islands; Spratly Islands.

Mainland Affairs Council (MAC) (ta-lu wei-yuan-hui). Cabinet-level body created in October 1989 at the request of President Lee Teng-hui (q.v.), to, among other things, draft rules to formalize contacts between Taiwan (q.v.) and China and for planning, coordinating, evaluating, and, in some part implementing, policy toward the mainland. Members of MAC include most cabinet ministers and related commissioners. In August 1997, MAC proclaimed "shared sovereignty, divided jurisdictions" as an idea to describe the situation between Taipei (q.v.) and Beijing following a Presidential Office press statement that talked about "pursuing the unification of China based on the reality of separate jurisdictions." See also National Unification Council; Straits Exchange Foundation.

Mainland Chinese (wai-sheng-jen). Also called "Mainlanders" or "later immigrants," (in Chinese, "outside province person") this term refers to Chinese who migrated to Taiwan from China after 1945, though most went in 1949 at the time of the Communist victory over the Nationalists, plus their sons and daughters, even if born in Taiwan (q.v.). Most were government officials or military personnel; some were businessmen. They hailed from "various parts of China, but more came from the coastal provinces and south China.

They speak Mandarin (q.v.) Chinese, the official language of both China and Taiwan, but most also speak their provincial dialects (q.v.). Many younger ones and those born in Taiwan, especially outside of Taipei (q.v.), now speak Taiwanese. Until recent years they occupied the majority of positions in the government and in education. Their political power, as well as their social status, however, has diminished with democratization and Taiwanization. They make up about 15 percent of Taiwan's population.

Mandarin (kuo-yu). The official language of both Taiwan (q.v.) and the People's Republic of China, and derivative of the Peking dialect. Formerly it was the court language of China but came into widespread use in China in the early part of this century. However, it was not spoken much in Taiwan before 1945, when it was made the national language by the government of the Republic of China. With its use since World War II in the educational system and elsewhere, it is now spoken by most of the population of Taiwan, although many residents also speak Taiwanese and Hakka (qq.v.).

In recent years, Mandarin—which is called *kuo yu*, or "national language"—has been influenced by English and some other foreign languages and by popular culture in Taiwan. In the People's Republic of China, it is called *pu tong hua* or the "ordinary language." There it has undergone change influenced by Communism and Communist ideology. Though some terms used in Taiwan are not understood by Chinese in China and vice versa, residents of the two places can usually communicate without difficulty. In recent years, with greater contacts across the Taiwan Strait, the differences in Mandarin spoken in China and Taiwan have diminished.

Martial law (chieh-yen-fa). Initially declared by the Nationalist government in China in 1934, it was applied in Taiwan (q.v.) by executive order in December 1949. That order was activated by Chiang Kai-shek (q.v.) in January 1950. Subsequently the Garrison Command (q.v.) was created to take charge of matters concerning the implementation of martial law rules, which included regulating foreign travel, overseeing emigration and customs, reviewing publications and broadcasts and much more. Under martial law, 10 categories of criminal offenses were transferred to jurisdiction to military courts, thus allowing civilians to be tried in military courts. Though many martial law rules (such as the Garrison Command's control over local administrative and judicial matters) were never implemented or were not applied in full, many felt martial law nevertheless constituted a serious encroachment on civil and political liberties because it canceled important constitutional protections in the realms of basic civil and political rights, and was used by the government and the ruling Nationalist Party (q.v) to maintain control over the population and sustain an authoritarian political system. Many thus saw it as antithetical to the development of democracy. Others, however, argued that it was necessary and by maintaining national security, it made Taiwan's miraculous economic growth and even democracy possible. Whereas public opinion polls long indicated that a large majority of the population did not feel inconvenienced by martial law and most favored keeping it, in October 1986 President Chiang Ching-kuo (q.v.) promised to terminate it, reasoning that it nominally, if not in other ways, distracted from democratization and was not good for Taiwan's image abroad. Indeed Western news reporters often cited it in a negative way suggesting it was a trapping of an undemocratic regime. Martial law was formally ended on July 15, 1987. See also *Chieh Yen Fa.*

Matsu (ma-szu). One of the Offshore Islands (q.v.) that remained in Nationalist Chinese hands after 1949 and which became a locus of international tension, in particular a dispute between Taipei (q.v.) and Beijing and involving the United States, in 1954-55 and again in 1958. See also Quemoy.

May the Fourth Movement (wu-sz yun-tung). A protest that occurred in Peking in 1919 in response to China being "sold out" in the Treaty of Versailles. It is said to have been the beginning of Chinese nationalism. Its pro-Western leaders, such as Hu Shih (q.v.), went to Taiwan (q.v.) and continued their advocacy and support of democratic change. The May the Fourth "group"—which also includes Lei Chen (q.v.)—is said to be the first significant advocacy group of democratization in Taiwan.

May 20, 1988 Incident (wu-er-ling shih-chien). Massive street demonstrations on that date organized by the Democratic Progressive Party (DPP) (q.v.) and the Labor Party together with fruit and chicken farmers to protest government agricultural policies. They caused considerable chaos and were said at the time to reflect the ability of opposition political parties, especially the DPP, to use street politics or demonstrations to rally people to their causes.

Meilitao. Literally "beautiful island" this term is sometimes considered the Chinese translation of Formosa (q.v.).

"Message to Compatriots in Taiwan from the Standing Committee of the Fifth National People's Congress." A document published by the People's Republic of China (PRC) on New Year's Day in 1979 just at the time the United States established formal diplomatic ties with Beijing. It reflected the fact that PRC leader Deng Xiaoping made the resolution of the "Taiwan issue" one of three main tasks for the 1980s. It also mirrored confidence among Chinese leaders in the PRC that Taiwan could be pressured to negotiate unification. It called on Taiwan (q.v.) to be pragmatic and allow families to be reunited, and for businesses in Taiwan to participate in China's economic development. PRC leaders promised Taiwan that China would respect the status quo on the island and the opinions of a broad range of people. Taipei (q.v.), however, did not respond in a positive way.

Military Aid and Advisory Group (MAAG) (chun-shih ku-wen-t'uan). Group of U.S. military advisors who helped rebuild the Nationalist forces in the early 1950s and stayed on until

Washington and Taipei (q.v.) broke diplomatic relations in 1979. The group grew from around four hundred in 1952 to several thousand in the 1960s.

Min-Ch'uan. "People's Rights" or democracy. See Three Principles of the People.

Minnan. Term that refers to the southern part of Fukien Province in China, from which most of the early Chinese immigrants hailed. It also refers to the Fukien Taiwanese (q.v.) and their language. Minnan is *Hoklo* in Fukienese or Taiwanese.

Min-Sheng. "People's Livelihood." See Three Principles of the People.

Min-Tsu. "People's Nationhood" or nationalism. See Three Principles of the People.

Mirage 2000-5 (huan-shang liang-ch'ien wu). Sophisticated high-performance fighter aircraft sold to Taiwan (q.v.) by France in 1992. Taiwan decided to purchase 60 of these planes to augment its air defenses, even though it was building its own plane, the Indigenous Defense Fighter (IDF) (q.v.) and had been authorized to purchase 150 F-16 (q.v.) fighter planes from the United States at the time. The deal caused friction between France and China. The Mirage 2000-5s are stationed in Hsinchu and are intended to provide high altitude defense of the island together with the F-16s.

Mountain People. See Aborigines.

Musha Rebellion (wu-she shih-chien). A joint Aborigine-Taiwanese (qq.v.) uprising in 1930 that resulted in the deaths of several hundred Japanese police and government officials. The rebellion was led by an aborigine named Moldanao.

- N -

Nansha Islands. See Spratly Islands.

National Affairs Conference (kuo-shih hui-yi). A "Constitutional"-style meeting held from June 28 to July 4, 1990, in Taipei to discuss various political reforms, including the direct election of the president and the mayors of Taipei and Kaohsiung (qq.v.); the recomposition of the National Assembly and Legislative Yuan (qq.v.); and relations between the president, premier, and cabinet. Participants included a crosssection of Taiwan's political interest groups, even opposition politicians who had recently been released from jail. President Lee Teng-hui (q.v.) called the meeting after students demonstrated in opposition to the undemocratic composition of theNational Assembly in the spring. Tsiang Yien-si and Shih Chi-yang (qq.v.) were the co-conveners of the conference. The conference was preceded by more than a hundred discussion meetings with more than 13,000 people attending and produced a number of suggestions on political reform, including the termination of the Temporary Provisions (q.v.), the retirement of senior parliamentarians (q.v.), new policies toward China, and amendments to the Constitution (q.v.). Most of the suggestions for reform were adopted in the following months. See also National Development Conference.

National Assembly (kuo-min ta-hui). Organ of the central government whose functions as set forth in the Constitution (q.v.) (before it was amended) were to elect or recall the president and vice president and amend the Constitution. It met in regular session every six years. Extraordinary sessions could be called by a vote of not less than two-fifths of the delegates or by the president to discuss initiatives or referendum measures to impeach the president or vice president, or when an amendment to the Constitution is proposed by the Legislative Yuan (q.v.). Two extraordinary sessions had been called since the government of the Republic of China moved to Taiwan (q.v.)—the latest in April 1991 to discuss constitutional revision ending the Temporary Provisions (q.v.).

Like the Legislative Yuan and the Control Yuan (qq.v.) (the other two elective bodies of government before the Constitution was amended), the National Assembly's makeup or representation was based on the claim that the government of the Republic of China represents "all of China" and thus had holdovers from the 1947 election frozen in office or replacements hailing from the same province. Since supplemental elections had affected its membership less than they had affected the Legislative Yuan and the Control Yuan, as of 1989 it was still nearly 90 percent composed of members representing areas not under the control of the government. In 1989, as part of Taiwan's democratization, a law was passed to rectify this situation and delegates were offered retirement bonuses. Only a few, however, accepted the offer.

In 1990, the National Assembly met and tried to expand its powers and play a special role in the election of the president. This evoked public outcries and demonstrations in opposition, including thousands of college and university students staging a sit-in protest, thereby provoking a political crisis. Debate about the role and powers of the National Assembly and other issues followed. (See National Affairs Conference.) Later, in 1990, the Council of Grand Justices (q.v.) ruled that the senior parliamentarians (q.v.) had to step down by the end of 1991, and they did. Thus, in December 1991, an election was held to elect a "new" National Assembly.

In 1992, the National Assembly made important changes in the Constitution. Subsequently more amendments were passed, including provision for the direct election of the president, which eliminated one of the major functions of the National Assembly. There were subsequently proposals made to eliminate the National Assembly, turn it into an electoral college similar to that in the United States, or merge it with the Legislative Yuan—making that body a bicameral legislature. None of these proposals, however, was realized.

In 1997, the National Assembly made additional changes to the Constitution, during which time there was heated debate over eliminating the provincial government. Friction also developed with the Legislative Yuan over the powers of each and their mutual relationship, in addition to other issues.

National Chengchi University (cheng-chih ta-hsueh). Located in Mucha outside of Taipei (q.v.), it is generally regarded as one of the nation's best universities. It specializes in politics, journalism, and several other fields.

National Chiang Kai-shek Cultural Center (chung-cheng Chi-nien-t'ang). Large center in Taipei (q.v.) that includes the Chiang

Kai-shek Memorial Hall and Park and the National Concert Hall, it is a memorial to the late President Chiang Kai-shek (q.v.). The hall was completed in 1980; the theaters in 1987. It has since become one of Taiwan's major tourist attractions. In March 1990, thousands of college and university students staged a sit-in demonstration there protesting the National Assembly's (q.v.) effort to expand its powers. The students departed peacefully after having a meeting with President Lee Teng-hui (q.v.).

National Democratic Independent Political Alliance (NDIPA) (chuan-kuo min-chu tu-li cheng-chih lien-meng). Political "party" formed by a group of independent candidates prior to the 1991 National Assembly (q.v.) election. The NDIPA claimed to be made up of "non-party" politicians, yet the alliance became one of four political parties that qualified for television time during the campaign, having nominated more than 10 candidates. The alliance, however, got just over 2 percent of the popular vote, not enough to qualify for national seats allocated by party. The alliance's platform was vague and its future uncertain after the election. It subsequently faded from Taiwan's political scene. The NDIPA was founded by Kao Tse-min.

National Development Conference (kuo-chia fa-chan hui-yi). A meeting convened in December 1996 to discuss and debate constitutional reform, economic development, and relations with the People's Republic of China following generally the format of the 1990 National Affairs Conference (q.v.). The Ministry of Interior, the Council for Economic Planning and Development (q.v.), and the Mainland Affairs Council (q.v.) provided working papers. Some 170 individuals participated, including members of the three main political parties, government officials, and scholars.

President Lee called "consensus building" the most important objective of the meeting. However, the meeting evoked potent controversy and division over a number of issues, in particular the recommendation to reduce, if not eliminate, the provincial and village levels of the Republic of China's (q.v.) four levels of government. Also controversial was the plan to strengthen the presidency in its relations with the Legislative Yuan (q.v.). The Democratic Progressive Party (q.v.) generally supported the ruling Nationalist Party (q.v.), which presented the reforms. The New Party (q.v.) did not, and boycotted the meeting.

Provincial Governor Soong Chu-yu (q.v.) tendered his resignation over the issue of downsizing or eliminating the provincial government, though it was not accepted by Premier Lien Chan (q.v.), and Soong remained on the job. Subsequent talks between Soong and President Lee Teng-hui (q.v.), however, did not produce any visible compromise, and according to many observers the two became alienated after that.

Critics of President Lee said that his objectives showed him to be less than a supporter of democracy and that acting to eliminate the provincial government revealed that he supported Taiwan independence. Supporters said that the overlap in government between the national and provincial government was expensive and that eliminating the other local level of government would help resolve the serious problems of corruption, especially vote-buying. Taiwan's political system also needed revamping for other reasons, especially in view of the reality of party politics and coalition government.

Some of the proposals coming out of the meeting were written into constitutional amendments proposed and passed later in the year and have had an impact on the political system. The political reforms discussed at the meeting overshadowed the debate about both economic policy and relations with the mainland, and few changes were made in the latter two areas as a result of the conference.

National General Mobilization Law. See Martial law.

National Health Insurance (chuan-min chien-pao). A national program providing universal health care to virtually all citizens of the Republic of China (q.v.) made effective in March 1995. Prior to this only 59 percent of the population had health insurance. The program incorporated health care coverage provided by 13 existing plans and extended coverage to an additional 7.5 million people. The main beneficiaries were the elderly, children, students, and housewives. Participation in the program is mandatory under the Health Insurance Law.

Employees pay 30 percent of the premiums, employers 60 percent, and the government 10 percent. People over age 70 and the disabled pay no premium. The program pays 70 to 95 percent of costs for patients admitted to hospitals.

The program became controversial due to its cost, and disagreements over who would pay for it. The Nationalist Party (q.v.) promoted the plan and took credit for its implementation, though delays and scandals over doctors asking for additional payments somewhat sullied its accomplishment.

National Independent Labor Federation (chuan-kuo tu-li lao-tung tsung-hui). Established in 1988 by the Taiwan Association for Labor Movement (q.v.), its unions represent workers in the petrochemical and synthetic fiber industries. Its unions' members mostly support the Democratic Progressive Party (q.v.).

National Mobilization Law (ch'uan-kuo tsung-tung-yuan-fa). A law which regulates labor in Taiwan (q.v.), including banning strikes.

National Palace Museum (kuo-li ku-kuan po-wu-yuan). Located in suburban Taipei (q.v.), it is generally recognized as the best Chinese museum in the world. It contains artifacts and art objects from 5,000 years of Chinese history, most of which were brought from the mainland in 1949 by Dr. Han Lih-wu (q.v.). The 134,000-square-foot, five-story building also houses a library, lecture hall, and research rooms. It opened in 1965.

National Party Congress (ch'uan-kuo tang-tai-piao ta-hui). Theoretically the highest decision-making organ of the Nationalist Party (q.v.). However, it meets infrequently and it delegates power to its Central Committee (q.v.), which in turn selects the Central Standing Committee (q.v.) of the party, where real decision-making power resides. At the 13th Party Congress, unlike past congresses, most delegates were democratically chosen. The Nationalist Party's most recent National Party Congress, the 15th, was held in August 1997.

National Police Administration (nai-cheng-pu ching-cheng-hsu). The nation's highest public security authority, rising to that status after the dissolution of the Taiwan Garrison Command (q.v.) or Garrison Guard Headquarters in 1992.

National Science Council (NSC) (kuo-chia k'o-hsueh wei-yuan-hui). An organ of the Executive Yuan (q.v.) that is considered the highest government agency responsible for planning scientific and technological development and setting relevant policies, recruiting experts, and funding research. It is composed of eight divisions: biological, agricultural, and medical sciences; natural sciences and mathematics; engineering and applied sciences; humanities and social sciences; planning, coordination, and evaluation; science education; program administration; and international programs. Heads of government offices dealing with science and technology, ministers without portfolio, the president of Academia Sinica (q.v.), the secretary-general of the Executive Yuan, and noted scientists are members. The NSC's budget in 1997 was U.S.$5.4 million. Sixty-five percent was spent on research projects in cooperation with academic and other institutions, buildings, and faculty procurement.

National Security Bureau (NSB) (kuo-an-chu). Established in 1954, the NSB is considered the highest intelligence organization in Taiwan. Employing an estimated 1,500 people, it directs and coordinates all intelligence activities, both external and internal, and is regarded as the core body of the National Security Council (q.v.). The NSB comprises six departments: Mainland Operations, Overseas Operations, Internal Security Intelligence, Research and Production, Communications, and Cipher, plus an Intelligence Staff Training Center and a VIP Security Task Force. In 1991, the NSB was put under the jurisdiction of the National Security Council, which is controlled by the president. In 1993, the redefining of the National Security Council's missions resulted in narrowing its functions to relate primarily to foreign intelligence work.

National Security Council (NSC) (kuo-chia an-ch'uan hui-yi). Established by presidential order in 1967 as a special organ attached to the Executive Yuan (q.v.), its status was altered and made more official in 1987 after passage of the National Security Act. The NSC makes policy decisions concerning national defense issues. Early in its history the NSC controlled the Taiwan Garrison Command, the National Security Bureau (qq.v.), the Investigation Bureau and other intelligence agencies that often operated beyond the law and represented the repressive side of martial law (q.v.) in Taiwan. Its status was changed in 1993 from that of an advisory body to the president to a constitutionally mandated organization made part of the Executive Yuan and subject to oversight by the Legislative Yuan (q.v.). The Intelligence Committee of the Legislative Yuan approves its budget, though parts of it remain secret. The NSC's responsibilities include helping formulate defense and foreign policy, overseeing domestic security and counterintelligence, and making policy toward the mainland. Members of the NSC include the president (who is the NSC's chairman), vice president, secretary-general of the Office of the President, chief of the President's Military Staff, premier, vice-premier, minister of defense, minister of foreign affairs, minister of finance, minister of economic affairs, chief of the general staff, NSC secretary-general, chairman of the National Reconstruction Research Committee, and chairman of the Committee for Science Development. The latter two organs are adjunct bodies of the NSC.

National Security Law (kuo-chia an-ch'uan fa). A law passed after martial law (q.v.) was ended in July 1987 that supporters said was needed to retain the provisions guaranteeing the nation's security found in the martial law decree. They also argued the law was very similar to such laws in most other countries including Western democracies and, therefore, was not antithetical to democracy. Critics said, however, including leaders of the Democratic Progressive Party (q.v.) who mobilized supporters to protest and oppose the law, that it was "old wine in new bottles" or martial law in disguise. Most controversial was a provision that disallowed an appeal of civilian cases tried by military courts under martial law.

National Security Report No. 48-1 (kuo-chia an-ch'uan pao-kao-shu). A report presented to the U.S. National Security Council on December 23, 1949, which stated that "logistical support of the present Nationalist island regime cannot ensure its indefinite survival as a non-communist base. Failing U.S. military occupation and control, a non-communist regime on Taiwan will probably succumb to the Chinese Communists by the end of 1950." The report followed a joint chiefs of staff assessment which concluded that Taiwan's strategic importance did not justify overt U.S. military action to protect it, and a State Department memorandum stating that intervention would provide the Chinese Communists with a potent "ideological issue." The report served as the basis for a U.S. policy of reduced support to the Nationalist government on Taiwan (q.v.), and subsequently to a policy of what some called the "abandonment of Chiang Kai-shek (q.v.)." This policy was, of course, abandoned with the onset of the Korean War. National Security Report No. 48-1 became public with the publication of the *Pentagon Papers* in 1971.

National Sports Council (t'i-yu wei-yuan-hui). Established in 1997 within the Executive Yuan (q.v.), this body seeks to promote and regulate sports.

National Taiwan University (t'ai-wan ta-hsueh). Taiwan's best-regarded institution of higher learning, located in Taipei (q.v.). See also Taihoku Imperial University.

National Unification Council (NUC) (kuo-chia t'ung-yi wei-yuan-hui). A government organization founded in October 1990 by President Lee Teng-hui (q.v.) to advise the president and conduct research and write policy statements. It is attached to the Office of the President, and the president is its chairman. The NUC's membership comprises 32 people from various fields who serve for one year. Members include representatives of the opposition parties, since the NUC seeks to forge a consensus among various parties and groups on the issue of China's reunification. The NUC is organized into task forces or groups. In March 1991 the NUC promulgated a three-phase program for the unification of Taiwan with China, called the National Unification Guidelines (q.v.). However, conditions were attached leading most analysts to think that unification would not be likely for some time. In the summer of 1992, the NUC engaged in a four-month-long debate on the definition of the one-China (q.v.) policy, opting for a policy of one China, two areas or "one country with two equal political entities" (q.v.) in an effort to give the two sides equal status and to offer an alternative to Beijing's "one country, two systems" (see One country, two entities) formula for reunification.

National Unification Guidelines (kuo-chia t'ung-yi kang-ling). A set of policies proposed by President Lee Teng-hui (q.v.), adopted by the National Unification Council (q.v.) and approved by the Executive Yuan (q.v.) in early 1991, according to which the

Republic of China (ROC) (q.v.) will be unified with the People's Republic of China (PRC) in three phases: (1) unofficial contacts through people-to-people exchanges and activities that benefit mutual understanding, (2) opening "three links" (postal, air and sea, and trade), and (3) negotiations on unification based on political democracy, economic freedom, and social equality. The country is presently said to be in the first stage, emphasizing "four exchanges": tourist, academic, cultural, and sports, though some links cited in phase two may be said to have already been established because of the large volume of trade and the considerable amount of investment from Taiwan (q.v.) in China. Moving from step one to step two is contingent upon Beijing not denying Taiwan's status as a "political entity," and its pursuing economic and political reforms, settling disputes through peaceful means, and respecting Taipei's rights in the international community. The DPP, even the more moderate Formosa faction (q.v.), rejected the guidelines when they were proposed and formalized. Some observers said that the formulation of this policy would not have any immediate impact, if any impact at all, and was President Lee's way of parrying criticism that he supported Taiwan's independence, especially by the Non-Mainstream faction (q.v.) of the Nationalist Party (q.v.).

The National Unification Guidelines were important for another reason: They constituted a formal abandonment of Taipei's claim to sovereignty and jurisdiction over territory ruled by the government of the People's Republic of China. Ironically, some said, Beijing did not reply to this in a positive way. The Guidelines, on the other hand, paved the way for increased contacts between the populations of the ROC and the PRC. Reference was made to "one China" (q.v.), but also to two political entities and unification based on parity. The idea of two political entities was opposed by Beijing; one-China was not.

Nationalist Party (Kuomintang, or KMT) (kuo-min-tang). The largest and currently the ruling political party in Taiwan (q.v.), which traces its origins to several political organizations founded and/or led by Sun Yat-sen (q.v.), including the Hsing Chung Hui or the Society for Regenerating China that he founded in November 1894 in Hawaii. The party, in fact, sees that occasion as its birth and thus claims to be more than one hundred years old—having celebrated its 100th anniversary on

November 24, 1994. Sun's, and the party's, goals at that time were to end Manchu rule of China and unify the country. Sun's followers staged a number of uprisings before one in Wu-chang, Hupei Province, in October 1911 succeeded. Sun became president of the newly formed Republic of China (q.v.), but stepped down almost immediately in order to prevent conflict and what some said might have been a civil war.

After Sun died the party experienced a split between left and right factions. Chiang Kai-shek (q.v.), leader of the rightist faction, won control of the party's leadership after a power struggle against the leftist faction, which had the support of the Communists. After the successful Northern Expedition led by Chiang in 1928 the party ruled China. The Nationalist Partyled military tried to completely unify the country and fought both the Japanese and the Communists in ensuing years. It moved to Taiwan in 1949 with the government of the Republic of China and the Nationalist military after the defeat of Nationalist forces by Mao and his Communist forces.

Sun Yat-sen holds the honorary title of president (*tsung li*) of the Nationalist Party; Chiang Kai-shek holds the title of director-general (*tsung tsai*). Chiang Kai-shek led the party until his death in 1975.

Chiang Ching-kuo (q.v.) was elected chairman of the party after his father's death. Lee Teng-hui (q.v.) became acting chairman upon Chiang Ching-kuo's death in January 1988, and was formally elected chairman at the 13th Party Congress in July 1988, again at the 14th Party Congress in 1993, and once more at the 15th Party Congress in 1997.

The National Party Congress (q.v.) is theoretically the highest decision-making organ of the party, but it is too large to deliberate seriously on policy issues, and therefore delegates power to its Central Committee (q.v.). Real power, however, resides in the 33-member Standing Committee or Central Standing Committee (q.v.).

The Nationalist Party is considered a mass party, with a membership of around 2.5 million members or about 12 percent of the Republic of China's population. Its membership represents virtually all social classes and segments of the population. Though sometimes thought of as a party of Mainland Chinese (q.v.), which it was during the early years of its role in Taiwan, its membership had become 70 percent Taiwanese (q.v.) by the early 1980s. In fact, some now claim that the Nationalist Party is the only multiethnic party in Taiwan, the Democratic Progressive Party (q.v.) being almost exclusively composed of Taiwanese, and the New Party (q.v.) being made up mostly of Mainland Chinese.

The party's work is carried out by several departments and commissions. Departments include: Organizational Affairs, Social Affairs, Youth Activities, and Women's Activities. There are commissions dealing with financial affairs, party history, and discipline. The party has operated a number of businesses, including several in the media area and several in the cultural field, including the Central News Agency, the *Central Daily News*, and the Broadcasting Corporation of China (qq.v.). The party is indirectly linked—through the China Development Corporation (q.v.), the holding of stocks, or members' control of boards—to many more companies in Taiwan. Its vast holdings, in fact, have earned the KMT the reputation of being the richest political party in the world, and this among other reasons, has prompted the other parties in Taiwan to criticize the Nationalist Party for its use of money in buying elections and its unfair or illegitimate ties to many businesses.

Until the 1980s, typical of a one-party system, the Nationalist Party and the government were in many ways synonymous, and their functions to a large extent overlapped. With the growth of democracy and formation of new, opposition political parties this has ceased to be the case. The Nationalist Party, in fact, has distanced itself from the government in many ways.

Similarly, the Nationalist Party is no longer the dominant political party in Taiwan. In recent years, especially since 1995, it has had to seek support from the Democratic Progressive Party and/or the New Party to pass legislation and write and pass constitutional amendments.

New KMT Alliance (hsin kuo-min-tang chen-hsien). A caucus group formed within the Nationalist Party (q.v.) in 1988, led by Jaw

Shau-kong (q.v.)., which reflected the views of younger Mainlander Chinese (q.v.) and represented more progressive KMT members' views on a number of issues, such as democratization. Members alleged that President Lee Teng-hui (q.v.) had concentrated too much power in his own hands and supported Taiwan's independence. The New KMT Alliance was considered more of a party faction than its predecessor the Breakfast Club (q.v.). The New KMT Alliance supported the Non-Mainstream faction (q.v.) of the party. Most of its members joined the New Party (q.v.) in 1993, and soon after it faded from the political scene.

New Movement faction (hsin ch'iao-liu hsi). See New Tide faction.

New Party (NP) (hsin-tang). A political party formed in August 1993 at the time of the Nationalist Party's (q.v.) 14th Party Congress by members of the Non-Mainstream faction (q.v.) of the KMT. The important founding members included six members of the Legislative Yuan (q.v.) and one former member. The two most important founders and leaders of the NP at this time were Jaw Shau-kong and Wang Chien-shien (qq.v.). The NP criticized the KMT's performance in elections, corruption, and what it members considered its weak stance (pointing especially to Lee Teng-hui [q.v.]) against Taiwan's independence. Its platform included more strict adherence to the teachings of Sun Yat-sen (q.v.), social justice, and clean politics.

The NP is organized differently from the Nationalist Party and the Democratic Progressive Party (DPP) (q.v.), stressing the leadership roles of those holding public office. In the 1994 election the NP did well in the Taipei City Council (q.v.) race and Jaw Shau-kong garnered the second largest number of votes for Taipei mayor, some saying at the time that the KMT helped the DPP candidate win. In 1995, the NP tripled its seats in the Legislative Yuan (q.v.) and in 1996 improved its position in the National Assembly (q.v.). Since then it has not performed so well in election contests. In fact, its bad performance at the polls has recently engendered speculation concerning its survival.

The NP is regarded by many observers as being a regional party (in the Taipei region) since it has very little support in many parts of the country. It is permanently relegated to the role of a lesser party, many say, because it represents Mainland Chinese (q.v.), who are a minority of the population. The party, on the other hand, has won the support of many intellectuals and younger people, especially in Taipei (q.v.) and has made a convincing case that it is a clean party. It is also the only opposition party, other than the DPP, that is considered as a serious party. Many label the NP a right of center or conservative party (compared to the DPP which is a liberal party and the KMT which is moderate or center), but this view stems mainly from its origin from the right wing of the Nationalist Party and its stance on the one China issue. The NP's stance on money politics, foreign policy, and a number of issues has also given it the label of a progressive party.

New People's Society (hsin-min-hui). Also called the Taiwan Cultural Society, this organization was formed in 1920 in Japan by Taiwanese (q.v.) who sought a means to promote Taiwan's cultural identity. Lin Hsien-t'ang (q.v.) was its president for a time. The organization published the magazine *Taiwan_Youth*. The New People's Society opposed both assimilation by Japan and ties with China.

New Tide faction (hsin ch'iao-liu hsi). A faction of the Democratic Progressive Party (DPP) (q.v.), members of which came mainly from the Formosa group (q.v.). It is considered the more extreme segment of the DPP, compared to the Formosa faction (q.v.). It unequivocally advocates the independence of Taiwan and uses street demonstrations as a main tactic for attaining this and other objectives. Its philosophical position is that there can be no democracy in Taiwan (q.v.) until it is formally independent of China, and that the DPP should regard itself as a "revolutionary party" before independence is realized. Its members propose the use of Philippine-style "people's power" to overthrow the government. Its agenda also includes changing the name of the Republic of China (q.v.) to Republic of Taiwan (q..v) and obtaining a new constitution, flag, and national anthem. The New Tide faction (q.v.) also promotes the idea that Taiwan should be an operations center for multinational businesses and opposes more extensive trade and commercial relations with the People's Republic of China, saying that political talks with the PRC are as important as economic negotiations. It refutes the notion of interdependence in dealing with the issue of relations with China as well as the idea of "Greater China" (q.v.). The New Tide faction has sought the support of farmers, workers, and students—the so-called "deprived social groups"—but with only limited success. Chiou I-jen (q.v.) is head of the New Tide faction.

Nine-Point Proposal (Yeh chiu-tien). Set forth in a speech by Ye Jianying, chairman of the Standing Committee of the National People's Congress in the People's Republic of China (PRC) in September 1981. Ye also suggested talks between the Chinese Communist Party and the Nationalist Party (q.v.). His most important points concerned: the establishment of trade, mail, and shipping ties; cultural and sports exchanges; and visits by relatives. He promised that, after reunification, Taiwan (q.v.) could keep its socioeconomic system and would enjoy a high degree of autonomy as a special administrative region of the PRC.

Taipei (q.v.) responded coolly, saying that it had "nothing to gain and everything to lose" if it accepted the proposal. It jeered the offer of economic help, noting that Taiwan was rich and China was poor. Taipei responded with its "Three No's Policy" (q.v.). Leaders in Taiwan subsequently pointed out that the proposal included autonomy for the Republic of China's (q.v.) armed forces, yet PRC leaders sought to pressure the United States to end arms sales to Taipei. See also Six-Point Supplement.

Nitobe Inazo. A Japanese agricultural specialist who was made director of the Bureau of Industry in Taiwan very soon after it was incorporated into the Japanese empire. He turned Taiwan's agriculture into a very efficient and productive part of the economy, developed new strains of rice, and encouraged trade in food commodities.

No haste policy (chieh-chi yung-jen cheng-tse). Also called the "no haste, be patient strategy" it is a tenet of Taiwan's foreign policy initiated by President Lee Teng-hui (q.v.) in 1995 following missile tests conducted by China's People's Liberation Army in the Taiwan Strait (q.v.) to intimidate Taiwan (q.v.). Lee admonished businessmen at that time not to invest too much money in the mainland in view of strained relations between Taipei (q.v.) and Beijing. In 1996, after more missile tests which further strained relations, Lee repeated this statement. In late 1997, speaking to a National Unification Council (q.v.) plenum meeting, Lee reiterated this policy and used the term "no haste, be patient" in dealing with China. In early 1998, Premier Vincent Siew (q.v.) said the policy was aimed at pushing Beijing to review and reconsider its irrational policy toward Taiwan. Chang King-yu (q.v.), chairman of the Mainland Affairs Council (q.v.), however, said that it was intended to restrict investment in high technology industries, infrastructure projects, and some massive investment projects only. The policy has been interpreted to ban investments of more than U.S.$50 million or financial involvement in infrastructure projects. See also Go South policy.

Nogi Maresuke. Third Japanese governor-general of Taiwan, who served from 1896 to 1898. Though a lieutenant-general in the Japanese army, Nogi brought civilian government to Taiwan and restricted the power and authority of the army there.

Non-Mainstream faction (fei chu-liu p'ai). A group of Nationalist Party (q.v.) members that opposed President Lee Teng-hui's (q.v.) nomination of Li Yuan-zu (q.v.) as vice president in 1990. The group supported Lin Yang-kang and Chiang Wei-kuo (qq.v.), respectively, for president and vice president. Members of the group included important political figures such as Chen Li-an (q.v.), Kuan Chung (q.v.), and even (later) Premier Hau Pei-tsun (q.v.). This group continued to exist after the challenge to President Lee failed, but not as a formal organization or faction. In 1993, a number of members of the faction left the Nationalist Party and formed the New Party (q.v.). The faction continues to oppose many of President Lee's policies and views his stand against Taiwan's independence as weak and even false. Its members are mostly Mainland Chinese (q.v.).

Normalization Agreement (cheng-ch'ang-hua hsieh-yi). Communiqué signed between the United States and the People's Republic of China (PRC) in December 1978, which formalized diplomatic relations between the two countries as of January 1, 1979. At that time the United States severed relations with the Republic of China (q.v.). In the agreement the United States acknowledged the position of the government of the PRC regarding Taiwan: that there is but one China, and Taiwan is part of China. On the other hand, the agreement stated that the

United States would "maintain cultural, commercial and other unofficial relations with the People of Taiwan." Congress was dissatisfied with the way the Carter Administration treated Taipei in this agreement and subsequently wrote the Taiwan Relations Act (q.v.).

The agreement was said to have represented a departure from ambiguity in U.S. China policy and a policy of favoring the People's Republic of China. It also had a marked negative effect on Taipei's diplomatic situation, causing other nations to also break relations. It likewise led to the U.S. terminating, after a one-year hiatus, the United States-Republic of China Defense Treaty (q.v.).

- O -

Office of the President. See President.

Office for Private Investment (szu-jen t'ou-szu-chu). Established in 1958 within the USAID mission organization, it sought to encourage the development of private industry in Taiwan (q.v.) and the privatization of the economy. Its aims were furthered by the Industrial Development and Investment Center and the China Productivity Center.

Offshore Islands. Term referring to several island groups close to the mainland that were or still are controlled by the Republic of China (q.v.), including Quemoy (q.v.), Matsu (q.v.), and some other islands. These islands were not captured by Communist forces in 1949 when Mao defeated Nationalist forces on the mainland and established the People's Republic of China. The islands became an issue of international attention when the People's Liberation Army attacked Quemoy in 1954-55 and again in 1958. During the former crisis Taipei (q.v.) abandoned some of the smaller, less important islands for strategic reasons. The United States did not include the islands in the United States-Republic of China Defense Treaty (q.v.), but did subsequently cite them in the Formosa Resolution (q.v.) by which Congress gave the president discretionary authority to protect them. Taipei for a number of years considered the islands important in its plan to counterattack the mainland and liberate it from communism. It kept one-third of its military forces on the island for some years—against the counsel of U.S. military advisors. The Republic of China currently maintains jurisdiction over the islands. Leaders of the Democratic Progressive Party (q.v.) have suggested at times that the islands are not part of Taiwan and should be abandoned, but have found that position unpopular.

One China (yi-ke chung-kuo). The idea that Taiwan (q.v.) is or should be a part of China for historical, cultural, political, and a variety of other reasons. From the points of view of Chiang Kai-shek and Chiang Ching-kuo (qq.v.), this was a state concept, the Republic of China (ROC); in other words they claimed to be the legitimate government of China and claimed territory under the jurisdiction of the People's Republic of China (PRC), plus Outer Mongolia and some other territory. PRC leaders also adhered to the one-China (q.v.) idea, but claimed one China meant the People's Republic of China and asserted the ROC did not constitute a legitimate or sovereign nation. They still maintain this view, although they have veered somewhat from it at times apparently to encourage Taipei (q.v.) to negotiate reunification.

Under Lee Teng-hui (q.v.), one China has come to refer to a historical or a cultural China and not a Chinese nation-state, thereby allowing separate (at least temporarily) Chinese governments. (See One country, two entities.) The PRC frequently accuses Taiwan, including President Lee, of not supporting the one China principle. Clearly the Democratic Progressive Party (q.v.) opposes it, saying so in its platform. (See One China, one Taiwan.) The New Party (q.v.) supports it but does not call for immediate action to unite the two parts of China. The Nationalist Party (KMT) (q.v.) formally supports it, but many KMT members as well as outside observers say President Lee does not really support it and is only paying lip service to the idea. Others say Lee's policy is undecided or is a wait and see policy. (See No haste policy.) Opinion polls reflect low support for both separation or independence and unification; most people support instead the status quo, which many say is President Lee's view.

One China is also said to be the policy of the United States and most other nations of the world. However, most nations have simply "taken note of" or "acknowledged" Beijing's claim to Taiwan rather than "recognizing" its sovereignty over the ROC's territory, and none have taken any tangible actions to help the PRC reclaim this objective.

One China, one Taiwan (yi-chung yi-t'ai). The idea that Taiwan (q.v.) and China are separate, or should be, based on history, culture, language, and other differences, and are or should be legally and politically two states, both with sovereignty. Some who support this idea say that the Republic of China is synonymous with Taiwan (q.v.) and that this is both a legal and practical reality. Others say a Republic of Taiwan (q.v.) should be declared to realize the idea of one China and one Taiwan. The more radical members of the Democratic Progressive Party (q.v.) espouse the latter position; most in the New Party (q.v.) oppose it strongly.

Some say this is, in fact, the policy of most nations of the world since they deal with Taiwan separately from China and support its right to choose its future because of its successful democratization and because they support the idea of self-determination. See also One China.

One country, two areas (yi-kuo liang-ke-di-fang). A idea for dealing with the situation of two Chinas that was passed in the form of a resolution by Legislative Yuan (q.v.) in July 1992. See also One country, two entities; One country, two governments.

One country, two entities (yi-kuo liang-ke-cheng-chih shih-t'i). A formula advanced by some in Taiwan (q.v.) in the 1990s for dealing with the situation of two Chinas or the separation of Taiwan from China by using "creative ambiguity" and referring to both sides as "political entities." Some say it originated because President Lee Teng-hui (q.v.) had earlier referred to the People's Republic of China as a political entity. See also One country, two governments; one country, two areas.

One country, two governments (yi-kuo liang-fu). A formula advanced by some Republic of China (ROC) (q.v.) officials to deal with the problem of the existence of two Chinas or the separation of the ROC and the People's Republic of China (PRC). Those advocating the formula support the sovereignty of the Republic of China but also the principle of one China (q.v.). This concept or idea is rejected by both Beijing and most opposition politicians in Taiwan (q.v.). PRC leaders promote another formula. (See One country, two systems.) Most members and supporters of the Democratic Progressive Party (q.v.) take the position that Taiwan and China are equal political entities, each with sovereignty, and are separate— therefore such a formula does not apply. See also One China, one Taiwan; One country, two areas; One country, two entities.

One country, two systems (yi-kuo liang-chih). A formula advanced by leaders of the People's Republic of China (PRC) to resolve the problem of two Chinas or one Taiwan (q.v.), one China, or bring about the reunification of China. The concept is attributed to Deng Xiaoping, although both Deng and other Chinese leaders had talked about it before Deng first began to promote it in 1982 and it was put in China's constitution (though phrased somewhat vaguely). It was applied to the reunification of Hong Kong in July 1997 and PRC leaders said at the time that it would be used as the basis for Taiwan's incorporation.

Taipei (q.v.) rejects this formula, stating that it is an attempt to make the government of the Republic of China (ROC) (q.v.) a local government under Beijing's control and take away its sovereignty. They add that it does not take into consideration Taiwan's history, its democratization, and the PRC's bad human rights record. They also point out that autonomous regions in the People's Republic of China, which Taiwan would become under the formula, are not positive examples of Beijing's rule, frequently citing the bad situation in Tibet. President Lee Teng-hui (q.v.) has rejected the formula stating that Hong Kong and Taiwan are two very different places, noting that Hong Kong was formerly a British colony and was not self-governing or sovereign, unlike the ROC. He has also declared that Taiwan, unlike Hong Kong, is capable of defending itself.

Operation Causeway. Invasion plan designed by U.S. Admiral Chester Nimitz in early 1944 based on a directive of the U.S. Joint Chiefs of Staff to investigate the feasibility of an invasion of Taiwan (q.v.). Because of successes against Japanese forces in the Central and Western Pacific together with doubts as to whether the Chinese residents of Taiwan would rise up and fight against the Japanese government and military, the plan was abandoned in October 1944.

Orchid Island (lan yü). A small island off Taiwan's southeast coast, home to about 3,000 Yami aborigines (q.v.). In 1980, a controversial nuclear waste facility was built there.

Ota Masahiro. The governor-general of Taiwan (q.v.) appointed in early 1931 following the Musha Rebellion (q.v.). His rule was a harsh one, and he was recalled after little more than a year following complaints by Home Rule leaders.

Overseas Alliance for Democratic Rule in Taiwan (t'ai-wan min-chu hai-wai lien-meng). Formed by Kuo Yu-hsin (q.v.) in 1978, mainly from members of the World United Formosans for Independence (q.v.), the organization advocated Taiwan's separation from China.

Overseas Chinese (hua-ch'iao). Term referring to people of Chinese descent living outside of the Republic of China (ROC) (q.v.), but more recently to Chinese not residing in either the People's Republic of China or the Republic of China. There are over 40 million Overseas Chinese, 80 percent of whom live in Southeast Asian countries. Over half of the rest live in the United States. Most hail from Kuangtung and Fukien provinces, but second are Taiwan (q.v.) and Shan-tung. Around 800,000 Chinese have migrated from Taiwan since 1950.

The ROC government considers the allegiance of Overseas Chinese, sometimes called "mothers of the revolution," very important because the Republic of China was created, in large measure, with their support and because of the past contest between Taipei (q.v.) and Beijing for recognition as the legal government of China. Taipei still considers the Overseas Chinese important for economic, public relations, and other reasons. (See Overseas Chinese Affairs Commission.)

Overseas Chinese representation in the ROC government is provided via provisions in an amendment to the Constitution (q.v.) in 1991. Twenty Overseas Chinese serve in the National Assembly (q.v.) and six in the Legislative Yuan (q.v.).

Overseas Chinese Affairs Commission (OCAC) (hua-ch'iao wei-yuan-hui). Established in 1926 as a commission of the Executive Yuan (q.v.), OCAC seeks to protect the welfare and interests of Overseas Chinese (q.v.). Its work consists of helping students, getting passports and visas for Overseas Chinese, and running the Overseas Chinese News Agency and the Chung Hua Correspondence School.

Overseas Economic Cooperation Fund (hai-wai ching-chi ho-tso chi-chin). A fund established in 1989 as a foreign assistance program to help "friendly developing countries." The government appropriated NT$2.5 billion in fiscal year 1989 and NT$3 billion in fiscal year 1990 for the fund. The fund will eventually have a total of NT$30 billion. By July 1991, 10 countries had applied for economic assistance from the fund. Fund activities include making loans and grants and facilitating capital transfers. According to government guidelines, the People's Republic of China cannot apply to the fund. Many observers say the main purpose of the fund is to upgrade Taiwan's diplomatic ties with Third World countries and influence some countries to grant diplomatic recognition to Taipei (q.v.).

- P -

Pakkan Tao. Literally "northern anchorage," this term was used by Chinese fishermen in the 13th century to refer to Taiwan (q.v.).

Palace Museum. See National Palace Museum.

Pao Chia (pao-chia chih-tu). System of social organization and control used in ancient China and also used in Taiwan (q.v.). According to the system, each of 10 households chooses a representative who meets with nine other similarly chosen representatives, that group also selecting a leader, and on and on. The system was abolished by Tokyo in 1895 when Taiwan became a Japanese colony. Goto Shimpei (q.v.), however, revived it in 1898. It was used primarily as a means of facilitating police control by making each individual person responsible for those in his or her unit and subject to punishment for crimes committed by those people. Thus it incorporated the idea of collective responsibility and collective punishment for crimes. Under Japanese governance, it evolved into a means of political control and record keeping as well.

Paracel Islands (hsi-sha chun-tao). A group of islands, called Hsisha in Chinese, in the South China Sea claimed as territory of the Republic of China (q.v.). See also Macclesfield Bank, Pratas Islands, and Spratly Islands.

Party of Taiwanese People (t'ai-wan min-chung-tang). A political party formed in Taiwan (q.v.) in 1927 when it came under Japanese colonial rule and which was the first ever legal political party in Taiwan. It functioned, however, for only four years, until the governor-general banned it. It cannot be correctly called an opposition party, however, since it did not oppose Japanese rule nor advocate conflict between Japanese and Taiwanese (q.v.). Nor did it help consolidate a fledgling political opposition in Taiwan, but rather resulted in a split among Taiwanese political activists.

Peng Ming-min (1923-). Known as the "father of Taiwan independence," when a professor at Taiwan National University (q.v.) in the mid-1960s, he began to agitate against the "Chiang clique." He, together with some of his students, wrote and published a manifesto advocating Taiwan's independence causing him to be arrested and incarcerated in 1964. He served 14 months in jail after which he was placed under house arrest. He escaped the country and for the next three-plus decades lived in the United States. While in the U.S. he founded the Formosan Association for Public Affairs (q.v.).

Peng returned to Taiwan in 1992 and in 1994 joined the Democratic Progressive Party (DPP) (q.v.). He was viewed as a symbol of past travails and sufferings of pro-independence advocates and because of that gained support in the opposition party. In 1996, he was nominated by the DPP to be its candidate for president, with Hsieh Chang-t'ing (q.v.) as his running mate. He was defeated, receiving 21.13 percent of the popular vote. Subsequently Peng's relationship with the DPP deteriorated and he experienced increasing isolation in the party due to his hardline position on independence. Peng subsequently organized the Nation Building Association which evolved into the Taiwan Independence Party (TAIP) (q.v.). Peng's political influence has waned dramatically in the last few years.

Period of National Mobilization for the Suppression of the Communist Rebellion (tung-yuan k'an-luan shih-ch'i). Declared in 1948, based on the Temporary Provisions to the Constitution (qq.v.), which canceled many of the Constitution's provisions guaranteeing individual rights and freedoms as well as limits on government power; it is now seen as the period when the Republic of China was staunchly anti-Communist and also a period when democracy was very limited. The "period" was terminated by President Lee Teng-hui (q.v.) in May 1991, restoring the original rights in the Constitution and technically ending the state of war between the Nationalist government and the Communist government as far as Taipei was concerned. Beijing, on the other hand, did not respond to this as a friendly gesture and did not reciprocate.

Pescadore Islands (p'eng-hu ch'un-tao). A group of islands or an archipelago off the southwestern coast of Taiwan (q.v.) in the Taiwan Strait (q.v.). There are 64 islands in all, comprising 126 square kilometers in area. Penghu, the largest island, accounts for about half of the land surface of the archipelago and 70 percent of its population. The islands form a natural demarcation between the East China Sea and the South China Sea.

The Pescadore Islands attracted the attention of Chinese fishermen in the 12th century and were the first among islands around Taiwan, and including Taiwan itself, to be settled by Chinese, which began at this time.

In 1622, the Dutch occupied the islands, and intended to use the islands as a base to control ship traffic in the Taiwan Strait, but two years later were forced to leave or, alternatively, negotiated with the Chinese government and traded the islands for the island of Taiwan, though the latter was not really controlled by China. The Dutch subsequently got control of the Pescadores again.

In 1895, the Pescadores, along with Taiwan and other surrounding islands, were transferred to Japan via the Treaty of Shimonoseki (q.v.). They were returned to the Republic of China (q.v.) with Taiwan and other surrounding islands at the end of World War II.

PFG-2 (chu-li chien-er-hao). The designation of Taiwan's home-built missile frigate also called the Perry Frigate, launched in October 1991. The Navy ordered it from China Shipbuilding Corporation (q.v.) in August 1989. Its design follows the U.S. PFG-7, but it has greater offensive capabilities. It will be used to defend Taiwan against an attack by China. The navy plans to have eight such ships.

Pingpu. A name that refers to the plains-dwelling aborigines (q.v.) in Taiwan (q.v.) who were driven from the flat lands or assimilated by the Chinese settlers after they began to populate the island. There were 10 tribes of Pingpu aborigines. They lived in houses built on stilts and cooked food and ate pickled vegetables. They worshipped nature, ghosts, and their ancestors. Women were responsible for tilling the fields and weaving, and the eldest daughter in the family became the heir, her husband usually adopting her family name.

Political parties (cheng-tang). Before 1986, Taiwan (q.v.) had a one-party system, although there were two token legal opposition parties before that: the Young China Party and the China Democratic Socialist Party (qq.v.). The political party system began to change in the late 1970s and early 1980s with the increasing number of independent candidates participating in elections and due to the formation of the *tangwai* (q.v.)—meaning outside the party, referring to the Nationalist Party (q.v.). In September 1986, the *tangwai* evolved into the Democratic Progressive Party (DPP) (q.v.). The DPP, though still technically an illegal organization, challenged the Nationalist Party in the 1986 election. After the lifting of the Emergency Decree or martial law (q.v.) in July 1987, more parties formed, although they did not become formally legal until January 1989 with the passage of the Law on Civic Organizations (q.v.). The DPP performed well in the December 1989 election, prompting some to say that a two-party system was evolving. Nevertheless, by the end of February 1990 there were more than 40 political parties registered. In the December 1991 election four political parties qualified for television time: the Nationalist Party, the Democratic Progressive Party, the Chinese Social Democratic

Party (q.v) and the National Democratic Independent Political Alliance (q.v.), whose leaders said this "organization" was not really a party. The results of the election again suggested to many observers that a two-party system was evolving as only the Nationalist Party and the Democratic Progressive Party did sufficiently well to win at-large delegates in the National Assembly (q.v.). Others noted that, because of the KMT's margin of victory and considerably better performance than in the 1989 election, the system was rather a one-party dominant system or a mixture of that and a multiparty system. This view was reversed in favor of a two-party system after the Legislative Yuan (q.v.) election in 1992 when the DPP did very well.

In 1993, the New Party (q.v.) formed and made a credible showing in the 1994 election and turned in an even better performance in the 1995 Legislative Yuan election. This prompted speculation that the political party system was a three-party system. That idea, however, was heard less after the 1996 presidential election and subsequent local elections and especially after the 1998 Legislative Yuan and metropolitan mayoral races; the NP did poorly in all of these elections.

Recently cooperation between the parties has been necessary to pass legislation and to amend the constitution, giving rise to coalition politics and to speculation about parties splitting, merging, etc. In short, the political party system in Taiwan seems to be still evolving.

Potsdam Declaration (po-sz-tan hsuen-yen). A formal agreement among the United States, the United Kingdom, and the Soviet Union in July 1945 (when Japan's defeat was imminent) that, among other things, confirmed the promise made in the Cairo Declaration (q.v.) that "Taiwan and other territories stolen by Japan" would be returned after the war. However, it was not stated in the declaration specifically to whom Taiwan (q.v.) was to be given. Rather this matter was to be resolved in a subsequent peace treaty. The Potsdam Declaration is frequently cited by those who argue that Taiwan belongs to the Republic of China (q.v.) and not the People's Republic of China (since the latter did not exist at the time). The fact that it is vague about Taiwan's future is cited by those who say Taiwan's status is yet to be decided.

Pragmatic diplomacy (wu-shih wai-ch'iao). A new style of diplomacy practiced by the Republic of China (q.v.) and attributed to Lee Teng-hui (q.v.) soon after he became president. It included efforts to: reinforce formal diplomatic ties; establish substantive relations with nations with which the Republic of China did not have formal ties; establish ties with communist nations; obtain admission or readmission to international organizations. The assumption was that the end of the Cold War provided new diplomatic opportunities and that the diplomatic war with the People's Republic of China was no longer a zero-sum contest. It was also the product of Taiwan's successful democratization and the fact that Taiwan (q.v.) had a good reputation in the world community and could capitalize on this. It likewise mirrored Taiwan's considerable investment in and trade with the mainland and the possibility of improved political relations with Beijing. Pragmatic diplomacy was originally undertaken, some say, as a response to charges by the opposition that the government was to blame for the Republic of China's loss of diplomatic relations and diplomatic status and in large part includes tenets of the Democratic Progressive Party's (q.v.) foreign policy agenda. It has been criticized as lacking principles and supporting Taiwan's separation from China or a two Chinas policy. See also Dollar Diplomacy; Flexible Diplomacy; Substantive Foreign Relations; Vacation diplomacy.

Pratas Islands (tung-sha ch'un-tao). Located in the eastern part of the South China Sea, these small islands include territory claimed by the Republic of China (q.v.), which maintains a small military force there. The islands are also claimed by the People's Republic of China, Vietnam, the Philippines, Malaysia, and Indonesia. They are considered strategically located and may be important because they lie near vital shipping lanes and their ownership is seen as the possible basis for legal claims to undersea resources in the vicinity.

Premier (hsing-cheng-yuan yuan-chang). The president of the Executive Yuan (q.v.), the premier has been considered the highest executive leader in the government of the Republic of China (q.v.) and generally its second most important political figure after the president (q.v.). When Chiang Ching-kuo (q.v.) was premier from 1975 to 1978, being also head of the ruling Nationalist Party (q.v.), most regarded him as the nation's most powerful political leader rather than Yen Chia-kan (q.v.), who was president, and the political system as more a cabinet or parliamentary one than a presidential one. Under President Lee Teng-hui (q.v.) the president and the premier became locked in dispute and the fact that the president could appoint the premier but could not fire him led to a mini constitutional crisis. It was resolved in practice when Premier Hau Pei-tsun (q.v.) either stepped down at Lee's behest or left with the cabinet (both interpretations have wide acceptance) following an election of the Legislative Yuan (q.v.) in 1995. The relationship between the president and the premier was formally altered as a result of amendments to the Constitution (q.v.) passed in 1997 which strengthened the presidency and pushed the system toward a presidential one. See list of premiers in appendix 1.

Presbyterian Church of Taiwan (PCT) (t'ai-wan chang-lao-ch'iao-hui). Established in 1865 by British and Canadian missionaries, it built a following that is today more than 200,000 strong, with over 1,000 congregations. In the nineteenth century, its missionaries developed a system for romanizing the Taiwanese dialect or language. During the Japanese period, the PCT was suppressed because the colonial government believed it was involved in stirring up the aborigines (q.v.).

The PCT has also been distrusted by the present government because of its sympathy with the Taiwan Independence Movement (q.v.). In the past it was the target of investigations and repression, and some of its foreign missionaries were expelled or deported. In 1971, the PCT issued a "Public Statement on Our National Fate"; this document advocated self-determination in the wake of Taipei's expulsion from the United Nations.

Critics of the PCT note that it is the only religious organization in Taiwan that is involved in politics or takes an unequivocal stand on political matters. Reverend Kao Chun-ming (q.v.) was, until 1979, the general secretary of the PCT. An acting head served after Kao was imprisoned for his role in helping one of the leaders of the Kaohsiung Incident (q.v.). The PCT has sometimes suffered from an internal division over its involvement in political issues between its Fukien Taiwanese (q.v.) membership and its aborigine (q.v.) membership.

Lee Teng-hui (q.v.) is a member of the PCT, as is Yao Chia-wen (q.v.), former head of the Democratic Progressive Party (q.v.).

President (tsung-t'ung). The highest official of the Republic of China, formerly elected by the National Assembly (q.v.) for a six-year term with a two-term limit (exempted by the Temporary Provisions [q.v.]). The president is now elected by direct election for a four-year term, the first direct election having been held in 1996. The president has the power to command the military forces, issue mandates, conclude treaties, represent the nation in foreign affairs, declare war or peace, effectuate martial law (q.v.), grant amnesties, make appointments—including the premier (q.v.); president, vice president, and grand justices of the Judicial Yuan (q.v.); president, vice president, auditor-general, and members of the Control Yuan (q.v.); and president and vice president and members of the Examination Yuan (q.v.). He or she also convenes the National Assembly, grants amnesty and commutations, appoints and removes civil service officers, and confers honors. The president may also intervene to resolve disputes between the Executive Yuan and the Legislative Yuan (q.v.) to resolve disputes.

The fact that past presidents have been the leaders of the ruling party enhanced the president's power beyond what was constitutionally given, and this, plus the perceived need for a strong leader in Taiwan, made the political system in practice a presidential one—even though the Constitution (q.v.) sets forth a mixed presidential and cabinet system (some say more the latter). Recently, through both practice and constitutional change, the president is now head of what most people say is a presidential system of government and the presidency is the locus of political power more than the premier or the head of the Nationalist Party (q.v.)—though the positions of chairman of the KMT and president are currently held by one person: Lee Teng-hui (q.v.).

The Office of the President consists of a secretary-general, advisors, military aides, Academia Sinica, Academia Historica, the National Unification Council and, since 1967, the National Security Council (qq.v.). The First Bureau of the Office of the President is in charge of drafting and promulgating laws and decrees; the Second Bureau handles information and documents; the Third Bureau is responsible for protocol, awards, honors, etc. The Code Office takes care of telegraphic correspondence and national archives. The Office of the Guards is in charge of security. The Department of Public Affairs manages public relations. See list of presidents in appendix 1.

Presidential and Vice Presidential Election and Recall Law (tsung-t'ung fu-tsung-t'ung hsuan-pa-fa). A law passed by the Legislative Yuan (q.v.) in July 1995, following after amendments were written to the Constitution (q.v.) which changed the method of electing the president (q.v.) to a direct system and which formalized the procedures and provided specific regulations for the direct election in March 1996. It states that the presidential and vice presidential candidates may be nominated by any political party gaining at least 5 percent of the vote in the most recent provincial-level or higher election, or by collecting the signatures of at least 1.5 percent of the eligible voters in the most recent parliamentary election. In addition, the Election Commission must provide 30 minutes of national television time for each candidate and funding for national televised debates when two or more candidates agree to participate. See also Public Officials Election and Recall Law.

Presidential Palace (tsung-t'ung-fu). A large office building located in downtown Taipei (q.v.) built by the Japanese which, during the colonial period, contained the offices of the governor-general and other high officials. It is now the site of the Office of the President (q.v.) and some other important agencies of government. On National Day, October 10, it is the scene of parades and celebrations and a presidential address.

Provintia. A fort and town or city that became the capital of the Dutch colonial government in 1650. At one time there were 600 Dutch officials living there, in addition to over 2,000 troops. It was called *hung mao lou*, or the "edifice of red-haired barbarians" in Chinese. It was located at the present city of Tainan. See also Zeelandia.

Provisional Amendments for the Period of Mobilization for the Suppression of Communist Rebellion (tung-yuan k'an-luan shih-ch'i ling-shih ti'ao-k'uan). A set of amendments promulgated on May 10, 1948, during the Chinese Civil War by the Nationalist Chinese government which canceled or held in abeyance a number of provisions of the Constitution (q.v.). They remained in effect when the government moved to Taiwan. Commonly known as the "Temporary Provisions," the amendments expanded the emergency powers given to the president (q.v.) in Articles 39 and 43 of the Constitution. They also permitted the president and vice president to exceed the constitutionally limited two terms in office and authorized the president to appoint members to the three elected bodies of government. Moreover, they canceled many of the political and civil rights guaranteed to individual citizens in the Constitution. Critics of the Temporary Provisions felt that, while they were perhaps justified at one time, they were long due for repeal and were an obstruction to constitutional government and democracy. The Temporary Provisions were altered three times, in 1960, 1966, and 1972, and were finally abolished in 1991.

Public Construction Commission (kung-kung kung-ch'eng wei-yuan-hui). Established in 1995 within the Executive Yuan (q.v.), this body is responsible for building and construction.

Public Law 96-8. See Taiwan Relations Act.

Public Officials Election and Recall Law (kung-chih jen-yuan hsuan-pa-fa). A new election law adopted on May 14, 1980, that laid the foundation for a competitive national election in December 1980. The law was the result of a series of meetings that involved government officials, scholars, the media, and others called after the Kaohsiung Incident (q.v.). Compromises were made between the government and the ruling party on the one hand and opposition politicians on the other so that democratization would be possible without causing political instability. The election law was amended in 1983 and again after that. It contains a set of elaborate rules on conducting elections and electing officials. It also guarantees the impartiality of the Central Election Commission (q.v.). Another set of laws was written for a direct presidential election in 1996. See also Presidential and Vice Presidential Election and Recall Law.

Public Opinion Research Foundation (min-yi tiao-ch'a chi-chin-hui). Founded in 1986 primarily to aid businesses to do market research, it now conducts opinion polls on a variety of subjects and does frequent opinion surveys on political issues and leaders.

- Q -

Qiandao Lake Incident (ch'ien-tao-hu shih-chien). A resort lake in Chekiang Province in China where, in March 1994, 24 tourists from Taiwan (q.v.) were murdered. The government of the People's Republic of China (PRC) labeled the incident an accident and refused a request by the Straits Exchange Foundation (q.v.) to send representatives to accompany family members of the victims and to help deal with the matter. PRC police then arrested three young men for the crime and they were immediately executed. To relatives and the public in Taiwan the handling of the matter was seen as a coverup—for the military that had been involved in a robbery and mass killing. The incident resulted in a sudden and marked drop in Taiwan investment in China. It was also followed by the highest recorded level of support for independence since that question had been asked by opinion pollsters in Taiwan.

Quemoy (chin-men). A small island (though the name also refers to a chain of islands) off the coast of China (called Kinmen in the local dialect of Chinese and in Taiwanese and sometimes in English). In 1949, Communist forces failed to defeat Nationalist armies there and left the island in Nationalist hands. (See Offshore Islands.) Quemoy was subsequently heavily fortified by the Nationalists and became the main "stepping-stone" in their plan to counterattack and liberate the mainland. In September 1954, shortly after the Geneva Conference on Indochina, Mao ordered an attack on the island. The United States came to Taipei's rescue, thus preventing the People's Liberation Army from taking the island. Three months later, Washington and Taipei (q.v.) signed the United States-Republic of China Defense Treaty (q.v.). A month after this a joint resolution of the U.S. Congress, called the Formosa Resolution (q.v.), put Quemoy and some other islands not far away under U.S. protection by giving the president discretionary authority to protect them. In 1958, another assault was made on Quemoy, again resulting in U.S. action —including the placing of an atomic cannon on the island (though it had no nuclear shells). Peking backed down, but shelled the island on alternate days after that until the United States granted diplomatic relations to the People's Republic of China on January 1, 1979. See also Matsu.

- R -

Republic of China (ROC) (chung-hua min-kuo). The term which refers to the government established in China after the 1911 revolution, which was inspired by Sun Yat-sen (q.v.) and which overthrew the Manchu government or Ch'ing Dynasty. In 1945, Taiwan (q.v.) was incorporated into the Republic of China. In 1949, Mao's forces defeated the Nationalist Chinese armies on the China mainland after which the ROC government and its military forces and the Nationalist Party (q.v.) fled to Taiwan. The government of the Republic of China and the Nationalist Party continued to claim to be the legitimate government of all of China, even though it ruled only Taiwan, the Pescadore Islands (q.v.), the Offshore Islands (q.v.), some other islands close to Taiwan, and some islands in the South China Sea.

This claim, however, became less credible over the years and was terminated in principle in 1991 when Taiwan ended the period of mobilization to suppress the Communist rebellion on the mainland and recognized the People's Republic of China as a legal "entity." Most now consider the Republic of China to consist only of the territory over which it has actual jurisdiction. Thus the term "Republic of China on Taiwan" has become commonly used. Some other terms have also been used for the Republic of China, such as "ROC, Taiwan," and just "Taiwan." President Lee Teng-hui (q.v.) recently used the term "ROC, Taiwan." Some opposition groups in Taiwan have contended, and still argue, that the term "Republic of China" is illegitimate and should be replaced by the "Republic of Taiwan" or some other name. See also Republic of Taiwan.

Republic of China Amateur Sports Federation (chung-hua-min-kuo t'i-yu yun-tung tsung-hui). An organization responsible for upgrading athletic skills and promoting sports activities among the public in Taiwan.

Republic of China Professional Baseball League (chung-hua chih-pang lien-meng). Making Taiwan the sixth country with a professional baseball league in 1990, the league has four teams and plays a season of games in Taipei (q.v.), Taichung, and Kaohsiung (q.v.).

Republic of China-United States Trade Committee (chung-hua mao-yi hsieh-hui). An ad hoc cabinet-level committee that deals with economic issues, especially trade between Taiwan and the United States.

Republic of Taiwan (t'ai-wan kung-ho-kuo). The term used after the Sino-Japanese War in 1895 by an independence movement which sought to resist Japanese rule of Taiwan (q.v.) and create a new nation. The Republic of Taiwan, however, lasted only 10 days. It, incidentally, was not recognized by Ch'ing Dynasty rulers in China.

Since World War II the term has also been used by advocates of Taiwan's independence for the nation they would like to create after either defeating the Nationalist Party (q.v.) at the polls or ending its rule by force. In 1989, Lin Yi-hsiung (q.v.) wrote a draft law for a Republic of Taiwan. In recent years the term has been used more frequently to support Taiwan independence aimed at Beijing. See also Republic of China.

Research, Development, and Evaluation Commission (yen-chiu fa-chan wei-yuan-hui). An organ of the Executive Yuan (q.v.) responsible for the coordination of research and research projects. It has five departments: research and development, overall planning, control and evaluation, information systems management, and documentation and publication. The commission has been known also for its opinion surveys and for its role in advising the premier.

Resolution 31 (san-yi chueh-yi-an). A resolution proposed by U.S. Senators Alan Cranston and Edward Kennedy during the congressional debates on the Taiwan Relations Act (TRA) (q.v.) in 1979. It pledged actions, though unspecified, by the United States in the event of a threat to Taiwan (q.v.) or to

America's interests in Taiwan. This resolution reflected a serious concern on the part of Congress about Taiwan's security in the wake of the United States breaking diplomatic relations with the Republic of China (q.v.). Resolution 31 was also a reaction to President Jimmy Carter concluding the Normalization Agreement (q.v.) with the People's Republic of China, which iterated an unequivocal one-China (q.v.) policy and declared that the United States-Republic of China Defense Treaty (q.v.) would be terminated after one year. The authors of the resolution sought to strengthen the U.S. commitment to Taiwan in this context. Competing resolutions at the time linked an attack on Taiwan to U.S. security interests, but less specifically. Vice president Walter Mondale and lobbyist Frank Moore convinced Congress to weaken provisions in this resolution and, as a result, somewhat less clear security provisions are found in the TRA.

Reyerszoon, Cornelis. Dutch military leader who attacked Macao in 1622 and, after failing to hold it, retreated to the Pescadores (q.v.) and built a large fort there. He subsequently negotiated with Chinese officials to give up the Pescadores in return for China giving Taiwan (q.v.) to Holland.

- S -

Sakuma Sakuma. A Japanese army general who became governorgeneral of Taiwan in 1906 and served until 1915. He was appointed after 40 years of military service, mostly as a military policeman. His rule was characterized by policies to pacify the population and bring hostile aboriginal (q.v.) areas under the government's control. His tough and often brutal tactics engendered local opposition to Japanese rule.

Senior parliamentarians (tse-shen min-yi tai-piao). Also called elder parliamentarians, or "old thieves" by opposition politicians, they served as representatives or delegates to the National Assembly, Legislative Yuan, and the Control Yuan (qq.v.) prior to 1991 when they stepped down in advance of plenary elections to the National Assembly and the Legislative Yuan. The senior parliamentarians consisted of delegates who were elected when the government was located on the mainland,

and replacements appointed thereafter. Supplemental elections (q.v.) were held to add to the representation in the parliamentary bodies of government from Taiwan beginning in 1969, but they were insufficient to reduce the influence of the senior parliamentarians fast enough to suit many people in the context of the rapid democratization of the country in subsequent years. By the 1980s, many of the senior parliamentarians were old and in bad health, and newly elected representatives often dominated debates. Still they were seen as an impediment to democracy and were pressured by the Nationalist Party (q.v.), and then the opposition, to step down. They refused to give up their positions in spite of pressure to get them to leave because they felt they were in office constitutionally, they reaffirmed the nation's one-China (q.v.) policy, and because of the reluctance of their critics to force them out due to respect for age in Taiwan. In January 1989, the Legislative Yuan passed a bill on their "voluntary retirement" to force them to step down, but few did. In June 1990, the Council of Grand Justices (q.v.) rendered an interpretation of the Constitution (q.v.) terminating their tenure in office, after which they retired.

Separation of Trial from Prosecution Reform Act (shen-pan ch'i fen-li kai-k'e fa-an). A legislative act which, in 1980, made the Judicial Yuan (q.v.) more independent.

Shan, Paul (1923-). Appointed cardinal by Pope John Paul II in January 1998, Shan is the first in Taiwan to have this rank since Cardinal Yu Pin died in 1978. He was also the only cardinal appointed in Asia in 1998 and is only the fifth Chinese cardinal ever. Shan was born in Hepei province. In 1979, he was chosen bishop of Hualien. In 1991 he became bishop of the Kaohsiung (q.v.) diocese.

Shanghai Communiqué (shang-hai kung-pao). Also called the Joint U.S.-China Communiqué or First Shanghai Communiqué, this agreement was concluded during President Richard Nixon's visit to China. Signed on February 28, 1972, the communiqué signified a marked warming of relations between the United States and the People's Republic of China (PRC). While the document contains more statements of each side's views and reflects as much disagreement as agreement, it nevertheless mirrored a "meeting of the minds" and an effort to deal with the "Taiwan question." China's stated position was that the

People's Republic of China is the sole legal government of China; that Taiwan (q.v.) is a province of China; that the liberation of Taiwan is an internal affair; that U.S. forces and military installations must be withdrawn from Taiwan. The United States declared that the settlement of the Taiwan matter must be peaceful, a long-held policy of the United States. Regarding the PRC's claim that Taiwan is part of China, the U.S. side said that it "does not challenge" this position—suggesting to some that it concurred and to others that it disagreed but did not want to make issue of Taiwan in the context of seeking a better relationship with China due to the rapidly increasing "Soviet threat," or an arms race with the Soviet Union, which the United States was not winning due to the Vietnam War. Clearly the phrase "does not challenge" is ambiguous, probably purposely so. The U.S. side further stated that "all Chinese on either side of the Taiwan Strait (q.v.) maintain there is but one China and Taiwan is part of China." This use of incorrect English and the fact that the statement was only speculation, or was patently false, again suggests the United States sought to create ambiguity.

In any event, the Shanghai Communiqué became one of the documents making up the formal basis of U.S. China policy in subsequent years. The United States agreed in the Shanghai Communiqué to withdraw U.S. military forces and installations from Taiwan and did so. The Shanghai Communiqué was later said to be the basis for the United States to establish formal diplomatic relations, though some doubted that this followed especially in the way President Carter did it in 1979.

Taipei (q.v.) was not happy with the Shanghai Communiqué at the time that it was signed and later. It was seen as very detrimental to its national interests. U.S. officials, including top decision-makers in both the Nixon administration and subsequent administrations, however, maintained that the agreement did not damage or threaten Taiwan's interests, because a better relationship between the United States and the People's Republic of China would make Taiwan more secure.

Shen Chang-huan (1913-1998). Sometimes called the "godfather" of Taiwan's diplomacy, he was minister of foreign affairs from 1960 to 1966 and 1972 to 1979, secretary of the national security council from 1979 to 1984, and after that secretarygeneral to the president. He was considered a hard-liner regarding relations with the Soviet Union and in other ways. He was not active politically after 1988.

Shieh Tung-min (1907-). The governor of Taiwan Province from 1972 to 1978 and vice president from 1978 to 1984 under President Chiang Ching-kuo (q.v.), for some time he was the highest-ranking Taiwanese (q.v.) official in the government. Shieh was also one of the few Taiwanese at one time to have membership in the Nationalist Party's Central Standing Committee (qq.v.). However, he was not seen by many Taiwanese as a true Taiwanese representative or a competent official. In 1976, activists in the Taiwan Independence Movement (q.v.) sent a letter bomb to Shieh which exploded when he opened it, injuring his hand and causing its subsequent amputation.

Shih Chi-yang (1935-). Former president of the Judicial Yuan (q.v.), Shih served as vice-premier from 1988, having served as minister of justice from 1984 to 1988.

Shih Ming (1918-). A noted Taiwanese historian, who joined the Red Army during World War II and fought against the Japanese, he founded the Association for Taiwan Independence (q.v.) in 1967.

Shih Ming-teh (1941-). A member of the Legislative Yuan (q.v.) and former chairman of the Democratic Progressive Party (DPP) (q.v.) from 1993 to 1996. Shih was a famous dissident, having been imprisoned from 1962 to 1977 for sedition and from 1980 to 1990 for his part—some said a key leadership role—in the Kaohsiung Incident (q.v.). After release from prison he became leader of the DPP's New Tide faction (q.v.). Shih, however, was not so radical after he became head of the DPP and seemingly did not bear a grudge against the Nationalist Party (q.v.) or government for his years in prison. He later proposed a "Greater Chinese Commonwealth" similar to the British Commonwealth as a formula to deal with China or the issue of Taiwan's relationship with the People's Republic of China. In December 1998, he was elected to a seat in the Legislative Yuan (q.v.).

Shimonoseki (Treaty of) (ma-kuan t'iao-yueh). Treaty signed in the Japanese city of that name on April 17, 1895, ending the Sino-Japanese War. Japan, victor in the war, got from China payment of an indemnity for the war and the cession of territory, including Taiwan and the Pescadores (qq.v.), to Japan "in perpetuity." The Western powers viewed the treaty as legal and thus saw Taiwan's transfer to Japan as legitimate. Neither the Chinese administration on Taiwan nor the population was consulted at the time of the signing of the treaty. In Taiwan, there were forces both for and against the transfer. Two attempts to form a republic at this time, however, failed. See Republic of Taiwan.

Sidewinder missile (hsiang-wei-she fei-tan). An air-to-air missile the United States provided to the Republic of China's (q.v.) Air Force in 1958, during the second Offshore Islands (q.v.) crisis. The transfer was intended to help Taipei defend the islands and preclude an invasion of Taiwan (q.v.) which many at the time feared was Peking's next objective after taking some or all of the Offshore Islands. Others, however, question whether Peking actually had this intent.

Siew, Vincent C. (1939-). Premier of the Republic of China (q.v.) since August 1997, having served previously as director-general of the Board of Foreign Trade of the Ministry of Foreign Affairs, chairman of the Mainland Affairs Council (q.v.), minister of economic affairs, and member of the Legislative Yuan (q.v.). Siew is considered to be an economic expert, a diplomat (having represented the country at various economic conferences), a man of the people (coming from a poor family), and a good politician (having defeated a strong Democratic Progressive Party (q.v.) incumbent in the 1996 Legislative Yuan election). Siew played a key role in the passage of constitutional amendments in 1997. He is considered to be close to both President Lee Teng-hui and Vice President Lien Chan (qq.v.). Many regard him as a strong possibility for president in the future.

"Singapore solution" (hsin-chia-po mo-shih). A model sometimes cited to resolve the "Taiwan issue." Advocates suggest that Taiwan (q.v.) should be regarded as a "Chinese nation-state" but with sovereignty, and separate from China —as is the case of Singapore. See also German formula.

Sino-American Mutual Defense Treaty (chung-mei kung-t'ung fang-yü tiao-yue). See United States-Republic of China Defense Treaty.

Six Assurances (liu-hsiang pao-cheng). Provisions in a statement made by the American Institute in Taiwan (q.v.) to President Chiang Ching-quo (q.v.) on July 14, 1982, prior to the August Communiqué (q.v.) in which the United States agreed (with Beijing) to reduce and eventually end arms aid to Taiwan (q.v.). The assurances were that the United States would: (1) not set a specific date to end arms sales to Taiwan; (2) not hold talks with the People's Republic of China (PRC) regarding arms sales to Taiwan; (3) not play a mediating role between the two; (4) not revise the Taiwan Relations Act (q.v.); (5) not change its position regarding the sovereignty of Taiwan; and (6) not pressure Taiwan to negotiate with the PRC. Although the Six Assurances were not conveyed in written form, they were subsequently mentioned by the U.S. assistant secretary of state for East Asian and Pacific Affairs in testimony before the Senate Foreign Relations Committee.

Six-Point Proposal (li liu-tian). Points made in a speech by President Lee Teng-hui (q.v.) to the National Unification Council (q.v.) in April 1995 in response to Jiang Zemin's Eight-Point Proposal (q.v.). Lee spoke of unification but in "gradual phases." He also said that Beijing must accept the "reality" of the government of the Republic of China (q.v.) and accept equality and agree to negotiate with Taipei (q.v.). The People's Republic of China did not respond in a positive way to Lee's points.

Six-Point Rejoinder (liu-tian hui-ying). Made by Premier Sun Yuan-suan (q.v.) on June 10, 1982, in reply to the People's Republic of China's just announced Nine-Point Proposal (q.v.). He stated that Taiwan was unwilling to negotiate for the following reasons: (1) the Nationalist Party (q.v.) had had a bad experience with the Chinese Communists in the past; (2) the Chinese Communist Party had lost credibility by its handling of Tibetan unification in the 1950s and 1960s; (3) the People's Republic of China continued to try to isolate the Republic of China (q.v.) in the world community; (4) Taiwan's domestic political situation would not allow the Nationalist Party to negotiate on such a highly publicized and controversial issue; (5) Peking's guarantees of Taiwan's autonomy after unification lacked credibility, and (6) the People's Republic of China had a history of shifts and reversals in policy. Sun's statements were eventually accepted by most in Taiwan, including various opposition leaders.

Six-Point Supplement (liu-tian pu-ch'ung). "Concessionary points" made by Deng Xiaoping to U.S. professor Winston Yang in June 1983, broadening Ye Jianying's earlier Nine-Point Proposal (q.v.). Deng, however, still excluded autonomy for Taiwan's armed forces, security, intelligence, and foreign affairs organs. More important, the offer was not considered an attractive one because it did not consider the Republic of China to have sovereignty.

Six-Year Development Plan (liu-nien fa-chan chi-hua). A plan approved by the government in 1991 to improve the country's economic infrastructure during the six-year period to 1996. Over U.S.$300 billion was allocated for 779 projects, including roads, rail and subway systems, petrochemical and other heavy industries, and pollution-control facilities. It was reported that the plan would put Taiwan in the top 20 countries in the world by per capita income before the year 2000.

Sky Bow missile (t'ian-kung fei-tan). A surface-to-air missile produced in Taiwan by the military's Chungshan Institute of Science and Technology (q.v.) to defend the country against invading aircraft from the People's Republic of China. It was successfully tested in March 1986. The Tienkung II, an upgraded version, was tested in 1998 and was said to be equivalent to the U.S. Patriot missile and would be used to defend the country against missile attacks.

Sky Sword missile (t'ian-chien fei-tan). An air-to-air missile made in Taiwan and carried on locally built (under contract) F-5E (q.v.) jet fighter planes. It resembles the Sidewinder missile (q.v.). It was test fired in April 1986.

Sonk, Maarten. Dutch military leader who replaced Cornelis Reyerszoon (q.v.) in 1624 and finalized negotiations that involved trading the Pescadores for Taiwan (qq.v.). He subsequently became the first Dutch governor of Taiwan, though it was not until years later that Holland was the exclusive colonizer of the island.

Soong Chu-yu (1942-). Also known as James Soong, he was secretary-general of the Nationalist Party (q.v.) from 1988 to 1993, having served as director-general of the Government Information Office (q.v.) from 1979 to 1984 and later as head of the party's Department of Cultural Affairs from 1984 to 1987. Soong took a strong stand in support of President Lee Teng-hui (q.v.) to head the Nationalist Party after Chiang Ching-kuo's (q.v.) death in January 1988, arguing that Lee should be made formal head of the party and that not doing so would send the wrong signal about Taiwan's democratization and would result in divided government. At the time Lee's opponents wanted to make him only temporarily head of the ruling party or make him only one of several party chairmen. Soong also strongly supported Lee during another challenge in early 1990 when Lee was reelected by the National Assembly (q.v.).

In 1994, Soong was elected the first governor of Taiwan in a strong victory with President Lee's support. Soong and Lee subsequently came into disagreement, however, primarily over the issue of eliminating the provincial government. In 1996, Soong resigned, creating a crisis in the government and the ruling party. Though his resignation was not accepted and he stayed on as governor until December 1998 when the position as an elected office was abolished, the crisis was not resolved amicably. The dispute between Soong and Lee was particularly apparent at the Nationalist Party's 15th Party Congress in 1997, even though Soong was absent from the meeting, and continued in the form of public statements after that.

Soong is widely considered a very popular and charismatic figure, a man of the people and a politician with a future—though his disagreements with President Lee and also Vice President Lien Chan (q.v.) as well as the fact that he is Mainland Chinese (q.v.) (even though he gets along very well with Taiwanese [q.v.] and has considerable Taiwanese support) have cast some doubts on what official position he can attain after 1998. Recent public opinion polls, on the other hand, indicate that he has greater public support than any other politician in Taiwan.

Soong Mayling (1898-). Also known as Madam Chiang Kai-shek, she has held a number of political and extrapolitical positions and has had considerable political influence in the Nationalist government and the Nationalist Party (KMT) (q.v.), both during her husband's life and after. At the time of World War II she was one of only two foreigners ever to address a joint session of the U.S. Congress, appealing for help from the United States on behalf of the Nationalist cause at that time. In 1988, after Chiang Ching-kuo (q.v.), died she sided with those who sought to prevent Lee Teng-hui (q.v.) from gaining leadership of the KMT. Since then she has been politically inactive and has resided in the United States. Her sister was married to Sun Yat-sen (q.v.), but instead of leaving with the Nationalists in 1949, stayed in China and served in a high position in that government. Her brother was minister of finance when the Nationalists ruled China. She has no children.

South (nan). A "New left" Marxist-humanist magazine that began publication in 1986. Many of its articles criticized Taiwan's capitalist economic development and what the magazine's editors regarded as resultant social problems in Taiwan (q.v.).

Southern strategy. See Go South policy.

Spratly Islands (nan-sha chun-tao). Also known as Nansha (in Chinese) and located in the South China Sea, these small islands are territory claimed by the Republic of China (q.v.). Taipei maintains a small military force on one of the islands. The islands are also claimed by the People's Republic of China, Vietnam, the Philippines, Malaysia, and Indonesia. They are considered strategically located in terms of controlling vital sea lanes, and their ownership could possibly be the basis for legal claim to undersea resources in the vicinity.

Statute on the Voluntary Retirement of Senior Parliamen-tarians (tse-shen min-yi tai-piao t'ui-chih t'iao-li). Passed into law in 1989, this law was intended to force members of the Control Yuan, Legislative Yuan and National Assembly (qq.v.) who were elected in the 1947 election or subsequently appointed to positions in these parliamentary organs of government, to resign. Most of the senior parliamentarians (q.v.) refused to abide by this law and stayed in office. It was not until a decision was rendered by the Council of Grand Justices (q.v.) that they stepped down, although the Statute on the Voluntary Retirement of Senior Parliamentarians may have had some influence on their decisions.

Straits Exchange Foundation (SEF) (hai-hsia ch'iao-liu chi-chin-hui). A private organization established in early 1991 to manage contacts with the People's Republic of China. However, since it has ties with the Mainland Affairs Council (q.v.) and receives much of its budget from the government it is considered quasi-official. On the other hand, being technically private it has been able to deal with officials in China without such contacts being regarded as formal negotiations or government to government talks. The SEF is chaired by Koo Chen-fu (q.v.). The SEF's counterpart organization is the Association for Relations Across the Taiwan Strait (ARATS) (q.v.). Talks were held between the two organizations in 1992, but little was accomplished because of differing definitions of "one China (q.v.)." Also there were problems because Beijing treated the talks as a matter of domestic affairs while Taipei treated them as diplomatic in nature. In 1993, the SEF helped engineer the Koo-Wang talks (q.v.) that led to what many called a breakthrough in Taipei-Beijing relations. In 1995, however, following President Lee Teng-hui's (q.v.) visit to the United States which angered leaders in Beijing, cross-strait meetings between the SEF and ARATS were suspended. Talks were, however, resumed in October 1998. See Koo-Wang talks. See also Mainland Affairs Council; National Unification Council.

Substantive Foreign Relations (shih-chih wai-ch'iao). A policy of the government of the Republic of China (q.v.) to promote bilateral or multilateral nondiplomatic relations, such as sports, culture, science, technology, trade, and investment, in lieu of formal diplomatic ties. This term came into common usage in the 1970s as a result of Taipei's loss of diplomatic ties following its expulsion from the United Nations in 1971 and President Richard Nixon's trip to Beijing in 1972 and a shift in diplomatic policy by the ROC.

Sun Li-jen (1900-1990). A Nationalist general trained at the Virginia Military Institute in the United States, Sun served under General Joseph Stilwell in the Burma campaign during World War II. Later, he became commander in chief of Nationalist Chinese ground forces. In August 1955, Chiang Ching-kuo (q.v.) placed Sun under arrest for organizing a coup against the government. Sun had been critical of Chiang Kai-shek (q.v.) and Chiang Ching-kuo's commissar system and may have secretly sought support in the United States for an alternative to Chiang Kai-shek. He remained under detention or house arrest until 1988 even though the Control Yuan (q.v.) had exonerated him of any plot against Chiang Kai-shek or the government.

Sun Yat-sen (1866-1925). Known as the father of the Republic of China (q.v.), the founder of the Nationalist Party (q.v.), and the most famous advocate of Chinese nationalism in the early part of the century, Sun was born in Kuangtung or Canton province. At the age of 13 Sun went to Hawaii where he attended middle school, high school, and college. He subsequently returned to China and to Hong Kong, where he graduated from Hong Kong Medical College in 1892. He practiced medicine briefly in Macao before he moved to Kuangchou. There he gave up medicine to devote his time and energy to the overthrow of the Manchu government in China. In 1894, following a failed uprising, he fled to Japan. In 1897, while in Japan, Sun gave a series of lectures which were later published as the book *Three Principles of the People.* (See Three Principles of the People.) Sun advocated revolution in contrast to most other Chinese intellectuals and officials of the time who advocated political reform.

During his early career as a revolutionary Sun spent most of his time abroad seeking support for the cause of overthrowing the Manchu government and establishing a democratic system of government in China, while his followers in China sought actively and aggressively to spark revolution. In 1894, he founded the Hsing Chung Hui (Revive China Society) in Hawaii and in 1905 the Tung Meng Hui (Revolutionary Alliance) in Japan. On October 10, 1911, Sun's supporters finally succeeded, ending the Manchu rule of China.

In January 1912, Sun was inaugurated the provisional president of the Republic of China which was established the previous year. However, he subsequently abdicated in order to prevent a civil war in China. (Yuan Shih-kai in the meantime had consolidated power in Peking and had won the allegiance and support of the Western powers.) Subsequently Sun, because of disappointment with the West, invited Soviet representatives to China who advised him on party organization and other matters, thus accounting for the fact that the Nationalist Party (q.v.) has a Leninist organizational structure. In the 1920s, Sun made still other attempts to establish a democratic government in China, but failed.

During his lifetime Sun wrote about politics, political philosophy, and political development. His political ideals or political philosophy are summarized in his *San Min Chu I* or Three Principles of the People—his most famous treatise. Sun's "Principles" became the ideological basis of the Nationalist Party and the government of the Republic of China when it ruled China and later after it moved to Taiwan. Sun's thinking and writings were highly influenced by American democracy and political thought.

Sun visited Taiwan for the first time in 1900 and built a base of support there, though this did not survive the Japanese colonial period very well. His political thinking and writings, however, had a strong influence in Taiwan after it became part of the Republic of China in 1945 and even more after the government moved to Taiwan in 1949. His teachings and writings are taught in schools in Taiwan at all levels and his works are widely read by government and Nationalist Party officials. Some also say Sun's writings about economic and political development, and the interrelationship between the two, are the first of their kind and also that they provided the design or framework for Taiwan's economic and political modernization.

Sun Yat-sen's Birthday (kuo-fu yen-chen chi-nien-jih). November 12, an official holiday.

Sun Yun-suan (1913-1984). Premier from 1978 to 1984, having previously served in a number of top government positions and having a high rank in the Nationalist Party (q.v.), he was minister of communications from 1967 to 1969 and minister of economic affairs from 1969 to 1978. Throughout 1983, Sun was thought to be Chiang Ching-kuo's (q.v.) choice for vice president in 1984 and ultimately his successor. Chiang, however, picked Lee Teng-hui (q.v.). In February 1984, Sun suffered from a serious stroke, thus ending his political career. See also Six-Point Rejoinder.

Supplemental elections (tseng-pu hsüan). National elections that increased the representation of Taiwan in the Legislative Yuan and the National Assembly (qq.v.). These elections were necessary because the delegates to these two parliamentary bodies and also the Control Yuan (q.v.) represented all of China and when the government of the Republic of China (q.v.) moved to Taiwan, elected officials representing districts on the mainland were frozen in office or their replacements appointed. (See Senior Parliamentarians.) The first supplemental election was held in 1969. National elections through 1989 were nonsupplemental, though more and more seats were added over time to represent Taiwan. Supplemental elections ended when the senior parliamentarians stepped down in 1991 and nonsupplemental elections were held in 1991 and 1992, respectively, for the National Assembly and the Legislative Yuan.

"Switzerland of the Orient" (tung-fang jui-shih). A term used by some to refer to Taiwan (q.v.)—because of its size, mountainous terrain, and high standard of living. Some use the term also to suggest that Taiwan should pursue a policy of neutrality.

Sworn brotherhoods (hsiung-ta-hui). Secret alliances of friendship that became an important part of social life for many early Chinese settlers on Taiwan. Members were usually males in their late teens and early twenties but came from all walks of life: soldiers, merchants, vagabonds, peasants, and even scholars. Gambling, banditry, and fighting were common activities among the members. Beginning in 1683, the Ch'ing government attempted to suppress the groups but was unsuccessful. The brotherhoods had become powerful elements by the mid-1800s in both the rural and the urban areas of Taiwan.

- T -

Taichung. Meaning "stage of the center" in Chinese, and located in the middle of Taiwan (q.v.), it is one of Taiwan's five large cities administered by Taiwan Province. It is located near Taichung

Harbor, which is the site of many of the projects associated with Taiwan's effort to become a regional business hub.

Taihoku Imperial University (t'ai-wan t'i-kuo ta-hsueh). The first university established in Taiwan (in Taipei) in 1927 and generally regarded as its best. After 1945, it was renamed National Taiwan University (q.v.).

Tainan. Meaning "stage of the south" in Chinese, and located in the southern part of the island, it is one of Taiwan's five large cities administered by Taiwan Province. It was the capital of Taiwan (q.v.) when it was ruled by Cheng Ch'eng-kung (q.v.).

Taipei (tai-pei). Meaning "stage of the north" in Chinese, it is the largest city in Taiwan (q.v.). There is little or no historical record of the area, however, before it was settled in the 1700s. It became a major river port city on the Tamsui River (q.v.) in the 1800s, bringing prosperity to the city and increasing its population markedly. In 1875, it became an administrative district under the jurisdiction of the government in Peking. In 1892, walls around the city were completed. When Taiwan became part of the Japanese Empire, Taipei was the administrative center of Taiwan. In 1945, it became the capital of Taiwan Province under the jurisdiction of the Republic of China (q.v.), and, in 1949, the provisional capital of the Republic of China. In 1967, it was given the status of special municipality under the jurisdiction of the Executive Yuan (q.v.).

Taipei City Council (t'ai-pei shih-yi-hui). Established in 1946 as a provisional legislative organ, it became a formal body after the institutionalization of local self-government in 1950. There were six elections of members from 1950 to 1967 at which time Taipei (q.v.) was made a special municipality. The next election was held in 1969, following which there have been elections at four-year intervals. There are 40 seats for the first one million residents and one additional for each additional 100,000 people. Elections are conducted in five precincts and one woman is required for each seven members. In 1994, 52 members were elected including many from the Democratic Progressive Party and the New Party (qq.v.), causing the Nationalist Party (q.v.) to lose control of the Council. It regained control after the 1998 election.

Taipei City Government (t'ai-pei shih-cheng-fu). Established in 1945 as an executive organ when Taipei (q.v.) was designated a city under provincial jurisdiction, it governed 10 administrative districts (*chu*). In 1967, Taipei, because of its growth and importance, was made a special municipality under the Executive Yuan (q.v.)—although critics said it was to preclude the mayorship from becoming a springboard for a popular Taiwanese leader. In 1968, six suburbs were incorporated: Chingmei, Mucha, Nankang, Neihu, Shihlin, and Peitou. In 1994, the mayor once again became an elected official.

Taipei Economic and Cultural Representative Office (TECRO) (t'ai-pei ching-chi wen-hua tai-piao-ch'u). Representing a name change in 1994 from the former Coordination Council for North American Affairs (q.v.), TECRO represents the Republic of China (q.v.) in the realms of diplomatic, cultural, economic and military affairs in Washington, D.C. Local offices are referred to as Taipei Economic and Cultural Office (TECO). The name change was seen by some to mirror an upgrading of Taiwan's status by the United States following a "review" of U.S. Taiwan policy by the Clinton administration after considerable pressure was felt from the Republicancontrolled Congress that perceived that Taiwan was not being treated well. See also Taiwan policy review.

Taipei International Convention Center (t'ai-pei kuo-chi hui-yi chung-hsin). Large facility that opened in 1991 for conferences and exhibits and is considered one of the best of its kind in the world. It is operated by the China External Trade Development Council (q.v.). It operates the adjoining World Trade Center, which promotes business in Taiwan (q.v.), especially trade.

Taiwan (t'ai-wan). Literally "stage," or "terrace bay," the origin of the term is uncertain, though in the 17th century it referred to a small islet where the Dutch established their early colonial base. They subsequently used the word to designate what is now the island of Taiwan. The word currently refers—depending on one's point of view—to simply the island of Taiwan, a Chinese province (belonging either to the Republic of China [q.v.] or the People's Republic of China), territory constituting most of the Republic of China, or a nation-state (meaning that it should be synonymous with or substituted for the term the "Republic of China").

Taiwan Association for Labor Movement (lao-tung yun-tung t'ai-wan lien-meng). An organization established in 1984 to provide workers with free legal assistance and help in organizing free trade unions. In 1988, it established the National Independent Labor Federation, consisting of 12 unions and representing 12,000 workers.

Taiwan Benevolent Association of America (mei-kuo-ti-ch'u t'ai-wan tse-shan hsieh-hui). An organization established in the U.S., composed of Chinese from Taiwan. It is pro-Nationalist.

Taiwan Church News **(t'ai-wan ch'iao-hui-pao).** A publication of the Presbyterian Church in Taiwan (q.v.), it was Taiwan's first newspaper. It publishes both religious and political news.

Taiwan Communist Party (TCP) (t'ai-wan kung-chan-tang). Formed in 1928, the TCP existed until 1931 as a local branch of the Japan Communist Party. At that time it supported the creation of an independent, socialist Taiwan (q.v.), reflecting the positions of both the Japan Communist Party and the Chinese Communist Party. It subsequently became inactive and was suppressed during the subsequent era of militarism in Japan. It has been rumored that President Lee Teng-hui (q.v.) was once a member, and his opponents have on a number of occasions publicly accused him of this, including during the 1996 election campaign. Lee denies the charge and says that his age and place of birth do not fit the person described.

Taiwan Democratic Movement Overseas (hai-wai t'ai-wan min-chu yun-tung). An organization started by Hsu Hsin- liang (q.v.) when the Democratic Progressive Party (q.v.) rebuffed Hsu in his attempt to represent the DPP abroad and decided not to establish overseas units.

Taiwan Democratic Self-Government League (t'ai-wan min-chu tse-chih cheng-fu lien-meng). Established in Shanghai in 1947 by Ms. Hsieh Hsueh-hong and other Taiwanese Communists in China. In 1949, it became one of the "satellite parties" that worked with the Chinese Communist Party. It established branches in Japan that opposed Liao Wen-yi's (q.v.) work there, especially his call for a U.N.- sponsored plebiscite to decide Taiwan's future. The league's position, like the Chinese Communist Party, was that American and Japanese "imperialists" sought to keep Taiwan (q.v.) independent, and the Taiwanese Independence Movement (q.v.) was their tool.

Taiwan Development Company (t'ai-wan k'ai-fa kung-szu). The largest landholder in Taiwan (q.v.) before the end of World War II. It held 230,000 acres of land. It was Japanese-owned. In the 1950s, this land was sold to tiller-farmers by the Nationalist government in conformance with the land reform (q.v.) program.

Taiwan economic miracle (t'ai-wan ching-chi ch'i). A term frequently used to describe Taiwan's (q.v.) very impressive economic development after the mid-1960s, but also employed to recognize that Taiwan was able to do so well in promoting economic development in spite of a bleak outlook in the late 1940s and 1950s and what were seen at that time as extremely serious handicaps to economic growth. Also, Taiwan saw very rapid growth and yet incomes were very equitable, which is often not the case using the capitalist model of economic development. The "economic miracle" is frequently said to be the basis for the "Taiwan model" or the "Taiwan experience" (q.v.).

In 1949, when the Nationalist government moved to Taiwan, many economists described Taiwan's economic prospects in very dim or pessimistic terms. Some even called Taiwan an economic "basketcase" and opined that Taiwan had little hope to grow economically, that it would always be poor. The reasons usually given were Taiwan's lack of natural resources; its very bad population to land ratio; its lack of capital; and an inefficient, corrupt and discredited government. Some also mentioned the fact that U.S. economic assistance had been terminated and that Taiwan lacked technological skills and its population was not well educated.

These evaluations proved wrong and, instead, Taiwan grew very rapidly—averaging 10 percent annual growth (often called miracle growth) from the mid-1960s to the early 1980s, notwithstanding two oil crises which caused economic instability and slowed growth. This rate of growth made Taiwan the number one performing economy in the world during this period. Taiwan's economic growth subsequently slowed, but over a period of thirty-five years it is still the best of any developing country in the world.

Taiwan's economic success has been attributed to a number of factors, including: land reform (q.v.) in the 1950s; U.S. economic assistance (which for some years was the largest to any country in the world not at war, but which, unlike aid to most other recipients, was used effectively— when it was terminated Taiwan's economy "took off"); an intelligent import substitution plan (which was wisely terminated after a brief period, as many countries have failed to do); export promotion policies; high rates of savings; privatization; improvements in education geared to create a better work force; export processing zones (q.v.); intelligent government planning and oversight of a free market economy. (See Ten Projects; Twelve Projects; Fourteen Projects.)

Taiwan pursued economic growth based on free market, free trade principles and invited foreign investment while rejecting dependency theory (q.v.). Many large state-owned or controlled industries that were in the early years felt to be best kept in the public sector due to their vital connections to national defense were privatized. Unionization was discouraged, crime controlled, taxes kept low, and economic freedom and opportunities provided generously by the government. It was a clear case of promoting business and viewing economic development as rightly preceding political change.

The term "economic miracle" has also been used to describe the fact that Taiwan was not affected very much by the so-called Asian economic meltdown that began in July 1997. Taiwan's economy was not hurt by this phenomenon as were many other countries in East Asia. (See also Taiwan political miracle.)

Taiwan Environmental Protection Agency (t'ai-wan huan-ching pao-hu-chu). Established in 1987 by local environmental groups, it became affiliated with the U.S.-based International Environmental Protection Association. This organization, in contrast to the official government agency, focuses its attention primarily on nuclear power, the petrochemical industry, forest ecology, and land use. See also Environmental Protection Administration.

"Taiwan experience" (t'ai-wan ching-yen). A term used frequently in recent years to refer to Taiwan's successful economic, social, and political modernization and the lessons that might be adopted by other countries, including the People's Republic of China. The term is also used by the government in Taipei (q.v.) to refer to efforts to promote democracy on the mainland. (See Taiwan economic miracle; Taiwan political miracle.)

Taiwan Garrison Command General Headquarters. See Garrison Command.

Taiwan Human Rights Association (t'ai-wan jen-ch'uan hsieh-hui). A human rights organization founded in Taiwan (q.v.) in the 1970s. It is concerned with local human rights problems and often reflects the views of opposition political candidates. See also Chinese Association for Human Rights.

Taiwan Independence Movement (t'ai-wan tu-li yun-tung). A term that in the late 1950s and 1960s referred to the provisional government of the Republic of Formosa founded in 1956 by Liao Wen-yi (q.v.) (Thomas Liao). But as that organization faded in importance and others were established, the term came to mean generally organizations that support a separate and independent Taiwan (q.v.) and/or one ruled by Taiwanese rather than Mainland Chinese (qq.v.). The various organizations disagreed about how to accomplish "independence" or even whether that should be considered a goal in view of the fact Taiwan was already independent, given that it was generally considered to have sovereignty in the name of the Republic of China (q.v.). They also differed in opinion about what to do with approximately 15 percent of the population or the three million Mainlanders living in Taiwan: whether they should be forced leave, be assimilated, or simply, made to share political power. Nearly all of the Taiwan Independence Movement groups were illegal in Taiwan since advocating an independent Taiwan was considered treason. In fact, a number of supporters of independence were imprisoned.

Several of the groups, especially those which were most active in the United States, were antagonistic toward other groups. Also their relationship with politicians and groups with similar views in Taiwan were not always cordial. Some supported opposition candidates in Taiwan, but this was not as frequent as might have been expected since many politicians in Taiwan keep their distance from these groups.

The World United Formosans for Independence and the Formosan Association for Public Affairs (qq.v.) were the most active of the groups supporting Taiwan independence.

In recent years, due to democratization, independence has been widely discussed and advocated in political debates and in election campaigns in Taiwan. An independent Taiwan is favored and openly advocated (in fact, being in the party platform) by the Democratic Progressive Party (DPP) (q.v.), though there are disagreements in the DPP as to whether it should prevail over other objectives, whether it is a short-term or long-term goal, and if it is a prerequisite to democracy. (See Formosa faction and New Tide faction.) The Taiwan Independence Party (q.v.), in fact, was formed in 1996 by some DPP members who felt the party was abandoning the cause.

The New Party (q.v.) strongly opposes Taiwan's independence. The Nationalist Party (q.v.) technically opposes independence, but critics of President Lee Teng-hui (q.v.), especially those in the ruling party's Non-Mainstream faction (q.v.) and the NP say he secretly supports it. Leaders in the People's Republic of China say they will launch a military attack on Taiwan if the government openly or officially adopts a policy of independence.

Taiwan Independence Party (TAIP) (chien-kuo-tang). A political party formed in October 1996 by a splinter group from the Democratic Progressive Party (DPP) (q.v.) that was disappointed with what it considered the DPP's weakening stand on Taiwan independence. The TAIP grew out of the Nation Building Association, founded by Peng Ming-min (q.v.) immediately after his defeat in the March 1996 presidential election. Some have called the TAIP Taiwan's "fourth force" or fourth meaningful political party. However, to date it has not had much political influence and has suffered from internal disagreements.

Taiwan policy review (t'ai-wan cheng-tse hui-ku). A process set in motion in the United States as a result of Congress calling on the White House for an upgrading of relations with Taiwan (q.v.) and which the Clinton administration put into effect, though some say reluctantly. It was proposed by Congress in the Authorization Act for 1994 and 1995.

It provided for more direct contacts between high officials from the United States and the Republic of China (ROC) (q.v.), supported Taipei's entry into the World Trade Organization (WTO) and the use of the term "Taipei" in the name of the ROC's representative offices in the United States. See also Taipei Economic and Cultural Representative Office.

Taiwan political miracle (t'ai-wan cheng-chih ch'i-chi). A term used to describe the Republic of China's (q.v.) rapid political modernization that began in the early or mid-1980s and which, within a decade or two turned Taiwan into a genuine or fullfledged democracy. It was called a miracle by many because Taiwan had been widely regarded as a hard authoritarian dictatorship that resisted reform and was frequently labeled a pariah nation for that, but was subsequently seen as a real, working democracy. The transition to a democratic system was made, moreover, without the benefit of a colonial experience that prepared Taiwan for the change, it was accomplished in a very short period of time compared to Western democracies, and it happened without bloodshed. It also occurred at a time when the nation was technically at war and was certainly under threat. Taiwan's experience is unique in these respects, and as a result it has been viewed as a model for other countries seeking to democratize. (See Taiwan experience.) Taiwan's political modernization and transition to democracy were also more difficult, according to some scholars, because of the fact that its authoritarian control was built on the rule of a single party rather than the military, which could simply "return to the barracks." Party control of the media, judiciary, and the government bureaucracy was, in other words, difficult to break. Also, the military and security organizations had to be depoliticized and their ties with the party broken, and this was not an easy task.

The factors contributing to the Taiwan "political miracle" include land reform (q.v.), which destroyed the feudal landlord-tenant ties and which fostered the development of local democracy; rapid development with equity (see Taiwan economic miracle); urbanization (which led to the creation of interest groups); the growth of competing political parties (q.v.); elections; enlightened leaders, especially Chiang Ching-kuo and Lee Teng-hui (qq.v.); pressure by the United States; and efforts by the government to build a better image in the international community in the face of efforts by the People's Republic of China to force Taiwan to negotiate reunification.

The Taiwan political miracle, or its democratization, is often seen as the major obstacle to reunification and hostile relations with Beijing. It is often cited by Taipei (q.v.) as the reason that Taiwan cannot unify with China, since the People's Republic of China has not democratized.

Taiwan Political Review *(t'ai-wan cheng-chih hui-ku).* An opposition publication started by Kang Ning-hsiang (q.v.) in 1975. It published only five issues and was closed by the government. Kang then launched the magazine *Eighties* (q.v.).

Taiwan Power Company (t'ai-wan tian-li kung-szu). A state corporation founded in 1946 and owned mainly by the central government (66.7 percent) and the provincial government and Taipei (q.v.) municipal government, plus financial institutions and individuals in Taiwan, Taipower is responsible for developing, generating, supplying, and marketing electric power throughout the country. In the 1950s and 1960s, the cheap electricity it supplied, much of which was generated by hydropower, helped spur Taiwan's industrialization and its economic growth. Now hydropower makes up less than 10 percent of Taiwan's total usage; coal, oil, and nuclear plants each account for about a third of electricity generated. All three of these have been controversial because they have to be imported, and because the first two cause pollution. Nuclear power has provoked serious political controversy and protest in recent years. Taipower operates 60 power plants, including three nuclear plants that generate more than 20,000 megawatts of electricity annually. It is ranked the 14th largest power generating company in the world. Taipower will be privatized in 2001.

Taiwan Production Board (t'ai-wan chih-tsao-chu). Estab-lished in 1949 by the Taiwan Provincial Government (q.v.) to stabilize the economy, reduce inflation, and develop various companies and enterprises, it was absorbed by the Economic Stabilization Board (q.v.) in 1953.

Taiwan Provincial Assembly (t'ai-wan sheng-yi-hui. A "local" representative legislative body in Taiwan (q.v.) that, because the government of the Republic of China controls only Taiwan plus some outlying islands, paralleled or duplicated in large part the functions of the Legislative Yuan (q.v.). It was established by law in 1959, its predecessors being the Provincial People's Political Council (1946-51) and the Taiwan Provisional Provincial Assembly (1951-59).

The Taiwan Provincial Assembly was long considered more democratic than the Legislative Yuan because all of its members were elected by voters in Taiwan. Members also were involved much more than Legislative Yuan (q.v.) members in serving their constituents and in legislative work (which in the case of the Legislative Yuan was frequently done in caucuses of Nationalist Party [q.v.] members in advance). On the other hand the Nationalist Party held a majority in the assembly, and, thus, controlled most debates and votes. The assembly, moreover, was not allowed to encroach on duties and powers of the Legislative Yuan.

The members of the Taiwan Provincial Assembly were elected to four-year terms and were eligible to be reelected. Sessions lasted for no more than 80 days in a six-month period, though extensions were possible. The Assembly eleced a speaker who maintained order on the floor and led debates and proceedings. This position was considered a powerful and important political position. There were five speakers: Huang Ch'ao-ch'in (1946-63), Shieh Tung-min (1963-70), Ts'ai Hung-wen (1970-81), Kao Yu-jen (1981-1990), and Huang Chen-yueh (1990-98). The Taiwan Provincial Assembly had six standing committees: agriculture and forestry, civil affairs, education, finance, reconstruction, and transportation. The last three dealt with large amounts of funds and were generally considered more important.

With the downsizing of the provincial government in 1998 the Provincial Assembly was abolished and many of its members ran successfully for positions in the Legislative Yuan (q.v.).

Taiwan Provincial Government (t'ai-wan sheng-cheng-fu). Established in May 1947 to replace the Office of the Governor-General, the Taiwan Provincial Government was for many years the highest organ of local government. It had jurisdiction over 16 counties and five cities and comprised 19 departments. It employed more than 300,000 people. It also controlled more than 30 businesses. The Taiwan Provincial Government Council was its policy-making body, which consisted of 23 members. Its executive head was the governor of Taiwan.

In 1988, with democratization, the Provincial Assembly was required to vote its approval of the person nominated by the premier to be governor. After 1994 and until 1998, it was headed by an elected governor (see Soong Chu-yu).

In 1996, the National Development Conference (q.v.) recommended that the provincial government be abolished or drastically downsized. Subsequently, the National Assembly passed a constitutional amendment to this effect. The Taiwan Provincial Government is now in the process of being cut and disestablished, though it will not be eliminated completely.

Taiwan Recovery Training Corps (t'ai-wan kuang-fu hsun-lien-t'uan). An organization established in China shortly after Mao came to power in 1949 to reeducate Taiwanese (q.v.) living in China and to train them for use in an invasion of Taiwan (q.v.). Ms. Chu Chen-tse was the director. Members of the Corps were sent to Taiwan in the 1950s as infiltrators and spies.

Taiwan Relations Act (TRA) (t'ai-wan kuan-hsi-fa). Legislation passed by the U.S. Congress in March 1979, and signed into law by President Jimmy Carter on April 10, 1979, the TRA reformalized or reconstituted relations between the United States and Taiwan (q.v.) in the absence of formal diplomatic relations. Draft legislation was submitted to the Congress by the White House after President Carter announced that the United States would derecognize the Republic of China (ROC) (q.v.) and establish formal diplomatic relations with the People's Republic of China (PRC), effective January 1,

1979. Congress viewed the draft legislation as inadequate and, in January and February, wrote the quite detailed TRA. It had strong bipartisan support and passed in the Senate by a majority of 85 to 4, and in the House by 339 to 50.

The TRA contains five sets of provisions regarding (1) Taiwan's sovereignty or nation-state status; (2) Taiwan's security; (3) Taiwan's economic health; (4) human rights and democracy in Taiwan; and (5) Congressional oversight. Unlike the Normalization Agreement (q.v.), which states that there is one China and Taiwan is a part of China, the TRA suggests that Taiwan is an independent, sovereign nation. For example, it states that laws of the United States that apply to other foreign countries also apply to Taiwan, and it mandates that treaties concluded with the government of the Republic of China remain in force. It provides for Taiwan's security by declaring that threats, including boycotts or embargoes, are of "grave concern to the United States." It furthermore commits the United States to maintaining military forces in the region to back up this provision. Though some say the defense clauses are ambiguous, others say they are better than those in the United States-Republic of China Defense Treaty (q.v.) that was canceled on January 1, 1980, because they cite boycotts and actions less serious than an invasion as requiring U.S. concern. Taiwan was allowed special economic advantages under the TRA, including Overseas Private Investment Corporation guarantees. The human rights provision has been interpreted to place a burden on the ROC government to democratize and to allow the people of Taiwan to decide their future. The act contained a provision requiring that it be reviewed by Congress.

The TRA is unique because it is the only instance of congressional legislation that regulates U.S. foreign relations with another country. It is important for its providing the foundation of U.S. relations with Taiwan. Along with the Shanghai Communiqué (q.v.), the Normalization Agreement, and the August Communiqué (q.v.), it is one of the four formal documents frequently cited in discussing U.S.- China policy. Unlike the other documents, however, which are of less legal standing, the TRA is a law. It contradicts the other documents in various ways, especially the latter two, causing some to say that U.S. China policy is unclear.

The TRA was not received happily in Taipei (q.v.) at the time because it referred throughout to Taiwan, instead of to the Republic of China. Since then it has had strong, but subtle, support from Taipei. Officials of the government of the People's Republic of China did not express serious opposition at the time of its passage by the Congress, probably because they were distracted by China's conflict with Vietnam, and Deng Xiaoping did not want to provoke the United States at the time. Later Beijing expressed strong opposition to the TRA. The PRC would like to see it abolished, diluted, or overshadowed by the communiqués.

Taiwan Revolutionary Party (t'ai-wan k'e-ming-tang). A political organization established in the United States by Hsu Hsin-liang (q.v.) in 1986, made up largely of the political left of the World United Formosans for Independence (q.v.). It soon became known as a radical organization that advocated revolutionary change in Taiwan. It was eclipsed in 1986, when Hsu announced the formation of the Taiwan Democratic Party and subsequently said he would return to Taiwan.

Taiwan Semiconductor Manufacturing Company, Ltd. One of Taiwan's largest and best regarded companies and its largest semiconductor producer, it has the largest integrated circuit foundry in the world. In 1997, it became the first Taiwan company to be listed on the New York Stock Exchange.

Taiwan Strait (t'ai-wan hai-hsia). The body of water west of Taiwan (q.v.), separating Taiwan from the Asia mainland. It is 85 miles wide at its narrowest point. It is also called the Formosa Strait.

Taiwan Television Enterprise (TTV) (t'ai-wan tian-shih kung-szu). Established in 1962 as a joint venture between the Taiwan Provincial Government (q.v.) and several Japanese corporations, it was the first television network in Taiwan (q.v.) and remains the largest.

Taiwan Tobacco and Wine Monopoly (t'ai-wan-sheng yen-chiu kung-mai-chu). A state-owned enterprise that sells tobacco and alcoholic beverages and which had a monopoly on these products until 1995. Earlier in Taiwan's history it accounted for a large share of government revenues.

Taiwan Youth Association (t'ai-wan ch'ing-nien-hui). Also known as the Formosan Association, it was established by Taiwanese (q.v.) in Japan, some formally associated with Liao Wen-yi's (q.v.) organizations. It later overshadowed Liao's organizations and for some time was the major representative of independence activities among Taiwanese in Japan. Wang Yu-teh was its first chairman.

Taiwanese (t'ai-wan-jen). A term used to refer to the Chinese who inhabited Taiwan (q.v.) before 1945, in contrast to the Mainland Chinese (q.v.,) or Mainlanders, who took up residence there after World War II. Taiwanese are sometimes called the "older Chinese" or "early arrival Chinese." They came from two parts of China: Fukien Province, just across the Taiwan Strait (q.v.), and Canton (or Kuangtung Province) further south. The Fukien Taiwanese are the larger of the two groups. The Hakkas (q.v.), who hail mostly from Canton, speak their own language and have a different culture from Fukien Taiwanese. The two groups of Taiwanese make up more than 85 percent of Taiwan's population. "Taiwanese" also connotes the language of the Fukien Taiwanese, which originates from the southern part of Fukien Province south of the Min River.

Taiwanese American Citizens League (t'ai-mei kung-min hsueh-hui). An organization established in the United States in the early 1980s to try to influence U.S. elections and thus U.S. policy toward Taiwan (q.v.). It was reported to have given financial support to Senator Edward Kennedy's 1980 presidential primary campaign in California and donations to Senator Clayborn Pell and Congressman Stephen Solarz. It was also involved in organizing Taiwanese (q.v.) to help support Matthew Martinez for a congressional seat from southern California in 1988 against Taiwan-born, but Mainland Chinese, Lilly Chen, causing her defeat. The League succeeded in getting U.S. census forms changed to distinguish between Taiwanese and Chinese.

Taiwanese American Society. A U.S.-based political organization formed in the 1970s by Peng Ming-min (q.v.), a former head of World United Formosans for Independence (q.v.).

Taiwanese Association of America (mei-kuo-ch'u t'ai-wan tung-hsiang-hui). Formed in the United States in the early 1960s from the Formosan Clubs in America, its membership was mainly Taiwanese living in the United States. It advocated self-determination, Taiwanese identity, and some other positions, but was not politically radical. It was said to be made up of 15,000 to 20,000 families. In 1974, it joined with similar groups in Japan, Canada, Western Europe, and Brazil to form the World Federation of Taiwanese Associations.

Taiwanese Home Rule Movement (t'ai-wan szu-chih yun-tung). A movement in Taiwan active during the Japanese period that advocated autonomy. In 1914, Sun Yat-sen (q.v.) supported the organization's objectives. In 1944, in the face of defeat, Japan declared Taiwan a full prefecture of Japan, as this organization had demanded.

Takasago. A major Japanese settlement on Taiwan before the Dutch established a presence nearby. It was a term used in Japanese records and maps for some time after to refer to Taiwan.

Tamsui River. A river which flows past Taipei (q.v.) and to the Taiwan Strait (q.v.). Taipei is a river port on the Tamsui River, though it is not currently of much commercial importance. The Tamsui is Taiwan's only navigable river.

Tangwai. Literally meaning "outside the party," the term refers to a group of opposition politicians, mostly Taiwanese (q.v.), who formed this informal or pseudo political party in the mid-1970s. In 1977, they won 21 of 77 seats in the Taiwan Provincial Assembly (q.v.) and some other fairly important elective offices. Though the formation of new political parties was illegal, they became for all intents and purposes an opposition party and campaigned against the Nationalist Party (q.v.) in the 1980 national election. Most members joined the Democratic Progressive Party (q.v.) in 1986.

Tangwai Research Association for Public Policy (TRAPP) (kung-kung cheng-tse tang-wai yen-chiu hsieh-hui). An organization formed in 1984 by and of moderate Tangwai (q.v.) politicians associated with Kang Ning- hsiang (q.v.), it became what many called a proto- political party. Members subsequently negotiated with Nationalist Party leaders concerning their right to open local offices and become a de facto party. In September 1986, leaders of TRAPP were instrumental in the formation of the Democratic Progressive Party (q.v.).

Teachers' Day (ch'iao-shih-chieh). September 28, also Confucius's birthday. An official national holiday in Taiwan (q.v.).

Temporary Provisions. See Provisional Amendments for the Period of Mobilization for the Suppression of Communist Rebellion.

Ten Projects (shih-ta chien-she). Major infrastructure projects launched by the government in 1973. They were completed in 1980, some ahead of schedule, at a cost of U.S.$5 billion. They include: Sun Yat-sen Freeway (225 miles in length extending from Keelung (q.v.) in the north to Kaohsiung (q.v.) in the south), North Link Railroad, railroad electrification, Chiang Kai-shek International Airport, Taichung Harbor, Suao Harbor, integrated steel mill, Kaohsiung Shipyard, petrochemical industry, and a nuclear power plant.

These projects underscored the government's role in facilitating economic development in what many considered an important exception to a laissez-faire approach by the government toward the economy. Some of the projects were not immediately successful, such as the steel mill and the shipyard, due to global competition. The Ten Projects were followed by the Twelve Projects and the Fourteen Projects (qq.v.).

Tengpu. An island located near Quemoy (q.v.). It was the site of a major battle between Nationalist and Communist forces on November 3, 1949—a week after the Battle of Kuningtou (q.v.). Nationalist forces won the battle, killing 3,700 Communist soldiers while losing 2,800 of their own.

Three empties (san k'ung). A strategy pursued, according to the foreign ministry in Taipei (q.v.), by the People's Republic of China (PRC) to restrict Taiwan's diplomatic space. The "empties" refers to measures taken by the PRC to reduce the Republic of China's (q.v.) diplomatic ties, block its efforts to join international organizations, and eliminate bargaining chips Taiwan (q.v.) has used to seek an equal relationship with Beijing. When Taiwan is empty of these, then it will negotiate reunification with Beijing. See also Three No's Policy.

Three links (san t'ung). A proposal made in the early 1980s by the People's Republic of China (PRC) that mail, trade, and transportation ties be established between the PRC and Taiwan (q.v.). In 1986, Deng Xiaoping suggested that the United States help in this effort. President Lee Teng-hui (q.v.) has stated that his no haste, be patient policy (q.v.) applies not only to investment in the mainland but also to the three links. Some businesspeople, including Chang Yung-fa (q.v.), do not agree with President Lee on this issue. The Democratic Progressive Party (q.v.), on the other hand, opposes the three links. Notwithstanding, postal and trade links have existed for some time. An agreement on transportation ties was reached in 1997 when the PRC accepted a proposal on direct shipping, and vessels have gone from port-to-port across the Taiwan Strait (q.v.). Other agreements still need to be worked out, however.

Three No's Policy (san pu cheng-tse). A policy of no contact, no negotiations, and no compromises, which was enunciated by President Chiang Ching-kuo (q.v.) at the Nationalist Party's (q.v.) 12th Party Congress in 1981 in response to Beijing's "reunification negotiation offensive." (See Nine Point-Proposal.) The government has since said it will abandon the Three No's when the People's Republic of China abandons its threats of military action against Taiwan (q.v.), its efforts to isolate Taiwan, and its "Four Cardinal Principles."

The term "three no's" has also been used to describe the policy of the government of the People's Republic of China regarding its desired U.S. China policy: no two Chinas; no one China, one Taiwan policy; and no admission of Taiwan to the United Nations. President Jiang Zemin pushed this policy when he met President Bill Clinton in Washington, D.C., in 1997, at which time the United States announced that this was its policy. It was reiterated in the form of a controversial public statement by President Clinton when he visited the People's Republic of China in 1998.

Three Principles of the People (san-min-chu-yi). Sometimes called the official ideology of the Republic of China (q.v.), the principles were advocated by Sun Yat-sen (q.v.) in a work of that title. The three principles are: nationalism, democracy, and people's livelihood. The first refers to nation building, Sun thinking China was a cultural entity more than a nation.

The second represents Sun's advocacy of a republican form of government. The third stresses economic development that would benefit the entire population. Sun, however, knew that democracy could not be realized quickly and advocated its promotion in stages: a military stage, a tutelage stage, and full democracy. For some years, the Nationalist government kept the democratization process at a slow pace based on the concept of tutelage. Antigovernment opposition groups for the most part have not attacked the Three Principles of the People; rather, they criticized officials of the government and the Nationalist Party (q.v.) for not living up to the ideals. Many have lauded the last, people's livelihood, which they equate with social programs and a welfare state.

Tiao Yu Tai (tiao-yu-t'ai). A group of small uninhabited islets, called Senkakus in Japanese and Tiao Yu Tai in Mandarin (or Diao Yu Islands in the People's Republic of China), 120 nautical miles northeast of Taiwan that were controlled by the United States after World War II. In 1972, they were returned to Japan along with Okinawa and the rest of the Ryukyu Islands, but not before provoking the first campus demonstrations in Taiwan in more than 20 years. Some described the student demonstrations as spontaneous; others said they were staged by the Nationalist Party (q.v.). Taipei (q.v.) claimed the islands based on use by fishermen from Taiwan and its claim to China (inasmuch as the islands are geologically part of China's continental shelf). Beijing also laid claim to them. The fact that there was speculation about large deposits of undersea oil in the area made them more important than they would otherwise have been. Japan's ownership of the islands in subsequent years was disputed periodically by both Taipei and Beijing even though the presence of meaningful deposits of oil was not subsequently proven.

In the fall of 1996, following Tokyo's declaring a 12-nautical-mile exclusion zone around the islands, and right-wing groups in Japan putting a beacon and a flag on one of the islands, protestors from Hong Kong and Taiwan organized a mission to tear down the symbols. One protester from Hong Kong was killed, drawing world attention to the dispute. However, the governments in both Beijing and Taipei sought to prevent a crisis regarding the islands. The Republic of China, in 1997, nevertheless reiterated its territorial claim to the islands.

Tienkung. See Sky Bow missile.

Ting Chih-chang (?-1882). Sent to govern Taiwan (q.v.) in 1875 when, because of Western interests in the island, Peking dropped its ban on immigration to Taiwan and made some efforts to help Taiwan's economic development. Ting led these efforts plus other reform measures, but they were short-lived. On the other hand, Ting's reforms helped lay the groundwork for a period of change and progress under Liu Ming-ch'uan (q.v.).

Tombsweeping Day (min-szu sao-mu-chieh). A holiday when people clean the graves of their ancestors. It falls on April 5 (April 4 in Leap Year). It is also an official national holiday commemorating the death of Chiang Kai-shek (q.v.).

Treaty of Shimonoseki. See Shimonoseki (Treaty of).

Ts'ai Pei-ho (1891-1986). An associate of Lin Hsien-t'ang (q.v.) and the editor of *Taiwan Youth*. He later established the League for the Establishment of a Formosan Parliament.

Tsai Wan-lin (1924-). The chairman of the Lin Yuan Group, which owns 70 percent of Taiwan's Cathay Life Insurance Company. Tsai is one of Taiwan's richest persons.

Tsiang Yien-si (1915-1998). Also known as Y.S. Tsiang, he held a number of high posts in the government and the Nationalist Party (q.v.) over an extended period of time. These include secretary-general of the Executive Yuan (q.v.) from 1967 to 1972, minister of education from 1972 to 1977, secretary general of the Office of the President (q.v.) in 1978, foreign minister from 1978 to 1979, secretary-general of the Central Committee of the Nationalist Party from 1979 to 1985, national policy advisor to the president from 1985 to 1989, and secretary general in the Office of the President from 1990 to 1994. Tsiang was regarded as a powerful insider.

Tungsha Islands. See Pratas Islands.

Twelve Projects (shih-er-hsiang chien-she). Infrastructure and development projects started in 1978 as a sequel to the Ten Projects (q.v.). They included the following: An around-the-island railroad, New Cross-Island Highway, Kaohsiung-Pingtung regional traffic improvement, China Steel expansion, a nuclear power project, Taichung Harbor expansion, new towns and housing, regional drainage, dike and levee construction, Pingtung-Olanpi Highway Widening Project, farm mechanization, and cultural centers. See also Fourteen Projects.

- U -

Uchida Kakichi. A civil administrator of Taiwan under Governor-General Sakuma Sakuma (q.v.) from 1910 to 1915. He later became governor-general but was removed in 1924, after serving less than a year, for shielding illegal narcotic trafficking.

United Daily News (lien-ho pao). One of the two largest newspapers in Taiwan, with a circulation over one million. Its owner, Wang Tih-wu, who holds a high rank in the Nationalist Party (q.v.), also owns the *Economic Daily News* and *Minsheng News*. *The World Journal*, the largest Chinese newspaper in North America, is operated by the *United Daily News*. The *United Daily News* is politically more conservative than its rival, the *China Times* (q.v.).

United Formosans for Independence (t'ai-wan tu-li lien-meng). A proindependence group formed from the group Formosans for Free Formosa (q.v.) in 1960. At that point it became a national organization in the United States. It was led by Chen I-te and advocated a United Nations trusteeship over Taiwan (q.v.). It later evolved into the United Formosans in America for Independence (q.v.).

United Formosans in America for Independence (t'ai-wan tu-li lien-meng mei-kuo fen-hui). A proindependence group that evolved from the United Formosans for Independence (q.v.). Like its predecessor organization it was also led by Chen I-te and advocated a United Nations trusteeship over Taiwan (q.v.) in the late 1960s. It merged with some other similar groups in 1970 to become the World United Formosans for Independence (q.v.).

United Microelectronics Corporation (lien tien). One of Taiwan's best known and regarded companies and its second- largest producer of semiconductors.

United States Mutual Security Agency (MSA) (chung-mei kung-t'ung an-chuan tai-piao-hsu). An American government agency with an office in Taipei (q.v.) through which U.S. decisions regarding Taiwan were articulated in the early post-World War II period. Its mission was to assist Nationalist forces to develop their military capabilities, but it often went far beyond that. MSA reports provided information on early U.S.-Republic of China relations. The MSA mission in Taiwan was later divided into two parts: Military Aid and Advisory Group (q.v.) and the Agency for International Development mission.

United States-Republic of China Defense Treaty (chung-mei fang-yu hsieh-ting). Signed by the two countries on December 2, 1954, it committed each to assist the other in the event of war or the threat of war. The treaty was part of a number of treaties and alliances built by the United States to surround and contain the People's Republic of China. Seen another way, the treaty was the direct outcome of an attack by Chinese Communist forces on Nationalist-held Quemoy (q.v.) in September 1954. Though the treaty mentioned U.S. commitments to only Taiwan and the Pescadores (qq.v.), it was subsequently extended to include the Offshore Islands (q.v.) with the Formosa Resolution (q.v.). In December 1978, President Jimmy Carter gave notification of the U.S. intent to terminate the treaty and it ended on January 1, 1980. Some say it was replaced by security provisions in the Taiwan Relations Act (q.v.).

Unsinkable aircraft carrier (yung-pu-ch'en-mo-di hang-k'ung-mu-chien). A name used by the Japanese to under-score Taiwan's geopolitical importance before and during World War II. General Douglas MacArthur used the same appellation in the early 1950s when the importance of Taiwan (q.v.) came up in debates over whether to aid Nationalist forces on Taiwan and keep the island from falling to Mao's forces.

- V -

Vacation diplomacy (chia-jih wai-ch'iao). A term used to describe golfing and other trips taken by President Lee Teng-hui, Premier Lien Chan (qq.v.) and other high Republic of China (ROC) (q.v.) officials to other countries, especially in Southeast Asia, with which the ROC does not have formal diplomatic ties, for the purpose of countering Beijing's efforts to isolate Taiwan. Some of the trips have been regarded by the Western media as quasi-official and have enhanced Taipei's (q.v.) diplomatic status. The trips have sometimes been assailed by officials in the People's Republic of China. Notable trips were made by President Lee to Indonesia, the Philippines, and Thailand in 1994. Other important trips have been made to Singapore and Malaysia. Vacation diplomacy has been linked to Taiwan's Go South policy (policy). See also Flexible diplomacy; Pragmatic diplomacy.

Vienna Convention on Treaties (1969) (er-nai-wau hui-yi). One of the most frequently cited conventions defining the legal basis of treaties, it has been cited by the People's Republic of China (PRC) when arguing that the Taiwan Relations Act (q.v.) could not be viewed as superior to or stronger legally than the Normalization Agreement (q.v.), which established formal diplomatic relations between the United States and the PRC.

- W -

Wang Chien-shien (1938-). A former Nationalist Party (q.v.) member who served as vice minister of economic affairs from 1989 to 1990 and, subsequently, finance minister. He resigned from the latter office after proposing an increase in the valueadded tax on property that had appreciated by a large amount. The increase did not receive the support of President Lee Teng-hui (q.v.) and thus was not enacted. He ran for a Legislative Yuan (q.v.) seat in 1992, winning big without the Nationalist Party's nomination. Wang was a member of the New KMT Alliance (q.v.) and in 1993 became one of the main forces behind the creation of the New Party (NP) (q.v.) and is considered one of its founders. In 1997, the NP nominated Wang as its presidential candidate but later shifted its support to Lin Yang-kang (q.v.). In 1998, Wang ran very unsuccessfully for mayor of Taipei (q.v.) representing the NP.

Wang Ching-feng (1952-). The vice presidential candidate in 1996 on the ticket with Chen Li-an (q.v.), Wang was the first female to attempt to win such a high office.

Wang Sheng (1917-). An Army general "purged" in 1983 after President Chiang Ching-kuo (q.v.) felt Wang was conspiring to become his successor. He was subsequently appointed the Republic of China's (q.v.) ambassador to Paraguay. Wang had a long and distinguished military career and had been close to the center of political power for many years. In mid-1992, Wang traveled to Beijing on what the press called a mission to improve relations.

Wang, Y.C. (1917-). The chairman of Formosa Plastics Group (q.v), and one of Taiwan's richest individuals, Wang has been called the "god of business management" in Taiwan. He became controversial in the 1990s after announcing a plan to build a plant in China that would involve an investment of several billion dollars. In August 1996, he announced an end to that plan and said his company would build offshore near Chiayi instead. Wang is the third recipient of the Republic of China's Order of Brilliant Star With Grand Cordon.

Wei Tao-ming (1901-1978). The second post-World War II governor of Taiwan (q.v.), Wei was appointed in April 1947 to deal with the bad situation on Taiwan created by his predecessor Chen Yi (q.v.). Wei had previously served as ambassador to the United States. Wei subsequently suggested that the United States support him in separating Taiwan from the mainland since the island could not be governed effectively; for that he was dismissed from his post by Chiang Kai-shek (q.v.) in December 1948.

White Paper on China (chung-kuo pai-p'i-shu). A report issued by the U.S. Department of State in August 1949, critical of Chiang Kai-shek and the Nationalist Party (qq.v.) for failures in China while indicting both for losing the civil war with the Communists. Corruption, lack of public support, and other problems were mentioned as the reasons. This report influenced President Harry Truman to announce the following January that the United States "would not pursue a policy that will lead to involvement in the civil conflict in China." Truman also declared that the United States would not provide military aid to Nationalist Chinese forces on Taiwan (q.v.), indicating that he was giving the Chinese Communists a free hand to invade Taiwan.

White Paper on Taiwan (t'ai-wan bai-p'I-shu). A major policy statement published by the Taiwan Affairs Office of the State Council in the People's Republic of China (PRC) in August 1993 called "The Taiwan Question and the Reunification of China." This report set forth the PRC's view on Taiwan's history, and in that connection why it is to be considered part of China. It also discussed Taiwan's legal status, relations across the Taiwan Strait (q.v.), questions about Taiwan in international relations, and other issues. The authors, not named, also explained why the PRC cannot accept the "German formula" (q.v.) to deal with the Taiwan issue. The document seemed to reflect Beijing's concerns about Taiwan's status in a changing international situation, especially its efforts to join the United Nations and its pragmatic diplomacy (q.v.).

White Terror (pai-se k'ung-pu). Term used to describe government oppression and the denial of basic freedoms prior to the end of martial law (q.v.). Special reference is often made to actions by the Garrison Command (q.v.) during this period. In 1998, the cabinet announced that it would establish a foundation to find and compensate approximately 10,000 people who were sentenced unjustly under martial law.

Wisdom Coalition (chi-shih-hui). A group of members of the Nationalist Party (q.v.), sometimes referred to as a caucus, faction, or subfaction of the party that was formed in 1988 by a number of Nationalist Party legislators. Wisdom Coalition members were dissatisfied with the pace of democratic reform and Taiwan's growing isolation in the world community. They advanced the "Taiwanization" of the party and supported the idea of "one China, one Taiwan" (q.v.). In 1991, the Wisdom Coalition advocated the direct election of the president (q.v.) and the abolition of the National Assembly and the Control Yuan (qq.v.). The Wisdom Coalition has been aligned with the Mainstream faction of the party and has supported Lee Teng-hui (q.v.).

World Taiwanese Association (shih-chieh t'ai-wan hui). An organization operating abroad, mainly in the United States and Japan, which advocates Taiwan's independence. In 1988, the organization held its annual meeting in Taiwan (q.v.) for the first time, and many of its members returned at the time. The movement's leader, Li Hsien-tung, who resides in Tokyo, did not return.

World Trade Center. See Taipei International Convention Center.

World United Formosans for Independence (WUFI) (shih-chieh t'ai-wan tu-li lien-meng). Founded in 1970 by Trong R. Chai, WUFI was more radical than its predecessor organizations, refusing to rule out armed struggle as a means of establishing a free, democratic, and independent Republic of Taiwan, while advocating the use of violence against the Nationalist Party (q.v.). Shortly after its founding, Peter Huang and Cheng Tzu-tai, WUFI's executive secretary, were indicted on charges of attempted murder for trying to assassinate Chiang Ching-kuo (q.v.) when he was in New York City. Because of this and subsequent bombing attacks attributed to the organization, including one which blew the hand off of the Taiwan provincial governor (see Shieh Tung-min), WUFI was labeled a terrorist organization by the State of California. Subsequently, a number of WUFI leaders left the organization to form other groups. WUFI continues to take a hard line on the issue of Taiwan's independence and advocates cutting all links, economic and otherwise, between Taiwan (q.v.) and the People's Republic of China. WUFI has been associated with the New Tide faction of the Democratic Progressive Party (qq.v.). See also Formosan Association for Public Affairs.

Wu, K.C. (1903-1984). The fourth governor of Taiwan, appointed in December 1949. He received his education at Princeton and was at one time mayor of Shanghai. He resigned from his position under protest in 1953 and went to the United States.

Wu Poh-hsiung (1939-). Secretary general of the Nationalist Party (q.v.) from 1996 to 1998, Wu served as mayor of Taipei (q.v.) from 1988 to 1990, minister of state from 1990 to 1991, minister of interior in 1994, and secretary general in the Office of the President (q.v.) from 1994 to 1996. Wu has long been considered one of Taiwan's leading Taiwanese (q.v.)

politicians and is thought by many to still have a political future.

- Y -

Yami. A tribe of aborigines (q.v.) that inhabits Orchid Island (q.v.). Tribal legend tells of kinship ties with tribes in the Batanes Archipelago in the Philippines, which, in addition to language and other strong similarities, supports the theory that Taiwan's native population hails from Southeast Asia.

Yang, C.K. (1933-). An aborigine (q.v.) known as the Iron Man of Asia. Yang broke the world's record in the decathlon at the Olympic Games in Rome in 1960.

Yangchow. The name used for Taiwan (q.v.) in early Chinese records— before the Han Dynasty.

Yao Chia-wen (1938-). The second chairman of the Democratic Progressive Party (q.v.), elected in November 1987. Yao had been a participant in the Kaohsiung Incident (q.v.) and was jailed, but was released in January 1987. In 1992, he was elected to the Legislative Yuan (q.v.), but failed in another bid in December 1998.

Yeh Kung-ch'iao (1904-1981). Minister of Foreign Affairs from 1949 to 1958 and Ambassador to the United States from 1958 to 1962, Yeh (also known as George Yeh) was involved in creating the Republic of China's foreign policy, especially regarding its relations with the United States, during very critical times. Chiang Kai-shek (q.v.) disciplined him over the matter of Outer Mongolia's representation in the United Nations and considered him too pro-U.S.

Yen Chia-kan (1905-). Born in Kiangsu Province, Yen rose to prominence in the government and the Nationalist Party (q.v.) on the mainland. In 1950, he became minister of economic affairs and subsequently held a number of other important posts including the position of governor of Taiwan (q.v.) from 1954 to 1957. From 1963 to 1972, he was premier and from 1966 to 1975 vice president. He became president upon the death of Chiang Kai-shek (q.v.) in 1975 and held that post until 1978. As president, however, he did not exercise the vast political authority and influence that other presidents had because Chiang Ching-kuo (q.v.), who was head of the ruling Nationalist Party (q.v.) and premier at the time he was president, wielded more political power than Yen.

Yen Yun-nien (1874-1923). Born in the Keelung (q.v.) area, Yen served as translator and intermediary to the Japanese in northern Taiwan (q.v.) in the late 1800s. Established in mining, Yen later signed an agreement with Fujita Gumi Company and developed mining in the area. In 1918, Mitsui, a large Japanese combine, developed a relationship with Yen to establish Keelung Coal Mining Company, helping to make Yen one of Taiwan's richest individuals. Yen was later appointed to the Governor-General's Advisory Council and helped in the development of Taiwan's railroads, forestry, retail stores, and credit institutions.

Yingchow. The name used for Taiwan (q.v.) in Chinese records during the Han Dynasty and for some years later.

You Ching (1942-). A lawyer and legal scholar who served as Shih Ming-teh's (q.v.) attorney during his trial after the Kaohsiung Incident (q.v.). You was subsequently elected to the Control Yuan (q.v.) and, in 1989, was elected magistrate of Taipei County—one of the most important victories for the Democratic Progressive Party (q.v.) in that election. In December 1998 he lost a bid for delegate to the Legislative Yuan (q.v.).

Young China Party (chung-kuo ch'ing-nien-tang). A political party formed in Paris in 1923 and subsequently active in Chinese politics before the Nationalist government moved to Taiwan. After 1949, the party broke many of its connections with the government and the Nationalist Party (q.v.) in order to become a real opposition party, but it never really succeeded in this effort. It maintained an anti-Communist stance and also opposed separatism. It had approximately 20,000 members. Its head was Li Huang, one of the original founders and a delegate to the San Francisco Conference in 1945. Following the formation of the Democratic Progressive Party (q.v.) the Young China Party lost support and has recently practically disappeared from Taiwan's political scene.

Youth Corps. See China Youth Corps.

Youth Day (ch'ing-nien-chieh). March 29, an official holiday in the Republic of China.

Yu Shan. Yu Shan, or Jade Mountain, is Taiwan's highest peak at 13,114 feet above sea level.

Yupin, Paul (1901-1978). The only Chinese cardinal of the Catholic Church when he died, he had been archbishop of Nanking before he fled to the United States in 1949. He was very outspoken about religious persecution in the People's Republic of China (PRC) and long opposed the Vatican establishing diplomatic relations with Beijing. Because of his views and actions he was on a list of "war criminals" in the PRC. In 1960, he went to Taiwan (q.v.) to head Fu Jen University.

- Z -

Zeelandia (an-p'ing ku-pao). A fort and town established in 1624 by the Dutch on the northern end of a small islet off the coast of southwest Taiwan (q.v.) near what is now the city of Anping. Zeelandia became the locus of considerable trade between Taiwan and both China and Japan as well as other cities in the region. It was the main Dutch settlement on Taiwan during its period of colonial rule of the island. The islet was then called Taiwan but later also became known as Zeelandia. In 1662, the fort was besieged by forces of Cheng Ch'eng-kung (q.v.) and fell, marking the end of the period of Dutch colonial rule of Taiwan. See also Provintia.

APPENDIX I

Presidents and Premiers of the Republic of China on Taiwan
(since 1949)

Presidents

Chiang Kai-shek	1949-75
Yen Chia-kan	1975-78
Chiang Ching-kuo	1978-88
Lee Teng-hui	1988-

Premiers

Yen Hsi-shan	1949-50
Chen Cheng	1950-54
Yu Hung-chun	1954-58
Chen Cheng	1958-63
Yen Chia-kan	1963-72
Chiang Ching-kuo	1972-78
Sun Yun-suan	1978-84
Yu Kuo-hua	1984-89
Lee Huan	1989-90
Hau Pei-tsun	1990-93
Lien Chan	1993-97
Vincent Siew	1997-

APPENDIX II

Statistical Data (as of December 1998)

Population (end of Nov. 1998):

Taiwan island proper	21,854,273
Kinmen & Matsu	57,830
Taiwan area total	21,912,103

Crude Birth Rate (per 1,000 population):

1995		15.50
1996		15.19
1997		15.07
1998	Aug.	12.49
	Sept.	12.18

Life Expectancy (years):

1993	Male	71.61
	Female	77.52
1994	Male	71.81
	Female	77.76
1995	Male	71.85
	Female	77.74
1996	Male	71.89
	Female	77.77

Medical Conditions (per 10,000 persons):

1993	No. of health personnel	52.17
	No. of hospital beds	47.90
1994	No. of health personnel	53.87
	No. of hospital beds	48.98
1995	No. of health personnel	55.37
	No. of hospital beds	52.77

1996	No. of health personnel	57.53
	No. of hospital beds	53.80
1997	No. of health personnel	66.72
	No. of hospital beds	55.87

Labor Force:

Labor participation rate (%):

1994		58.96
1995		58.71
1996		58.44
1997		58.33
1998	July	58.00
	Aug.	58.09
	Sept.	57.83

Unemployment Rate (%):

1994		1.56
1995		1.79
1996		2.60
1997		2.93
	Aug.	3.05
	Sept.	2.98

Percentage of Household Amenities (end of 1997):

Color TV	99.47
Telephone	93.99
Air conditioner	73.83
Video tape recorder/player	57.07
Motorcycle	80.19
Sedan vehicle	53.79
Newspaper	52.23
Personal computer	28.39

Education (1997 academic year):

Schools

Elementary	2,540
Junior High	719
Senior High	228
Vocational	204
College and University	78
Others	3,804

Students

Elementary	1,905,690
Junior High	1,074,588
Senior High	291,095
Vocational	509,064
College and University	373,072
Others	1,041,102

Percentage of population aged 6-21 enrolled in school:	79.26
Percentage of population aged 6-14 enrolled in school:	98.38

Economic Growth Rate (%):

1995	6.03
1996	5.67
1997	6.77
1998	5.07(f)
1999	5.24(f)

Changes in Price Indices (%):

Changes in wholesale price index

1994	2.16
1995	7.38

1996	-1.00
1997	-0.46
1998	0.68(f)
1999	-2.35(f)

Changes in consumer price index

1994	4.09
1995	3.68
1996	3.07
1997	0.90
1998	1.55(f)
1999	1.77(f)

Gross National Product (GNP) (at current prices in US$ million):

1995	262,978
1996	274,568
1997	284,777
1998	262,674(f)
1999	288,231(f)
2000	

Per Capita GNP (US$):

1995	12,396
1996	12,838
1997	13,198
1998	12,059(f)
1999	13,099(f)

Foreign Trade (US$ million):

Exports:

1995		111,659
1996		115,942
1997		122,081
1998	July	8,935(r)
	Aug.	9,646(p)
	Sept.	9,510(p)

Imports

1995		103,550
1996		102,370
1997		114,425
1998	July	7,901(r)
	Aug.	8,309(p)
	Sept.	8,412(p)

Tourism (persons):

Overseas Chinese & foreign visitors to Taiwan

1994		2,127,249
1995		2,331,934
1996		2,358,221
1997		2,372,232
1998	July	176,031
	Aug.	189,541
	Sept.	182,784

Chinese tourists going abroad

1994		4,744,434
1995		5,188,658
1996		5,713,535
1997		6,161,932
1998	July	587,653
	Aug.	588,707
	Sept.	443,591

Key:

(r): revised
(p): preliminary
(f): forecast

BIBLIOGRAPHY

GENERAL WORKS

BOOKS

Annual Review of Government Administration, Republic of China. Taipei: Research, Development and Education Commission, 1986.

Area Handbook for the Republic of China. Washington, DC: U.S. Government Printing Office, 1983.

Chang, Cecilia, ed. *The Republic of China on Taiwan, 1949-1988.* New York: St. John's University Press, 1991.

Chien, Frederick F. *Opportunity and Challenge.* Tempe, AZ: Arizona Historical Foundation, Arizona State University, 1995.

Clough, Ralph N. *Island China.* Cambridge, MA: Harvard University Press, 1978.

Cohen, Marc J. *Taiwan at the Crossroads: Human Rights, Political Development and Social Change on the Beautiful Island.* Washington, DC: Asia Resource Center, 1988.

Copper, John F. *Taiwan: Nation-State or Province?* (3rd Edition) Boulder, CO: Westview Press, 1999.

Foley, Frederic J. *The Great Formosan Imposter.* Beaverton, OR: International Specialized Book Services, 1980.

Furuya, Keiji. *Chiang Kai-Shek: His Life and Times.* New York: St. John's University Press, 1981.

Gates, Hill. *Chinese Working-Class Lives: Getting By in Taiwan.* Ithaca: Cornell University Press, 1987.

Han, Lih-wu. *Taiwan Today.* Taipei: Institute of International Relations, 1974.

Hsiung, James, ed. *Contemporary Republic of China: The Taiwan Experience, 1950-1980.* New York: Praeger, 1981.

Kennedy, Patrick J. *The Republic of China (Taiwan).* Washington, DC: American Association of College Registrars, 1977.

Kubek, Anthony. *Modernizing China: A Comparative Analysis of the Two Chinas.* Washington, DC: Regency Gateway, 1987.

Li, Victor C., ed. *The Future of Taiwan: A Difference of Opinion.* Armonk, NY: M.E. Sharpe, 1980.

Liu, Alan P.L. *Phoenix and the Lame Lion.* Stanford, CA: Hoover Institution Press, 1987.

Republic of China: A Reference Book. Taipei: Kwang Hwa Publishing Company, 1993.

The Republic of China on Taiwan Today: Views from Abroad. Taipei: Kwang Hwa Publishing Company, 1989.

Sutter, Robert G. *Taiwan: Entering the 21st Century.* Lanham, MD: University Press of America, 1988.

Williams, Jack F., ed. *The Future of Hong Kong and Taiwan.* East Lansing, MI: Asian Studies Center, Michigan State University, 1985.

ARTICLES

Boreham, Gordon F. "Two Chinas, One World," *International Perspectives,* July/August 1982.

Chan, L. "The Republic of China on Taiwan Belongs in the United Nations," *Orbis,* Fall 1993.

Chan, Lien. "A Pragmatic Strategy for China's Peaceful Reunification" *American Asian Review,* Spring 1996.

Chang, Parris H. "Taiwan in 1982: Diplomatic Setback Abroad and Demands for Reform at Home," *Asian Survey,* January 1983.

----------. "Taiwan in 1983: Setting the Stage for Power Transition," *Asian Survey,* January 1984.

----------. "Taiwan in 1985: Quest for a Brighter Day." In John S. Major, ed., *China Briefing, 1985.* Boulder, CO: Westview Press, 1985.

Cheng, Chu-yuan. "The Taiwan Development Model: Its Essence, Performance, and Implications," *American Journal of Chinese Studies,* October 1992.

Clark, Cal. "Taiwan Approaches the 21st Century: Past Successes Create Present Challenges," *American Asian Review,* Summer 1996.

Copper, John F. "Taiwan in 1980: Entering a New Decade," *Asian Survey,* January 1981.

----------. "Taiwan in 1981: In a Holding Pattern," *Asian Survey,* January 1982.

----------. "Taiwan in 1986: Back on Top Again," *Asian Survey,* January 1987.

----------. "Taiwan: Nation in Transition," *Current History,* April 1989.

----------. "Taiwan's Legal Status: A Multilevel Perspective," *Journal of Northeast Asian Studies,* December 1982.

Domes, Jurgen. "Taiwan in 1991: Search for Political Consensus," *Asian Survey,* January 1992.

Dreyer, June T. "Taiwan in 1989: Democratization and Economic Growth," *Asian Survey,* January 1990.

Dreyer, June T. "Taiwan in 1990: Finetuning the System," *Asian Survey,* January 1991.

Hsiung, James C. "The Hong Kong Settlement: Effects on Taiwan and Prospects for Peking's Reunification Bid," *Asian Affairs,* Summer 1985.

----------. "Taiwan in 1984: Festivity, New Hope and Caution," *Asian Survey,* January 1985.

----------. "Taiwan in 1985: Scandals and Setbacks," *Asian Survey,* January 1986.

Lam, W.F. "Institutional Design of Public Agencies and Co-production: A Study of Irrigation Associations in Taiwan," *World Development,* June 1996.

Lin, C.P. "China's Students Abroad: Rates of Return" *American Enterprise,* November/December 1994.

Selya, R.M. "Illegal Migration in Taiwan: A Preliminary Overview," *International Migration Review,* Fall 1992.

Seymour, James D. "Taiwan in 1987: A Year of Political Bombshells," *Asian Survey,* January 1988.

Seymour, James D. "Taiwan in 1988: No More Bandits," *Asian Survey,* January 1989.

"Taiwan: A Survey," *Economist,* 31 July 1982.

Weng, Byron S.J. "Taiwan and Hong Kong, 1987: A Review." In Anthony J. Kane, ed., *China Briefing, 1988.* Boulder, CO: Westview Press, 1988.

Williams, Jack F. "The Quality of Life in Taiwan: An Environmental Assessment," *American Asian Review,* Fall 1996.

Yahuda, M. "The International Standing of the Republic of China on Taiwan," *China Quarterly,* December 1996.

Zemin, Jiang. "Jiang Zemin's "Reunification" Speech of January 30, 1995," *Orbis,* Fall 1995.

BIBLIOGRAPHIES

Berton, Peter and Eugene Wu. *Contemporary China: A Research Guide.* Stanford, CA: Hoover Institution Press, 1967.

Jacobs, Bruce, et al. *Taiwan: A Comprehensive Bibliography of English-Language Publications.* New York: Columbia University East Asian Institute, 1984.

Lee, Wei-chin, ed., *Taiwan.* Santa Barbara: ABC-CLIO, 1990.

GEOGRAPHY

BOOKS

Knapp, Ronald G., ed. *China's Island Frontier: Studies in the Historical Geography of Taiwan.* Honolulu: University of Hawaii Press, 1980.

Lanier, Alison. *Update-Taiwan.* Yarmouth, ME: Intercultural Press, Inc., 1982.

Pannell, Clifton W. *T'ai-Chung, Taiwan: Structure and Function.* Chicago: University of Chicago Department of Geography, 1973.

Taiwan in Pictures. Minneapolis, MN: Lerner Publications Company, Department of Geography Staff, 1989.

Tomikel, John. *Taiwan Journal: Ten Historic Days.* Elgin, PA: Allegheny Press, 1979.

ARTICLES

Chiang, T.-L. "Deviation from the Carrying Capacity for Physicians and Growth Rate of the Physician Supply: The Taiwan Case," *Social Science and Medicine*, February 1995.

Hicks, N. "The Little Dragon: A Geographical Snapshot of Taiwan," *Geographic Magazine*, January 1993.

Knobel, H.H. et al. "Urban-Rural and Regional Differences in Infant Mortality in Taiwan," *Social Science and Medicine*, September 1994.

Williams, J.F. and C.Y. Chang, "Geography in Taiwan," *Professional Geographer,* May 1985.

HISTORY

BOOKS

Bing, Su. *Taiwan's 400 Year History: The Origins and Continuing Development of the Taiwanese Society and People.* Washington: Taiwanese Cultural Grassroots Association, 1986.

Campbell, William. *Formosa under the Dutch.* New York: AMS Press, 1967.

Chang, Kwang-Chih. *Fengpitou, Tepenkeng and the Prehistory of Taiwan.* New Haven: Yale University Publications in Anthropology, 1969.

Chiu, Hungdah, and Shao-Chuan Leng, eds. *China, Seventy Years after the 1911 Hsin-Hai Revolution.* Charlottesville: University of Virginia Press, 1984.

Crozier, Ralph C. *Koxinga and Chinese Nationalism: History, Myth and the Hero.* Cambridge: Harvard University Press, 1977.

Davidson, James W. *The Island of Formosa: Past and Present.* New York: AMS Press, (date not given).

Goddard, W.G. *Formosa: A Study in Chinese History.* East Lansing: Michigan State University Press, 1966.

Gordon, Leonard H., ed. *Taiwan: Studies in Chinese Local History.* New York: Columbia University Press, 1970.

Ho, S.P.S. *Economic Development in Taiwan, 1860-1970.* New Haven: Yale University Press, 1978.

Hsiung, James, ed. *The Taiwan Experience, 1950-1980.* New York: American Association for Chinese Studies, 1981.

Hutsebaut, Marc, ed., *The Authentic Story of Taiwan: An Illustrated History.* Taipei: SMC Publishers, 1991.

The Island of Formosa Past and Present. London: Oxford University Press, 1990.

Kierman, Frank Algerton. *The Fluke That Saved Formosa.* Cambridge: Massachusetts Institute of Technology, Center for International Studies, 1954.

Lai, Tse-han et al. *A Tragic Beginning: The Taiwan Uprising of February 28, 1947.* Stanford: Stanford University Press, 1991.

Lou Tsu-K'uang. *Personal Legends of Formosa.* Pasadena, CA: Oriental Book Store, 1975.

Lumley, F.A. *The Republic of China under Chiang Kai-shek.* London: Barrie and Jenkins, 1976.

MacKay, George L. *From Far Formosa: The Island, Its People, and Missions.* San Francisco: Chinese Materials Center, 1972.

Rubinstein, Murray A., ed. *The Protestant Community of Modern Taiwan: Mission, Seminary, and Church.* Armonk, NY: M.E. Sharpe, 1990.

Paul K.T. Sih, ed. *Sun Yat-sen and China.* New York: St. John's University Press, 1974.

----------. *Taiwan: A History.* Armonk, NY: M.E. Sharpe, 1998.

Takekoshi, Yosaburo. *Japanese Rule in Formosa.* Pasadena, CA: Oriental Book Store, 1978.

Tsurumi, E. Patricia. *Japanese Colonial Education in Taiwan, 1895-1945.* Cambridge, MA: Harvard University Press, 1977.

Wen, John L. *Elephant Embraces Dragon.* New York: Vantage Press, 1984.

ARTICLES

Anderton, L., and Barrett, R.E. "Demographic Seasonality and Development: The Effects of Agricultural Colonialism in Taiwan, 1906-1942," *Demography,* August 1990.

Chang, G.H. "To the Nuclear Brink: Eisenhower, Dulles, and the Quemoy-Matsu Crisis," *International Security,* Spring 1988.

Chen, J.R. "The Effects of Land Reform on the Rice Sector and Economic Development on Taiwan," *World Development,* November 1994.

Copper, John F. "The Fishing Islands Controversy," *Asian Quarterly* Number 3, 1972.

Dickson, B.J. "The Lessons of Defeat: The Reorganization of the Kuomintang on Taiwan, 1950-52," *China Quarterly,* March 1993.

Gregor, A. James. "Sun Yat-sen and Modern China," *American Journal of Chinese Studies,* October 1992.

Greiff, T.E. "The Principle of Human Rights in Nationalist China: John C.H. Wu and the Ideological Origins of the 1946 Constitution," *China Quarterly,* September 1985.

Hood, Steven J. "The Kuomintang and the Rise of Chiang Kai-shek," *American Journal of Chinese Studies,* October 1992.

Isett, C. M. "Sugar Manufacture and the Agrarian Economy of Nineteenth-Century Taiwan," *Modern China,* April 1995.

Jacobs, J.B. "Taiwanese and the Chinese Nationalists, 1937-1945: The Origins of Taiwan's 'Half-Mountain People,'" *Modern China,* January 1990.

Liu, Shia-ling. "Chiang Ching-kuo and the Republic of China," *American Journal of Chinese Studies,* October 1992.

Sun, C. et al. "Chronology," *World Affairs,* Fall 1992.

Unger, L. "Chiang Kai-shek's Second Chance: The Successful Chinese Revolution Was on Taiwan," *Policy Review,* Fall 1989.

Wang, Winston L.Y. "Taiwan under the Leadership of Lee Teng-hui, the Republic of China Since 1988," *American Journal of Chinese Studies,* October 1992.

CULTURE

BOOKS

An Anthology of Contemporary Chinese Literature Taiwan: 1949-1974. Taipei: National Institute for Compilation and Translation, 1975.

Adams, R.N. and R.D. Fogelson, eds. *The Anthropology of Power.* New York: Academic Press, 1977.

Aijmer, Goran. *The Religion of Taiwan Chinese in an Anthropological Perspective.* Gothenburg, Sweden: University of Gothenburg, 1976.

Barclay, George W. *Colonial Development and Population in Taiwan.* New York: Associated Faculty Press, 1971.

Chen, Chi-lu. *Material Culture of the Formosan Aborigines.* Taipei: The Taiwan Museum, 1968.

Chen, Chung-min. *Ancestor Worship and Clan Organization in a Rural Village of Taiwan.* Nankang, Taipei: Academia Sinica, Bulletin of the Institute of Ethnology, 1967.

Chiu, Ming-chung. *Two Types of Folk Piety: A Comparative Study of Two Folk Religions in Formosa.* Chicago: University of Chicago Press, 1970.

Cohen, Myron L. *House United, House Divided: The Chinese Family in Taiwan.* New York: Columbia University Press, 1976.

Cooke, David C. *Taiwan: Island China.* New York: Dodd, Mead & Company, 1975.

Diamond, Norma. *K'un Shen: A Taiwan Village.* New York: Holt, Rinehart and Winston, 1969.

Eberhard, Wolfram. *Moral and Social Values of the Chinese: Collected Essays.* San Francisco and Taipei: Chinese Materials and Research Aids Service Center, 1971.

----------. *Studies in Taiwanese Folktales.* Taipei: The Orient Cultural Service, 1974.

Elvin, Mark and G. William Skinner, eds. *The Chinese City Between Two Worlds.* Stanford: Stanford University Press, 1974.

Freedman, Ronald, and John Y. Takeshita. *Family Planning in Taiwan.* Princeton, NJ: Princeton University Press, 1969.

Gallin, Bernard. *Hsin Hising, Taiwan: A Chinese Village in Change.* Berkeley: University of California Press, 1966.

Goddard, W.G. *Formosa: A Study in Chinese History.* East Lansing: Michigan State University Press, 1966.

Gordon, Leonard H.D., ed. *Taiwan: Studies in Chinese Local History.* New York: Columbia University Press, 1970.

Hanson, Eric O. *Catholic Politics in China and Korea.* Maryknoll, NY: Orbis Books, 1980.

Harrell, Steven, and Chun-chieh Huang. *Cultural Change in Postwar Taiwan*. Boulder, CO: Westview Press, 1994.

Hsia, C.T. *A History of Modern Chinese Fiction*. 1st ed. New Haven: Yale University Press, 1961.

Jordan, David K. *Gods, Ghosts, and Ancestors: The Folk Religion of a Taiwanese Village*. Berkeley: University of California Press, 1972.

Joseph M. Kitagawa, ed. *Understanding Modern China*. Chicago: Quadrangle Books, 1969.

Lau, Joseph S.M., ed. *Chinese Stories from Taiwan 1960-1970*. New York: Columbia University Press, 1976.

Liao, David C.E. *The Unresponsive: Resistent or Neglected? The Hakka Chinese in Taiwan Illustrate a Common Mission Problem*. Chicago: Moody Press, 1972.

Long, Howard R. *The People of Musha: Life in a Taiwanese Village*. Columbia: University of Missouri Press, 1961.

Rubinstein, Murray A., ed. *The Protestant Community of Modern Taiwan: Mission, Seminary and Church*. Armonk, NY: M.E. Sharpe, 1990.

Sih, Paul K.T., ed. *China's Literary Image*. New York: St. John's University Press, 1975.

Swanson, Allen J. *The Church in Taiwan: Profile 1980, a Review of the Past, a Projection for the Future*. Pasadena, CA: William Carey Library Publishers, 1981.

Swartz, Mark M., Victor W. Turner, and Arthur Tuden, eds. *Political Anthropology*. Chicago: Aldine Publishing, 1966.

Thompson, Laurence G. *Chinese Religion: An Introduction*. 2nd ed. Encino, CA: Dickenson Publishing Company, 1975.

Tong, Hollington K. *Christianity in Taiwan: A History*. Taipei: Hollington Tong, 1961.

Walters, Jo Neher. *TaiwanXBeautiful Island*. New York: Exposition Press, 1972.

Arthur P. Wolf, ed. *Religion and Ritual in Chinese Society*. Stanford: Stanford University Press, 1974.

Wei, Yi-min (Henry) and Suzanne Coutanceau. *Wine for the Gods: An Account of the Religious Traditions and Beliefs of Taiwan*. Taipei: Ch'eng Wen Publishing Co., 1976.

Wolf, Margery. *The House of LimXA Study of a Chinese Farm Family*. New York: Appleton-Century-Crofts, 1968.

----------. *Women and the Family in Rural Taiwan*. Stanford: Stanford University Press, 1972.

Wu, Juu-huey. *The Continuity of China's Moral Heritage*. Taipei: Bureau of Cultural Affairs, Ministry of Education, Republic of China, 1972.

ARTICLES

Boretz, A.A. "Martial Gods and Magic Swords: Identity, Myth, and Violence in Chinese Popular Religion," *Journal of Popular Culture*, Summer 1995.

Bosco, Joseph. "The Emergence of a Taiwanese Popular Culture," *American Journal of Chinese Studies*, April 1992.

Bulbeck, C. "Sexual Dangers: Chinese Women's Experiences in Three Cultures—Beijing, Taipei and Hong Kong," *Women's Studies International Forum*, January/February 1994.

Chang, J.S. "What Do Education and Work Mean? Education, Nonfamilial Work/Living Experiences and Premarital Sex for Women in Taiwan," *Journal of Comparative Family Studies*, Spring 1996.

Chen, Yu-Ching. "Chinese Culture vs. Anti-Chinese Culture— Declaration of the Kuomintang on Its 80th Founding Anniversary," *Chinese Culture,* March 1975.

----------. "President Chiang Kai-shek and Chinese Cultural Renaissance," *Asian Culture Quarterly,* Spring 1975.

Chia, Sylvia Shih Heng. "The World of Classical Poets in Taiwan, R.O.C. in the 1950s," *American Journal of Chinese Studies*, October 1998.

Chu, Pao-tang. "Buddhist Organization in Taiwan," *Chinese Culture,* June 1969.

----------. "Dragon Boat Festival, May 8," *Asian Outlook,* June 1970.

----------. "Festivals in the Republic of China," *Asian Outlook,* February 1970.

Gallin, Bernard. "Rural to Urban Migration in Taiwan: Its Impact on Chinese Family and Kinship." In David C. Buxbaum, ed. *Chinese Family Law and Social Change in Historical and Comparative Perspective.* Seattle: University of Washington Press, 1978.

Gates, Hill. "Money for the Gods," *Modern China,* July 1987.

Gold, T.B. "Go with Your Feelings: Hong Kong and Taiwan Popular Culture in Greater China," *China Quarterly*, December 1993.

Greenhalgh, S. "DeOrientalizing the Chinese Family Firm," *American Ethnologist*, November 1994.

Hong, Junhao. "Opportunities, Needs, and Challenges: An Analysis of Media/Cultural Interactions among China, Taiwan, and Hong Kong," *American Journal of Chinese Studies*, October 1997.

Hsia, C.T. "The Continuing Obsession with China: Three Contemporary Writers." In Paul K.T. Sih, ed. *China's Literary Image.* New York: St. John's University Press, 1975.

Hung, Joe. "Religious Activities on Taiwan," *Asian Culture Quarterly,* Spring 1976.

Jacobs, J. Bruce. "A Preliminary Model of Particularistic Ties in Chinese Political Alliances: Kan-ch'ing and Kuan-hsi in a Rural Taiwanese Township," *China Quarterly,* June 1979.

Johnson, Irmgard. "Whatever Happened to Peking Opera?" *Asian Affairs,* July-August 1975.

Jordan, David K. "Language Choice and Interethnic Relations in Taiwan," *La Monda Lingro-Problemo,* 1973.

Kallgren, Joyce K. "Nationalist China: The Continuing Dilemma of the 'Mainland' Philosophy," *Asian Survey,* January 1963.

Lee, M. L, and T.H. Sun. "The Family and Demography in Contemporary Taiwan," *Journal of Contemporary Family Studies*, Spring 1995.

Lee, Wen-jer. "Taiwan and Dr. Sun's Revolution," *Free China Review,* November 1965

McBeath, Gerald A. "Roots of Regime Stability in the Taiwanese Family," *American Journal of Chinese Studies*, April 1987.

McCaghy, C.H., and C. Hou. "Family Affiliation and Prostitution in a Cultural Context: Career Onsets of Taiwanese Prostitutes," *Archives of Sexual Behavior*, June 1994.

Metzger, Thomas A. "On Chinese Political Culture," *Journal of Asian Studies,* November 1972.

O'Hara, Albert R. "A Factual Survey of Taipei's Temples and Their Functions," *Journal of Social Science,* July 1967.

Palandri, Angela Jung. "Current Trends in Taiwan Poetry: Creativeness Versus Conformity," *Literature East and West,* 1971.

Plummer, Mark. "Taiwan: Toward a Second Generation of Mainland Life," *Asian Survey,* January 1970.

Sangren, P. S. "Power and Transcendence in the Ma Tsu Pilgrimages of Taiwan," *American Ethnologist,* August 1993.

Saso, Michael. "The Taoist Tradition in Taiwan," *China Quarterly,* January-March 1971.

Stafford, C. "Good Sons and Virtuous Mothers: Kinship and Chinese Nationalism in Taiwan," *Man,* June 1992.

Starr, Kenneth. "Cultural Problems on Nationalist Taiwan," *France-Asie,* 1962.

Teng, Yuang Chung. "The Cultural Development of Taiwan, ROC during the Past Forty Years: A Study of Seven Chinese Views," *American Journal of Chinese Studies*, October 1992.

Tozer, Warren. "Taiwan's Cultural Renaissance: A Preliminary View," *China Quarterly,* July-September 1970.

Tsai, Wen-hui. "Folk Religion in Modernizing Taiwan, -*American Asian Review*," Fall 1996.

Uhalley, Stephen, Jr. "Taiwan's Response to the Cultural Revolution," *Asian Survey,* November 1967.

Wang, Sung-hsing. "Family Structure and Economic Development in Taiwan," *Bulletin of the Institute of Ethnology, Academia Sinica,* Autumn 1977.

Weller, R.P. "Bandits, Beggars, and Ghosts: The Failure of State Control over Religious Interpretation in Taiwan," *American Ethnologist,* February 1985.

Weller, R.P. "Social Contradiction and Symbolic Resolution: Practical and Idealized Affines in Taiwan," *Ethnology,* October 1984.

Yen, C.K. "Rotarianism and Confucianism," *Chinese Culture,* June 1975.

Yen, Yuan-shu. "New Trends in the Study of Classical Chinese Literature in the Republic of China." In Paul K.T. Sih, ed. *China's Literary Image.* New York: St. John's University Press, 1975.

----------. "Social Realism in Recent Chinese Fiction in Taiwan." In *Thirty Years of Turmoil in Asian Literature.* Taipei: The Taipei Chinese Center, International P.E.N., 1976.

Yip, Wai-lim, ed. "Chinese Arts and Literature: A Survey of Recent Trends," *Occasional Papers/Reprints Series in Contemporary Asian Studies,* No. 9, 1977.

Yu, Priscilla C. "Taiwan's International Exchange Program: A Study in Cultural Diplomacy." *Asian Affairs,* Summer 1985.

SOCIETY

BOOKS

Ahern, Emily M., and Hill Gates, eds. *The Anthropology of Taiwanese Society.* Stanford: Stanford University Press, 1981.

Barclay, George W. *Colonial Development and Population in Taiwan.* New York: Associated Faculty Press, 1971.

Bessac, Frank B. *An Example of Social Change in Taiwan Related to Land Reform.* Missoula: Department of Anthropology, University of Montana, 1967.

Brown, Melissa, ed., *Negotiating Ethnicities in China and Taiwan.* Berkeley: University of California, China Research Monographs, 1995.

Casterline, John B. *Nuptiality Transition and Its Causes: A Study of Taiwan, 1905-1976.* Boulder, CO: Westview Press, 1988.

The Changing Chinese Family Pattern in Taiwan. Pasadena, CA: Oriental Book Store, 1981.

Ch'en, Kou-Chun. *Studies in Marriage and Funerals of Taiwan Aborigines.* Pasadena, CA: Oriental Book Store, 1970 (Chinese).

Chou, Bih-er et al. *Women in Taiwanese Politics: Overcoming Barriers to Women's Participation in a Modernizing Society.* Boulder, CO: Lynne Rienner Publishers, 1989.

Cohen, Marc J. *Taiwan at the Crossroads: Human Rights, Political Development and Social Change on the Beautiful Island.* Washington, DC: Asia Resource Center, 1988.

Fetherling, Douglas. *The Other China: Journeys around Taiwan* Arsenal Pulp, 1996.

Gates, Hill. *Chinese Working-Class Lives: Getting by in Taiwan.* Ithaca: Cornell University Press, 1987.

Gold, Thomas B. *State and Society in the Taiwan Miracle.* Armonk, NY: M.E. Sharpe, 1986.

Grichting, Wolfgang. *The Value System on Taiwan, 1970.* Taipei: Privately printed, 1971.

Harrell, Steven. *Ploughshare Village: Culture and Context in Taiwan.* Seattle: University of Washington Press, 1982.

Ho Ting-Jui. *A Comparative Study of Myths and Legends of Formosan Aborigines.* Pasadena, CA: Oriental Book Store, 1972.

Hsiung, J.C., ed. *Contemporary Republic of China: The Taiwan Experience, 1950-1980.* New York: Praeger, 1981.

Ikeda, Toshio. *A Survey of Taiwanese Family-Life.* Pasadena, CA: Oriental Book Store, 1972.

Keijiro, Marui. *Survey of Taiwanese Religions in 1919.* 2 vols. Pasadena, CA: Oriental Book Store, 1974.

Li, William D.H. *Housing in Taiwan: Agency or Structure?* Brookfield, VT: Ashgate, 1998.

Liao, Cheng-hung, and Martin C. Yang. *Socioeconomic Change in Rural Taiwan, 1950-1978.* Taipei: Department of Agricultural Extension, National Taiwan University, 1979.

Liu, Alan P.L. *Social Change on Mainland China and Taiwan, 1949-80.* Baltimore: University of Maryland School of Law, 1982.

Long, Howard R. *The People of Musha: Life in a Taiwanese Village.* Columbia: University of Missouri Press, 1961.

Marsh, Robert M. *The Great Transformation: Social Change in Taipei, Taiwan since the 1960s.* Armonk, NY: M.E. Sharpe, 1996.

Moser, Michael J. *Law and Change in a Chinese Community: A Case Study from Rural Taiwan.* Dobbs Ferry, NY: Oceana Publications, 1983.

Murry, Stephen O., and Hong Keelung. *Taiwanese Culture, Taiwanese Society: A Critical Review of Social Science Research Done on Taiwan.* Lanham, MD: University Press of America, 1994.

O'Hara, Albert. *Social Problems: Focus on Taiwan.* Beaverton, OR: International Specialized Book Service, 1980.

Pasternak, Burton. *Kinship and Community in Two Chinese Villages.* Stanford: Stanford University Press, 1972.

Rubinstein, Murray A., ed. *The Protestant Community of Modern Taiwan: Mission, Seminary, and Church.* Armonk, NY: M.E. Sharpe, 1990.

Shee, Amy H.L. *Legal Protection of Children against Sexual Exploitation in Taiwan.* Brookfield, VT: Ashgate, 1998.

Speare, Alden, Jr., et al. *Urbanization and Development: The Rural-Urban Transition in Taiwan.* Boulder, CO: Westview Press, 1987.

Thornton, Arland, and Hui-sheng Lin. *Social Change and the Family in Taiwan.* Chicago: University of Chicago Press, 1994.

Tien, Hung-mao. *The Great Transition: Political and Social Change in the Republic of China.* Stanford, CA: Hoover Institution Press, 1989.

Wilson, Richard W., Amy A. Wilson, and Sidney L. Greenblatt, eds. *Value Change in Chinese Society.* New York: Praeger, 1979.

Wolf, Margery. *A Thrice-Told Tale: Feminism, Postmodernism and Ethnographic Responsibility.* Stanford: Stanford University Press, 1992.

Wu, Chen-Tau. *Studies on the Tea in Modern Taiwan.* Pasadena, CA: Oriental Book Store, 1977.

Wu, Tsong-shien. *Taiwan's Changing Rural Society.* 2 vols. Pasadena, CA: Oriental Book Store, 1972.

Wu, Tsong-shien. *The Value of Children: A Cross-National Study.* Honolulu: East-West Population Institute, 1977.

Yang, Chi-Ling. *Taiwan's Social Construction, Nineteen Forty-Five to Nineteen Seventy-Five.* Pasadena, CA: Oriental Book Store, 1976 (Chinese).

ARTICLES

Berndt, T.J. et al. "Perceptions of Parenting in Mainland China, Taiwan, and Hong Kong: Sex Differences and Societal Differences," *Developmental Psychology,* January 1993.

Bosco, J. "Taiwan Factions: Guanxi, Patronage, and the State in Local Politics," *Ethnology,* April 1992.

Brinton, M.C. et al. "Married Women's Employment in Rapidly Industrializing Societies: Examples from East Asia," *American Journal of Sociology,* March 1995.

Chen, Shao-hsing. "Trend Report of Studies in Social Stratification and Social Mobility in Taiwan," *East Asian Culture Studies,* March 1965.

Chen, Y.C.J. et al. "A Six-year Follow-up of Behavior and Activity Disorders in the Taiwan Yu-cheng Children," *American Journal of Public Health*, March 1994.

Chi, C. "Integrating Traditional Medicine into Modern Health Care Systems: Examining the Role of Chinese Medicine in Taiwan," *Social Science and Medicine*, August 1994.

Chi, C. et al. "The Practice of Chinese Medicine in Taiwan," *Social Science and Medicine,* November 1996.

Chou, Bih-er, Cal Clark, and Janet Clark. "Differences in the Political Attitudes of Women and Men Legislators in Taiwan," *American Asian Review*, Fall 1993.

Chu, Godwin C. "Impact of Mass Media on a Gemeinschaft-Like Social Structure," *Rural Sociology,* June 1968.

Clark, Cal. "Successful Structural Adjustment and Evolving State-Society Relations in Taiwan," *American Journal of Chinese Studies*, October 1994.

Clark, Janet, Cal Clark, and Bih-er Chou. "Assemblywomen in Taiwan: A Surprising Equality," *American Journal of Chinese Studies*, April 1992.

Clough, R.N. "The Enduring Influence of the Republic of China on Taiwan Today," *China Quarterly,* December 1996.

Davis, D.R., and S. Chan. "The Security-Welfare Relationship: Longitudinal Evidence from Taiwan," *Journal of Peace Research,* February 1990.

Davis, D.R., and M.D. Ward. "The Entrepreneurial State: Evidence from Taiwan," *Comparative Political Studies,* October 1990.

De Vos, S. "An Old Age Security Incentive for Children in the Philippines and Taiwan," *Economic Development and Cultural Change,* July 1985.

Diamond, Norma. "Women under the Kuomintang RuleXVariations on the Feminine Mystique," *Modern China,* January 1975.

Eberhard, Wolfram. "Labor Mobility in Taiwan," *Asian Survey,* May 1962.

Farris, Catherine S. "Women, Work, and Child Care in Taiwan: Changing Family Dynamics in a Chinese Society," *American Asian Review*, Fall 1993.

Gallin, R.S. "Women and Work in Rural Taiwan: Building a Contextual Model Linking Employment and Health," *Journal of Health and Social Behavior,* December 1989.

Gold, T.B. "Taiwan Society at the Fin de Siecle," *China Quarterly*, December 1996.

Goodkind, D.M. "New Zodiacal Influences on Chinese Family Formation: Taiwan, 1976," *Demography*, May 1993.

Greenhalgh, S. "Networks and Their Nodes: Urban Society in Taiwan," *China Quarterly* 99, 1984.

Harremann, R.W. "Family Planning in Taiwan: The Conflict between Ideologues and Technocrats," *Modern China,* April 1990.

Ho, Samuel P.S. "Decentralized Industrialization and Rural Development: Evidence from Taiwan," *Economic Development and Cultural Change,* October 1979.

----------. "Industrialization in Taiwan: Recent Trends and Problems," *Pacific Affairs,* Spring 1975.

Hsieh, C.R., and S.-J. Lin. "Health Information and the Demand for Preventive Care among the Elderly in Taiwan," *Journal of Human Resources*, Spring 1997.

Hsieh, H.C. "Women's Studies in Taiwan," *Women's Studies Quarterly*, Fall/Winter 1994.

Jochim, C. "Flowers, Fruit, and Incense Only: Elite versus Popular in Taiwan's Religion of the Yellow Emperor," *Modern China,* January 1990

Kao, C. et al. "Male-Female Wage Differentials in Taiwan: A Human Capital Approach," *Economic Development and Cultural Change*, January 1994.

Kao, C.H.C., and B.C. Liu. "Socioeconomic Advance in the Republic of China (Taiwan): An Intertemporal Analysis of Its Quality of Life Indicators," *American Journal of Economics and Sociology,* October 1984.

Knapp, R.G. "Rural Housing and Village Transformation in Taiwan and Fujian," *China Quarterly*, September 1996.

Kuang-Hua, H., and R.L. Burgess. "Marital Role Attitudes and Expected Role Behaviors of College Youth in Mainland China and Taiwan," *Journal of Family Issues*, September 1994.

Lavely, W. "Industrialization and Household Complexity in Rural Taiwan," *Social Forces,* September 1990.

Lee, Peter Ching-yung. "Social Welfare of Hong Kong, Singapore, and Taiwan: Progress and Challenge," *American Journal of Chinese Studies*, October 1996.

Lee, Y.J. et al. "Sons, Daughters, and Intergenerational Support in Taiwan," *American Journal of Sociology*, January 1994.

Lin, C.Y.G., and U.R. Fu. "A Comparison of Child Rearing Practices Among Chinese, Immigrant Chinese, and Caucasian-American Parents," *Child Development,* April 1990.

Lin, P.J., et al. "Category Typicality, Cultural Familiarity, and the Development of Category Knowledge," *Developmental Psychology,* September 1990.

Liu, H.C. et al. "Prevalence and Subtypes of Dementia in Taiwan: A Community Survey of 5297 Individuals," *Journal of the American Geriatric Society*, February 1995.

Ma, L. C., and K.B. Smith. "Education, Social Class, and Parental Values in Taiwan," *Journal of Social Psychology*, August 1993.

Ma, L.C., and K.B. Smith. "Social Correlates of Confucian Ethics in Taiwan," *Journal of Social Psychology*, October 1992.

Marsh, Robert M. "The Taiwanese of Taipei: Some Major Aspects of Their Social Structure and Attitudes," *Journal of Asian Studies*, May 1968.

Marsh, R.M., and C.-K. Hsu. "Changes in Norms and Behavior Concerning Extended Kin in Taipei, Taiwan, 1963-1991," *Journal of Comparative Family Studies*, Autumn 1995.

Olsen, Nancy J. "Social Class and Rural-Urban Patterning of Socialization in Taiwan," *Journal of Asian Studies*, May 1975.

Parish, W.L., and R.J. Willis. "Daughters, Education, and Family Budgets: Taiwan Experiences," *Journal of Human Resources*, Fall 1993.

Park, A., and B. Johnston. "Rural Development and Dynamic Externalities in Taiwan's Structural Transformation," *Economic Development and Cultural Change*, October 1995.

Schak, D.C. "Socioeconomic Mobility and the Urban Poor in Taiwan," *Modern China*, July 1989.

Shaw, T.A. "'We Like to Have Fun': Leisure and the Discovery of the Self in Taiwan's 'New' Middle Class," *Modern China*, October 1994.

Sih, Paul K.T. "Taiwan: A Modernizing Chinese Society," *Chinese Culture*, December, 1972.

Strom, R. et al. "Grandparents in Taiwan: A Three-Generational Study," *International Journal of Aging and Human Development*, 1996. 42, no.1.

Tang, T.L.P. "Factors Affecting Intrinsic Motivation Among University Students in Taiwan," *Journal of Social Psychology*, April 1990.

Thornton, A., et al. "Social and Economic Change, Intergenerational Relationships, and Family Formation in Taiwan," *Demography*, November 1984.

Tsai, S.L. et al. "Schooling Taiwan's Women: Educational Attainment in the Mid-20th Century," *Sociology of Education*, October 1994.

Tsai, Wen-hui. "From Tradition to Modernity: Social Change in the Republic of China," *American Journal of Chinese Studies*, October 1992.

----------. "Welfare Policies for the Aged on Both Sides of the Taiwan Straits: A Comparison," *American Asian Review*, Summer 1989.

Tu, E.J.C. et al. "Kinship and Family Support in Taiwan: A Microsimulation Approach," *Research on Aging*, December 1993.

Tu, E. J.C., and K. Chen. "Changes in Active Life Expectancy in Taiwan: Compression or Expansion?" *Social Science & Medicine*, December 1994.

Tyson, James. "Christians and the Taiwanese Independence Movement: A Commentary," *Asian Affairs*, Fall 1987.

Wang, Charlotte Shiang-yun. "Social Mobility in Taiwan," *Papers in Social Sciences*, no. 80-3. Taipei: Academia Sinica, 1980.

Wei, Hsian-Chuen, and Uwe Reischl. "Impact of Industrialization on Attitude Towards Parents and Children in Contemporary Taiwan," *Industry of Free China*, July 1983.

Wei, Yung. "Modernizing Process in Taiwan: An Allocative Analysis," *Asian Survey*, March 1976.

Weiming, Tu. "Cultural Identity and the Politics of Recognition in Contemporary Taiwan," *China Quarterly*, December 1996.

Weller, R.P. "Social Contradiction and Symbolic Resolution: Practical and Idealized Affines in Taiwan," *Ethnology*, October 1984.

Wilson, Richard W. "Some Rural-Urban Comparisons of Political Socialization in Taiwan," *Asian Studies*, April 1972.

Wolf, M. "The Woman Who Didn't Become a Shaman," *American Ethnology*, August 1990.

Wu, B. "The Declining Gender Difference in Crime: The Taiwanese Case," *International Journal of Offender Therapy and Comparative Criminality*, Winter 1995.

----------. "The Impact of an Antiamphetamine Law on Juvenile Delinquency on Taiwan," *International Journal of Offender Therapy and Comparative Criminality*, September 1996.

Yang, W.S. et al. "Gender Differences in Postneonatal Infant Mortality in Taiwan," *Social Science and Medicine*, November 1996.

Yen, E.C. et al. "Cultural and Family Effects on Fertility Decisions in Taiwan, R.O.C.: Traditional Values and Family Structure Are As Relevant As Income Measures," *American Journal of Economics and Sociology*, October 1989.

Yi, C.C. "Studying Social Change: The Case of Taiwanese Family Sociologists," *Current Sociology*, Spring 1993.

----------. "Urban Housing Satisfaction in a Transitional Society: A Case Study in Taichung, Taiwan," *Urban Studies*, February 1985.

Yuan, D.Y., and Edward G. Stockwell. "The Rural-Urban Continuum: A Case Study of Taiwan," *Rural Sociology*, September 1964.

Zveglich, J.E., Jr. et al. "The Persistence of Gender Earnings Inequality in Taiwan, 1978-1992," *Industrial Labor Relations Review*, July 1997.

EDUCATION

BOOKS

Barendsen, Robert Dale. *Higher Educational Institutions in Taiwan.* U.S. Office of Education, Bulletin No. 18. Washington, DC: Government Printing Office, 1966.

Kao, Charles H.C. *Brain Drain: A Case Study of China.* Taipei: Mei Ya Publications, Inc., 1971.

Kaser, Davis. *Book Pirating in Taiwan.* Philadelphia: University of Pennsylvania Press, 1969.

Smith, Douglas C. *Middle Education in the Middle Kingdom: The Chinese Junior High School in Modern Taiwan.* Westport, CT: Greenwood Press, 1997.

Thelin, Mark C., ed. *Two Taiwanese Villages.* New York: United Board for Christian Higher Education in Asia, 1976.

Tsurumi, E. Patricia. *Japanese Colonial Education in Taiwan, 1895-1945.* Cambridge, MA: Harvard University Press, 1977.

Wilson, Richard W. *Learning to Be Chinese: The Political Socialization of Children in Taiwan.* Cambridge, MA: M.I.T. Press, 1970.

ARTICLES

Appleton, S. "The Political Socialization of Taiwan's College Students," *Asian Survey,* October 1970.

Appleton, S. "Regime Support among Taiwan High School Students," *Asian Studies,* August 1973.

----------. "Silent Students and the Future of Taiwan," *Pacific Affairs,* Summer 1970.

----------. "The Social and Political Impact of Education in Taiwan," *Asian Survey,* August 1976.

Hong, L.K. "Taiwanese Students in the U.S.," *Social Psychology,* December, 1978.

Kao, Charles H.C. "An Evaluation of the Republic of China's Policy on Tuition for Public Higher Education," *Industry of Free China,* May 1984.

Lew, William J.F. "Education in Taiwan," *Asian Affairs,* May-June 1978.

Martin, Roberta. "The Socialization of Children in China and Taiwan: An Analysis of Elementary School Textbooks," *China Quarterly,* June 1975.

Stevenson, H.W. et al. "Cognitive Performance and Academic Achievement of Japanese, Chinese, and American Children," *Child Development,* June 1985.

Tien, Flora F. "Higher Education Reform in Taiwan: History, Development and the University Act," *American Asian Review*, Fall 1996.

ECONOMICS

BOOKS

Alam, M. Shahid. *Governments and Markets in Economic Development Strategies: Lessons from Korea, Taiwan, and Japan.* Westport, CT: Greenwood Press, 1989.

Barclay, George W. *Colonial Development and Population in Taiwan.* New York: Associated Faculty Press, 1971.

Behmron, Jack N., and Harvey W. Wallender. *Transfers of Manufacturing Technology with Multinational Enterprises.* Cambridge, MA: Ballinger, 1976.

Chan, S. and C. Clark. *Flexibility, Foresight, and Fortuna in Taiwan's Development: Navigating between Scylla and Charybdis.* London: Routledge, 1992.

Chen, Edward K.Y. *Hyper-growth in Asian Economics: A Comparative Study of Hong Kong, Japan, Korea, Singapore, and Taiwan.* New York: Holmes and Meier, 1979.

Chen, Shih-meng S. et al. *Disintegrating KMT-State Capitalism: A Closer Look at Privatizing Taiwan's State- and Party-Owned Enterprises.* Taipei: Taipei Society, 1991.

Chen, Tain-jy. *Taiwanese Firms in Southeast Asia.* Cheltenham, England: Edward Elgar Publishing, Ltd., 1998.

Cheng, Chen. *Land Reform in Taiwan.* Taipei: China Publishing, 1961.

Chi, Schive. *The Foreign Factor: The Multinational Corporation's Contribution to the Economic Modernization of the Republic of China.* Stanford, CA: Hoover Institution Press, 1990.

Chinese Taipei: The Origins of the Economic Miracle OECD, 1994.

Clark, Cal. *Taiwan's Development: Implications for Contending Political Economy Paradigms.* Westport, CT: Greenwood Press, 1989.

Council for Economic Planning and Development. *Taiwan Statistical Date Book, 1981.* Philadelphia, PA: International Publications Service, 1981.

Council for Economic Planning and Development. *Taiwan Statistical Date Book, 1982.* Philadelphia, PA: International Publications Service, 1982.

DeGlopper, Donald R. *Lukang: Commerce and Community in a Chinese City.* State University of New York Press, 1995.

Downen, Robert L. *To Bridge the Taiwan Strait.* Washington, DC: Council for Social and Economic Studies, 1982.

Fei, John, et al. *Growth with Equity: The Taiwan Case.* New York: Oxford University Press, 1979.

Ferdinand, Peter, ed., *Take-Off For Taiwan.* London: Pinter, 1996.

Galenson, Walter, ed. *Economic Growth and Structural Change in Taiwan: The Postwar Experience of the Republic of China.* Ithaca: Cornell University Press, 1979.

Grad, Andrew J. *Formosa Today: An Analysis of the Economic Development and Strategic Importance of Japan's Tropical Colony.* New York: AMS Press, Inc., 1978.

Greenhalgh, Susan M., and Edwin A. Winkler. *Approaches to the Poliical Economy of Taiwan.* Armonk, NY: M.E. Sharpe, 1987.

Gregor, A. James. *Ideology and Development: Sun Yat-sen and the Economic History of Taiwan.* Berkeley, CA: Institute of East Asian Studies, 1982.

Gregor, A. James, and Maria H. Chang, *Essays on Sun Yat-sen and the Economic Development of Taiwan.* Baltimore: University of Maryland School of Law, 1983.

Ho, Chi-min. *Agricultural Development of Taiwan, 1903-1970.* Nashville, TN: Vanderbilt University Press, 1966.

Ho, Samuel P.S. *Economic Development of Taiwan, 1860-1970.* New Haven: Yale University Press, 1978.

----------. *Small-Scale Enterprises in Korea and Taiwan.* Washington, DC: The World Bank, 1980.

Hou, Chi-ming, and Tzong-shian Yu, eds. *Modern Chinese Economic History.* Nankang, Taiwan: Institute of Economics, Academia Sinica, 1979.

Hsieh, S.C., and T.H. Lee. *Agricultural Development and Its Contributions to Economic Growth in TaiwanXInput-Output and Productivity Analysis of Taiwan Agricultural Development.* Taipei: Joint Commission on Rural Construction, 1966.

Hsing, Mo-huan. *Taiwan: Industrialization and Trade Policies.* London: Oxford University Press, 1971.

Hwang, Y. Dolly. *The Rise of a New World Economic Power: Postwar Taiwan.* Westport, CT: Greenwood Press, 1991.

Jacoby, Neil H. *U.S. Aid to Taiwan: A Study of Foreign Aid, Self-Help and Development.* New York: Praeger, 1966.

Kahn, Herman. *World Economic Development, 1979 and Beyond.* Boulder, CO: Westview Press, 1979.

Keefer, James F. *Taiwan's Agricultural Growth during the 1970's.* Washington, DC: Economic Research Service, U.S. Department of Agriculture, 1971.

Koo, Anthony Y.C. *The Role of Land Reform in Economic Development, a Case Study of Taiwan.* New York: Praeger, 1968.

Kuo, Shirley W.Y. *The Taiwan Economy in Transition.* Boulder, CO: Westview Press, 1983.

----------. *The Taiwan Success Story: Rapid Growth with Improved Distribution in the Republic of China, 1952-1979.* Boulder, CO: Westview Press, 1981.

Kuo, Wan Yong. "Technical Change, Foreign Investment and Growth in the Manufacturing Industries, 1952-1970." In Shinichi Ichimura, ed. *The Economic Development of East and Southeast Asia.* Honolulu: University of Hawaii Press, 1967.

Lee, Teng-hui. *Intersectoral Capital Flows in the Economic Development of Taiwan, 1895-1960.* Ithaca: Cornell University Press, 1971.

Leng, Tse-kang. *The Taiwan-China Economic Connection: Democracy and Development across the Taiwan Strait.* Boulder, CO: Westview Press, 1996.

Li, Kuo-ting. *The Evolution of Policy Behind Taiwan's Development Success.* New Haven: Yale University Press, 1988.

----------. *The Experience of Dynamic Economic Growth on Taiwan.* Beaverton, OR: International Specialized Book Services, 1980.

Li, Kwoh-ting, and Tzong-shian Yu, eds. *Experiences and Lessons of Economic Development on Taiwan.* Taipei: Academia Sinica, 1980.

Lin, Ching-yuan. *Industrialization in Taiwan, 1946-1972: Trade and Import Substitution Policies for Developing Countries.* New York: Praeger, 1973.

Lionberger, Herbert F., and H.C. Chang. *Farm Information for Modernizing Agriculture: The Taiwan System.* New York: Praeger, 1973.

McBeath, Gerald A. *Wealth and Freedom: Taiwan⎕s New Political Economy.* Abington, England: Brookfield, VT: Ashgate, 1998.

Metraux, Daniel E. *Taiwan's Political and Economic Growth in the Late Twentieth Century.* E. Mellen, 1991.

Mosher, Steven W., ed. *The United States and the Republic of China: Democratic Friends, Economic Partners and Strategic Allies.* New Brunswick, NJ: Transaction Publishers, 1990.

Negandhi, Anant R. *Management and Economic Development: The Case of Taiwan.* The Hague: Martinus Nijhoff, 1973.

Olson, Gary L. *U.S. Foreign Policy and the Third World Peasant: Land Reform in Asia and Latin America.* New York: Praeger, 1974.

Pasternak, Burton. *Kinship and Community in Two Chinese Villages.* Stanford: Stanford University Press, 1972.

Population Papers. Nankang, Taiwan: Institute of Economics, Academia Sinica, 1973.

Prybyla, Jan S. *The Societal Objective of Wealth, Growth, Stability and Equity in Taiwan*. Baltimore: University of Maryland School of Law, 1978.

Rabushka, Alvin. *The New China: Comparative Economic Development in Mainland China, Taiwan, and Hong Kong*. Boulder, CO: Westview Press, 1987.

Ranis, Gustav, Sheng Cheng Hu, and Yun-peng Chu, eds. *The Political Economy of Taiwan's Development into the 21st Century, Volume 2*. Cheltenham, England: Edward Elgar Publishing, Ltd., 1998.

Rostow, W.W. *The World Economy: History and Prospects*. Austin: University of Texas Press, 1978.

Schive, C. *The Foreign Factor: The Multinational Corporation's Contribution to the Economic Modernization of the Republic of China*. Stanford: Hoover Institution Press, 1990.

Selya, Roger M. *The Industrialization of Taiwan*. New Brunswick, NJ: Transaction Publishers, 1974.

Shen, T.H. *The Sino-American Joint Commission on Rural Reconstruction*. Ithaca: Cornell University Press, 1970.

Silin, R.H. *Leadership and Values: The Organization of Large-Scale Taiwanese Enterprises*. Cambridge: Harvard University Press, 1976.

Simon, Denis F. *Taiwan, Technology Transfer and Transnationalism: The Political Management of Dependency*. Boulder, CO: Westview Press, 1985.

Simon, Denis, and Michael Kau, eds. *Taiwan: Beyond the Economic Miracle*. Armonk, NY: M.E. Sharpe, 1992.

Steinhoff, Manfred. *Prestige and Profit: The Development of Entrepreneurial Abilities in Taiwan*. Miami: Australian National University Press, 1980.

Tai, Hung-chao. "The Kuomintang and Modernization in Taiwan" In Samuel P. Huntington and Clement H. Moore, eds. *Authoritarian Politics in Modern Society*. New York: Basic Books, 1970.

----------. *Land Reforms and Politics: A Comparative Analysis*. Berkeley: University of California Press, 1974.

Taiwan Buyer's Guide, 1982-83. Philadelphia: International Publications Service, 1982.

Taiwan Buyer's Guide, 1984-85. Philadelphia: International Publications Service, 1984.

Taiwan Buyer's Guide, 1986-87. Philadelphia: International Publications Service, 1986.

The Taiwan Development Experience and Its Relevance to Other Countries. Taipei: Kwang Hwa Publishing, 1988.

Wang, N.T., ed. *Taiwan's Enterprises in Global Perspective.* Armonk, NY: M.E.Sharpe, 1992.

Wheeler, Jimmy W., and Perry L. Wood. *Beyond Recrimination: Perspectives on U.S.-Taiwan Trade Tensions.* Indianapolis: Hudson Institute, 1987.

White, Gordon, ed. *Developmental States in East Asia.* New York: St. Martin's, 1988.

Willmott, W.E., ed. *Economic Organization in Chinese Society.* Stanford: Stanford University Press, 1972.

Winckler, Edwin A., and Susan M. Greenhalgh, eds. *Contending Approaches to the Political Economy of Taiwan.* Armonk, NY: M.E. Sharpe, 1987.

Wu, Kuang-hua, and Chiao Wei-cheng, eds. *JCRR and Agricultural Development in Taiwan.* Taipei: Joint Commission on Rural Construction, 1978.

Wu, Yuan-li. *Becoming an Industrialized Nation: ROC's Development on Taiwan.* New York: Praeger, 1985.

Wu, Yuan-li, and Kung-chia Yeh, eds. *Growth, Distribution and Social Change: Essays on the Economics of the Republic of China.* Baltimore: University of Maryland School of Law, 1978.

Yang, Martin M.C. *Socioeconomic Results of Land Reform in Taiwan.* Honolulu: East-West Center Press, 1970.

Yum, Kwang Sup. *Successful Economic Development of the Republic of China in Taiwan.* New York: Vantage Press, 1968.

ARTICLES

Adams, D.W. et al. "Differences in Uses of Rural Financial Markets in Taiwan and the Philippines," *World Development*, April 1993.

Andrews, J. "Transition on Trial: A Survey of Taiwan," *Economist,* maps, 5 March 1988.

Arnold, W. "Bureaucratic Politics, State Capacity, and Taiwan's Automobile Industrial Policy," *Modern China,* April 1989.

Ash, R.F., and Y.Y. Kueh. "Economic Integration within Greater China: Trade and Investment Flows between China, Hong Kong, and Taiwan," *China Quarterly*, December 1993.

Auty, R. M. "Competitive Industrial Policy and Macro Performance: Has South Korea Outperformed Taiwan?" *Journal of Development Studies*, April 1997.

Aw, B.Y. "An Empirical Model of Mark-ups in a Quality-Differentiated Export Market," *Journal of International Economics*, November 1992.

Aw, B.Y., and A. R. Hwang. "Productivity and the Export Market: A Firm-Level Analysis," *Journal of Development Economics*, August 1995.

Barnett, R.W. "China and Taiwan: The Economic Issues," *Foreign Affairs,* April 1972.

Benziger, V. "Small Fields, Big Money: Two Successful Programs in Helping Small Farmers Make the Transition to High Value-added Crops," *World Development,* November 1996.

Besley, T., and A.R. Levinson. "The Role of Informal Finance in Household Capital Accumulation: Evidence from Taiwan," *Economic Journal,* January 1996.

Bierling, J., and G. Murray. "The 'Emerging Powers': China, Singapore, Hong Kong, and Taiwan," *Current Sociology*, Summer 1995.

Brandt, K. "Economic Development: Lessons of Statecraft in Taiwan," *Orbis,* Winter 1968.

Brautigam, D.A. "What Can Africa Learn from Taiwan? Political Economy, Industrial Policy, and Adjustment," *Journal of Modern African Studies*, March 1994.

"A Brief Report on Taiwan's Economic Situation, 1981," *Industry of Free China,* June 1982.

"A Brief Report on Taiwan's Economic Situation, 1982," *Industry of Free China,* June 1983.

"A Brief Report on Taiwan's Economic Situation, 1984," *Industry of Free China,* Summer 1985.

Caldwell, J. Alexander. "The Financial System in Taiwan: Structure, Functions, and Issues for the Future," *Asian Survey,* August 1976.

Chan, S. "Defense Burden and Economic Growth: Unraveling the Taiwanese Enigma," *American Political Science Review,* September 1988.

----------. "The Mouse That Roared: Taiwan's Management of Trade Relations with the United States," *Comparative Political Studies,* October 1987.

Chan, S. et al. "State Entrepreneurship, Foreign Investment, Export Expansion, and Economic Growth: Grander Causality in Taiwan's Development," *Journal of Conflict Resolution,* March 1990.

Chan, Steve. "Peace by Pieces? The Economic and Social Bases for 'Greater China,'" *American Asian Review,* Summer 1996.

Chan, V.L. et al. "External Economies in Taiwan's Manufacturing Industries," *Contemporary Economic Policy*, October 1995.

Chang, Ching-huei. "The Limits of Statism in Taiwan: The Distortions of Policies Ignoring Small Enterprise Dynamism," *American Asian Review*, Summer 1996.

Chang, David W. "U.S. Aid and Economic Growth in Taiwan," *Asian Survey,* March 1965.

Chang, Kwang-shih. "The New Industrialized Countries in the Far East and Their International Position," *Industry of Free China,* February 1985.

Chang, P.L. et al. "Using Data Envelopment Analysis to Measure the Achievement and Change of Regional Development in Taiwan," *Journal of Environmental Management,* January 1995.

Chang, Ten-t'ien. "Taiwan: Economic Development and Population Policy." In Dun J. Li, ed. *Modern China.* New York: Charles Scribner's Sons, 1978.

Chao, Chieh-chien. "The Development of Trade and Cargo Flow between ROC and USA," *Industry of Free China,* June 1983.

----------. "Economic Growth, Trade Development and Foreign Investment in Taiwan, ROC," *Industry of Free China,* April 1985.

Chen, C.L. et al. "Farm Size and the Adoption of Rice Production Technologies in Taiwan," *Journal of Asian and African Studies,* July/October 1989.

Chen, J.R. "The Effects of Land Reform on the Rice Sector and Economic Development in Taiwan," *World Development,* November 1994.

Chen, Shyh-Jer, and Koji Taira. "Industrial Democracy, Economic Growth, and Income Distribution in Taiwan," *American Asian Review,* Winter 1995.

Chen, Sun. "The Republic of China and the Security of the Western Pacific: An Economic View," *International Commercial Bank of China Economic Review,* January/February 1982.

Chen, T.J., and D.P. Tang, "Export Performance and Productivity Growth: The Case of Taiwan," *Economic Development and Cultural Change,* April 1990.

Chen, Thomas P., and K. Thomas Liaw. "Bank Deposit Insurance Policies: An International Overview and Recommendations for Taiwan," *American Asian Review,* Winter 1993.

Chen, X. "Taiwan Investments in China and Southeast Asia: 'Go West, but Also Go South,'" *Asian Survey,* May 1996.

Cheng, Chu-yuan. "Economic Development in Taiwan and Mainland China: A Comparison of Strategies and Performance," *Asian Affairs,* Spring 1983.

----------. "Economic Relations across the Taiwan Straits: Progress, Effects and Prospects," *American Asian Review,* Spring 1997.

----------. "The Role of the ROC in International Economic and Financial Organizations," *American Asian Review,* Winter 1995.

----------. "Taiwan's Economy in Transition: New Challenges and Prospects," *Asian Outlook*, July-August 1991.

----------. "Taiwan's Economy in Transition: Structural Changes and Prospects," *American Asian Review*, Fall 1996.

----------. "United States-Taiwan Economic Relations: Trade and Investment," *Columbia Journal of World Business*, Spring 1986.

Cheng, Linsun. "Modern Banks and Government Debts in the Republican China," *American Journal of Chinese Studies*, October 1998.

Cheng, Peter P. "Taiwan: Protective Adjustment Economy," *Asian Survey*, January 1975.

Cheng, T.J. "Taiwan in 1996: From Euphoria to Melodrama," *Asian Survey*, January 1997.

"Chinese Communist Economic Development and Its Competition with Taiwan," *Asian Outlook*, February 1985.

Choi, Hak, and Chaw-hsia Tu. "ROC-US Trade Imbalance: Causes and Possible Solutions," *Industry of Free China*, July 1985.

Chow, Peter C.Y. "Money Market Segmentation and Financial Liberalization: A Revised Financial Repression Thesis in Taiwan," *American Journal of Chinese Studies*, April 1987.

----------. "The Role of Taiwan's Economy in the International Economic Community: The ROC's Bid for Memberships in the IMF and World Bank," *American Asian Review*, Summer 1997.

Chu, W.W. "Export-Led Growth and Import Dependence: The Case of Taiwan, 1969-81," *Journal of Development Economics*, March 1988.

----------. "Import Substitution and Exportled Growth: A Study of Taiwan's Petrochemical Industry," *World Development*, May 1994.

----------. "Causes of Growth: A Study of Taiwan's Bicycle Industry," *Cambridge Journal of Economics*, January 1997.

Chu, Yun-peng. "Growth, Distribution, and Stability in Taiwan," *Industry of Free China*, October 1984.

Chuang, Chi-an. "Special Characteristics of Taiwanese Entrepreneurship," *American Journal of Chinese Studies*, April 1994.

Chuang, Y.C. "Identifying the Sources of Growth in Taiwan's Manufacturing Industry," *Journal of Development Studies*, February 1996.

Clark, C. "Economic Development in Taiwan: A Model of a Political Economy" *Journal of Asian and African Studies*, January/April 1987.

----------. "The Taiwan Exception: Implications for Contending Political Economy Paradigms," *International Studies Quarterly*, September 1987.

Clark, Cal. "Dynamics of Development in Taiwan: Reconceptualizing State and Market in National Competitiveness," *American Journal of Chinese Studies*, April 1994.

"Contemporary Taiwan," *China Quarterly*, December 1996.

"Country Report: Taiwan," *Asian Finance,* October 1985.

Courtenay, P. "Taiwan's Hsinchu Science-Based Industrial Park," *Geography*, October 1993.

Cummings, Bruce. "The Origins and Development of the Northeast Asian Political Economy: Industrial Sectors, Product Cycles, and Political Consequences [Japan, South Korea, and Taiwan]," *International Organization,* Winter 1984.

"The Defarming of Taiwan," *Futurist*, January/February 1995.

De Melo, J., and L.A. Winters. "Do Exporters Gain from VERs?" *European Economic Review*, October 1993.

"Development and the Newly Industrializing Economies, 1965-86," *Finance Development,* March 1989.

"Economic Report: Taiwan's Great Leap Forward," *Asian Business,* December 1987.

Etherington, D M., and K. Foster. "The Structural Transformation of Taiwan's Tea Industry [1860 to the Present]," *World Development*, March 1992.

Fields, K.J. "Trading Companies in South Korea and Taiwan: Two Policy Approaches," *Asian Survey,* November 1989.

Fransman, Martin. "International Competitiveness, Technical Change, and the State: The Machine Tool Industry in Taiwan and Japan," *World Development,* December 1986.

Freeberne, Michael. "Lonely Taiwan Sows for the Future," *Geographical Magazine,* January 1972.

Gallin, Bernard. "Social Effects of Land Reform in Taiwan," *Human Organization,* Summer 1963.

Glass, Sheppard. "Some Effects of Formosa's Economic Growth," *China Quarterly,* July-September 1963.

Harding, H. "The Emergence of Greater China," *American Enterprise*, May/June 1992.

He, Jia, and Christina Liu. "Predictability of Taiwan Stock Returns Using World, Pacific-Basin, and Country-Specific Macro Variables," *American Asian Review*, Winter 1993.

Ho, Samuel P.S. "The Economic Development of Colonial Taiwan: Evidence and Interpretation," *Journal of Asian Studies,* February 1975.

Howe, C. "The Taiwan Economy: The Transition to Maturity and the Political Economy of Its Changing International Status," *China Quarterly*, December 1996.

Hsing, Y. "Blood, Thicker Than Water: Interpersonal Relations and Taiwanese Investment in Southern China," *Environment and Planning*, December 1996.

Hsu, D.Y.C., and J. T. Hwang. "Labor Shortage and Unutilized Labor Reserve in Taiwan," *Journal of Contemporary Asia*, 1992. 22, no. 4

Hu, J.C. "Taiwan: An Emerging Hub for the East Asian Regional Economy," *Journal of Social, Political, and Economic Studies*, Fall 1996.

Huang, C. "The State and Foreign Investment: The Cases of Taiwan and Singapore," *Comparative Political Studies* 22, 1989.

----------. "Joint Ventures between State Enterprises and Multinational Corporations in Taiwan," *International Studies Notes* 15, 1990.

Huang, S.W. "Structural Change in Taiwan's Agricultural Economy," *Economic Development and Cultural Change*, October 1993.

Hung, R. "The Great U-Turn in Taiwan: Economic Restructuring and a Surge in Inequality," *Journal of Contemporary Asia,* 1996. 26, no. 2.

Jenkins, R. "The Political Economy of Industrial Policy: Automobile Manufacture in the Newly Industrializing Economies," *Cambridge Journal of Economics*, October 1995.

Ka, C.M., and M. Selden. "Original Accumulation Equity and Late Industrialization: The Cases of Socialist China and Capitalist Taiwan," *World Development,* October/November 1986.

Kang, D.C. "South Korean and Taiwanese Development and the New Institutional Economics," *Industrial Organization*, Summer 1995.

Kau, Yin-mao. "The Power Structure in Taiwan's Political Economy," *Asian Survey*, March 1996.

Keng, C.W. Kenneth. "An 'Economic China': A Win-Win Strategy for Both Sides of the Taiwan Strait," *American Journal of Chinese Studies*, October 1998.

Klatt, Werner. "An Asian Success Story: Peaceful Agricultural Revolution in Taiwan," *Issues and Studies,* April 1972.

Kleingartner, Archie, and Hsueh-yu Peng. "Taiwan: An Exploration of Labor Relations in Transition," *British Journal of Industrial Relations* 29, no 3, 1991.

Lavrencic, Karl. "Taiwan: Will Politics Spoil the Economic Miracle?" *World Today,* January 1985.

Lee, Lai To. "Taiwan and Southeast Asia: Realpolitik Par Excellence?" *Contemporary Southeast Asia,* December 1985.

Lee, M.L. et al. "Growth and Equity with Endogenous Human Capital: Taiwan's Economic Miracle Revisited," *Southern Economic Journal*, October 1994.

Leng, Tse-Kang. "State-Business Relations and Taiwan's Mainland Economic Policy," *American Journal of Chinese Studies*, April 1994.

Levenson, A.R., and T. Besley. "The Anatomy of an Informal Financial Market: Rosca Participation in Taiwan," *Journal of Development Economics*, October 1996.

Li, C.P. "Trade Negotiation between the United States and Taiwan: Interest Structures in Two-Level Games," *Asian Survey*, August 1994.

Li, K.T. "Contributions of Women in the Labor Force to Economic Development in Taiwan, the Republic of China," *Industry of Free China,* August 1985.

----------. "The State of the Economic Contest," *Industry of Free China,* October 1982.

Liang, K.S., and C.I. Hou Liang. "Development Policy Formation and Future Policy Priorities in the Republic of China," *Economic Development and Cultural Change,* April 1988.

Liang, Kuo-shu. "Financial Reforms Recommended by the Economic Reform Committee, Republic of China," *Industry of Free China,* March 1986.

Lin, S.J., and Y.F. Chang. "Linkage Effects and Environmental Impacts from Oil Consumption Industries in Taiwan," *Journal of Environmental Management,* April 1997.

Liu, Fu-shan. "Agricultural Marketing Improvements in Taiwan," *Industry of Free China,* July 1983.

Liu, L.Y., and W.T. Woo. "Saving Behavior under Imperfect Financial Markets and the Current Account Consequences," *Economic Journal*, May 1994.

Liu, Paul K.C. "Technological Progress, Employment Structure and Income Distribution in Taiwan," *Industry of Free China,* August 1984.

Martellaro, Joseph A. "United States-Taiwan Trade Relations and the Trade Deficit," *Business Economy,* July 1987.

Mody, A. "Institutions and Dynamic Comparative Advantage: The Electronics Industry in South Korea and Taiwan," *Cambridge Journal of Economics,* September 1990.

Moll, T. "Mickey Mouse Numbers and Inequality Research in Developing Countries," *The Journal of Development Studies*, July 1992.

Moore, M. "Economic Structure and the Politics of Sectoral Bias: East Asian and Other Cases," *Journal of Development Studies*, July 1993.

Myers, Ramon H. "The Economic Development of Taiwan" In Hung-dah Chiu, ed. *China and the Question of Taiwan.* New York: Praeger, 1973.

Myers, Ramon H., and Norman Schroder. "America's Economic Stake in Taiwan," *Asian Affairs,* November-December 1975.

Niehoff, Justin D. "The Villager As Industrialist: Ideologies of Household Manufacturing in Rural Taiwan," *Modern China,* July 1987.

Noble, G.W. "Contending Forces in Taiwan's Economic Policymaking: The Case of Hua Tung Heavy Trucks," *Asian Survey,* June 1987.

O'Connor, James P. "Behind the Bull Markets in Korea and Taiwan," *Asian Affairs,* Summer 1988.

Ogawa, K. "Economic Development and Time Preference Schedule: The Case of Japan and East Asian NICs," *Journal of Development Economics,* October 1993.

Pan, Lien-fan. "The Urban Land Reform in the Republic of China," *Chinese Culture,* March 1975.

Pang, C.K. "The State and Socioeconomic Development in Taiwan since 1949," *Issues and Studies* 26. no. 5, 1990.

Pannell, Clifton W. "Urban Land Consolidation and City Growth in Taiwan," *Pacific Viewpoint,* September 1974.

Park, Y.C. "Development Lessons from Asia: The Role of Government in South Korea and Taiwan," *American Economic Review,* May 1990.

Prybyla, Jan S. "The Economy of Taiwan: A Study in Development," *Asian Affairs,* July-August 1976.

----------. "Some Reflections on Derecognition and the Economy of Taiwan." In *Taiwan: One Year after United States-China Normalization,* a workshop sponsored by the Committee on Foreign Relations, United States Senate and Congressional Research Service, Library of Congress, June 1980. Washington, DC: U.S. Government Printing Office, 1980.

----------. "Taiwan's Economy and Economic Development," *American Asian Review,* Spring 1996.

Reisen, H., and H. Yeches. "Time-varying Estimates on the Openness of the Capital Account in Korea and Taiwan," *Journal of Development Economics,* August 1993.

Rodrik, D. "The 'Paradoxes' of the Successful State," *European Economic Review,* April 1997.

Seth, Rama, and Robert N. McCauley. "Taiwan's Current Surplus and International Financial Market Linkages," *American Journal of Chinese Studies,* April 1994.

Silk, Mitchell A. "Reaching across the Water: Taiwan Traders and Investors Are Moving Cautiously toward the Mainland and

Being Greeted with Open Arms," *China Business Review,* November/December 1988.

Simon, D.F. "Charting Taiwan's Technological Future: The Impact of Globalization and Regionalization," *China Quarterly*, December 1996.

Sloane, Hugh. "Taiwan: Alternative Policies Are Needed to Promote Stronger Economic Growth," *Asian Monetary Monitor,* July/August 1985.

Speare, Alden, Jr. "Urbanization and Migration in Taiwan," *Economic Development and Cultural Change,* January 1974.

Sun, Chen. "Regional Economic Cooperation and Western Pacific Security: With Special Reference to the Role of the Republic of China," *Industry of Free China,* October 1984.

Tang, S.Y. "Informal Credit Markets and Economic Development in Taiwan," *World Development*, May 1995.

Tang, Wen-hui Anna. "State, Politics, and National Health Insurance on Taiwan," *American Asian Review*, Fall 1997.

Tsai, Steve Shih-teng. "The Improvement of ROC-USA Economic Ties," *Industry of Free China,* April 1984.

Tsay, C.L. "Industrial Restructuring and International Competition in Taiwan," *Environment and Planning A*, January 1993.

----------. "Labor Recruitment in Taiwan: A Corporate Strategy in Industrial Restructuring," *Environment and Planning*, April 1994.

Tsiu, T.K. "Taiwan's Approach to Economic Development," *Industry of Free China,* October 1984.

Underwood, Laurie. "Inside the Ruling Partys Moneymaking Machine —KMT, Inc.," *Topics*, April 1997.

von Gessel, Marinus. "American Businessmen's Views on the Investment Climate in Taiwan, ROC," *Industry of Free China,* April 1980.

Wade, Robert. "Asian Financial Systems As a Challenge to Economics; Lessons from Taiwan," *California Management Review,* Summer 1985.

----------. "Managing Trade: Taiwan and South Korea As Challenges to Economics and Political Science," *Comparative Politics*, January 1993.

----------. "What Can Economics Learn from East Asian Success?" *Annotated American Academy of Political and Social Science,* September 1989.

Wang, P., and C.K. Yip. "Macroeconomic Effects of Factor Taxation with Endogenous Human Capital Evolution: Theory and Evidence," *Southern Economic Journal*, January 1995.

Wang, Ping, and Yuan-li Wu. "Learning from the EC: The Implications of European Economic Integration for China and Taiwan," *American Journal of Chinese Studies*, October 1996.

Wang, V.W.C. "Developing the Information Industry in Taiwan: Entrepreneurial State, Guerrilla Capitalists, and Accommodative Technologists," *Pacific Affairs*, Winter 1995-1996.

Wang, Yan, and Zhi Wang. "The Impact of Opening Direct Trade Across the Taiwan Straits: A Quantitative Assessment, *American Journal of Chinese Studies*," October 1997.

Wang, Zhi, and Francis T. Tuan. "The Impact of China's and Taiwan's WTO Membership on World Trade—a Computable General Equilibrium Analysis," *American Journal of Chinese Studies*, October 1996.

Webb, L. "Taiwan: The Economic Prospects," *Australian Quarterly*, December 1956.

Webber, M. "Enter the Dragon: Lessons for Australia from Northeast Asia," *Environment and Planning*, January 1994.

Winn, J.K. "Relational Practices and the Marginalization of Law: Informal Financial Practices of Small Businesses in Taiwan," *Law and Society Review*, 28, no. 2, 1994.

Wu, Chung-lih. "Some Measures to Promote a More Balanced Bilateral Trade Relationship between the ROC and the USA— Economic and Political Implications," *International Commerce Bank of China Economic Review,* January/February 1988.

----------. "Trade Relations Between the ROC and European Countries in the Twentieth Century," *Industry of Free China,* December 1985.

Wu, Rong-I. "Taiwan's Success in Industrialization," *Industry of Free China,* November 1985.

Wu, Rong-I. "Trade Liberalization and Economic Development in Taiwan," *American Journal of Chinese Studies*, April 1987.

Wu, Y.S. "Taiwan in 1993: Attempting a Diplomatic Breakthrough," *Asian Survey*, January 1994.

Wu, Yuan-li and Yeh Kung-chia, eds. "Income Distribution in the Process of Economic Growth of the Republic of China.-- In Wu, Yuan-li and Yeh Kung-chia, eds. *Growth Distribution, and Societal Change: Essays on the Economy of the Republic of China.* Baltimore: University of Maryland School of Law, 1978.

----------. "The Survival of Development of Taiwan," *Asian Affairs,* September-October 1973.

Xu, D. "The KMT Party's Enterprises in Taiwan," *Modern Asian Studies*, May 1997.

Yin, Jason Z., and Charles C. Yen. "An Assessment of the Economic Relations between Taiwan and Mainland China," *American Asian Review*, Winter 1992.

Yip, C. K., and P. Wang. "Taxation and Economic Growth: The Case of Taiwan," *The American Journal of Economics and Sociology*, July 1992.

Young, Frank J. "Problems of Manpower Development in Taiwan," *Asian Survey*, August 1976.

Yu, Tzong-shian. "The Relationship between the Government and the Private Sector in the Process of Economic Development in Taiwan, ROC," *Industry of Free China*, October 1985.

Yuan, Mei-ling. "The Study of Labor-Management Conference in Taiwan," *Quarterly Journal of Labor* 102, 1991.

POLITICS

BOOKS

Aberbach, Joel, et al., eds. *The Role of the State in Taiwan's Development.* Armonk, NY: M.E. Sharpe, 1994.

Bader, William B., and Bergner, Jeffrey T., eds. *The Taiwan Relations Act: A Decade of Implementation.* Indianapolis: Hudson Institute, 1989.

Bate, H. Maclear. *Report from Formosa.* Philadelphia: Century Bookbindery, 1952.

Buxbaum, David C., ed. *Chinese Family Law and Social Change.* Seattle: University of Washington Press, 1978.

Chang, Cecelia S., ed. *The Republic of China on Taiwan, 1949-1988.* New York: St. John's University, Institute of Asian Studies, 1991.

Chang, King-yuh, ed. *The Democratization of the Republic of China: Process, System, and Impact.* Taipei: Institute of International Relations, 1992.

Chao, Linda, and Ramon H. Myers. *Democracy's New Leaders in the Republic of China.* Stanford: Hoover Institution Press, 1996.

Chao, Linda. and Ramon H. Myers. *The First Chinese Democracy: Political Life in the Republic of China on Taiwan.* Baltimore and London: The Johns Hopkins University Press, 1998.

Cheng, T.J., and S. Haggard, eds. *Political Change in Taiwan.* Boulder, CO: Lynne Rienner, 1992.

Chiu, Hungdah, ed. *China and the Taiwan Issue.* New York: Praeger Publishers, 1979.

Copper, John F. *A Quiet Revolution: Political Development in the Republic of China.* Washington, DC: Ethics and Public Policy Center, 1988.

----------. *Taiwan's Mid-1990s Elections: Taking the Final Steps to Democracy.* Westport, CT: Praeger Publisher, 1998.

----------. *Taiwan's Recent Elections: Fulfilling the Democratic Promise.* Baltimore: University of Maryland School of Law, 1990.

----------. *Taiwan's 1991 and 1992 Non-Supplemental Elections: Reaching a Higher State of Democracy.* Lanham, MD: University Press of America, 1994.

----------. *The Taiwan Political Miracle: Essays on Political Development, Elections and Foreign Relations.* Lanham, MD: University Press of America, 1997.

Copper, John F., with George P. Chen. *Taiwan's Elections: Political Development and Democratization in the Republic of China.* Baltimore: University of Maryland School of Law, 1985.

Cosway, R. et al. *Trade and Investment in Taiwan: The Legal Environment in the Republic of China.* Beaverton, OR: International Specialized Book Services, 1980.

Downen, Robert L. *Bridging the Taiwan Strait.* Washington, DC: Council on American Affairs, 1984.

Edmonds, L.G. *Taiwan—the Other China.* New York: Bobbs-Merrill, 1971.

Fa, Jyh-pin. *A Comparative Study of Judicial Review Under Nationalist Chinese and American Constitutional Law.* Baltimore: University of Maryland School of Law, 1980.

Fitch, Geraldine. *Formosa Beachhead.* Chicago: Henry Regnery, 1953.

Frost, Michael S. *Taiwan's Security and United States Policy: Executive and Congressional Strategies.* Baltimore: University of Maryland School of Law, 1982.

Gallin, Bernard. "Conflict Resolution in Changing Chinese Society: a Taiwanese Study." In M.J. Swartz, A. Tuden, and V.W. Turner, eds. *Political Anthropology.* Chicago: Aldine Publishing, 1966.

----------. "Mediation in Changing Chinese Society in Rural Taiwan," in D. Buxbaum, ed. *Traditional and Modern Legal Institutions in Asia and Africa.* Leiden, The Netherlands: Brill, 1967.

Gastil, Raymond D., ed. *Freedom in the World, 1983-1984: Political Rights and Civil Liberties.* Westport, CT: Greenwood Press, 1984.

Gregor, A. James. *Ideology and Development: Sun Yat-sen and the Economic History of Taiwan.* Berkeley, CA: Institute of East Asian Studies, 1982.

Gregor, A.J., and Maria H. Chang, *The Republic of China and U.S. Policy: A Study in Human Rights.* Washington DC: Ethics and Public Policy Center, 1983.

Hu, Jason C., ed. *Quiet Revolutions on Taiwan, Republic of China.* Taipei: Kwang Hwa Publishing Company, 1994.

Huang, Mab. *Intellectual Ferment for Political Reforms in Taiwan, 1971-1973.* Ann Arbor: University of Michigan Center for Chinese Studies, 1976 (Chinese).

Hughes, Christopher. *Taiwan and Chinese Nationalism: National Identity and Status in International Society.* London: Routledge, 1997.

Jo, Yung-hwan, ed. *Taiwan's Future.* Tempe: Arizona State University, 1974.

Kao, Ying-mao, and Hungdah Chiu. *The New Reforms Ahead of the Republic of China.* Long Island, NY: China Times Cultural Foundation, 1989.

Kerr, George. *Formosa Betrayed.* New York: Da Capo Press, 1976.

----------. *Formosa: Licensed Revolution and the Home Rule Movement.* Honolulu: University of Hawaii Press, 1974.

Lasater, Martin L. *Security of Taiwan: Unravelling the Dilemma.* Washington DC: Center for Strategic and International Studies, 1982.

Leng, Shao-chuan. *Chiang Ching-kuo's Leadership in the Development of the Republic of China on Taiwan.* Lanham, MD: University Press of American, 1993.

Lerman, Arthur J. *Taiwan's Politics: The Provincial Assemblymen's World.* Washington DC: University Press of America, 1978.

Li, Victor H., ed. *The Future of Taiwan: A Difference of Opinion.* Armonk, NY: M.E. Sharpe, 1980.

Linebarger, Paul M.A., Djang Chu, and Ardath W. Burks. *Far Eastern Government and Politics.* 2nd ed. Princeton: Van Nostrand, 1956.

Ma, Herbert H.P. "American Influence on the Formation of the Constitution and Constitutional Law of the Republic of China: Past History and Future Prospects." In Lawrence W. Beer, ed. *Constitutionalism in Asia: Views of the American Influence.* Berkeley: University of California Press, 1979.

Maguire, Keith, and Robert Gordon. *The Rise of Modern Taiwan: Government and Politics in the Republic of China.* Abington, England: Ashgate, 1998.

Mancall, Mark, ed. *Formosa Today.* New York: Praeger, 1964.

Mason, Bruce B. *Local Government in Taiwan: Some Observations.* Tempe: Bureau of Government Research, Arizona State University, 1964.

Mendel, Douglas. *The Politics of Formosan Nationalism.* Berkeley: University of California Press, 1970.

Moody, Peter R. *Opposition and Dissent in Contemporary China.* Stanford, CA: Hoover Institute Press, 1977.

----------. *Political Change in Taiwan: A Study of Ruling Party Adaptability*. New York: Praeger, 1992.

Peng, Ming-min. *A Taste of Freedom; Memoirs of a Formosan Independence Leader.* New York: Holt, Rinehart and Winston, 1972.

Rankin, Karl L. *China Assignment.* Seattle: University of Washington Press, 1967.

Riggs, Fred W. *Formosa under Chinese Nationalist Rule.* New York: Octagon Books, 1972.

Robinson, Thomas W., ed. *Democracy and Development in East Asia: Taiwan, Korea, and the Philippines.* Washington, DC: American Enterprise Institute, 1990.

Rudolph, Jorg M. *Media Coverage on Taiwan in the People's Republic of China.* Baltimore: University of Maryland School of Law, 1983.

Seymour, James D. "Republic of China." In Albert P. Blaustein and Gisbert H. Flanz, eds. *Constitutions of the Countries of the World.* Dobbs Ferry, NY: Oceana Publications, 1974.

Shaw, Yu-ming. *Beyond the Economic Miracle: Reflections on the Developmental Experience of the Republic of China on Taiwan.* Taipei: Kwang Hwa Publishing, 1988.

Shieh, Milton J.T. *The Kuomintang: Selected Historical Documents, 1894-1969.* New York: Center of Asian Studies, St. John's University, 1970.

The Truth about the February 28, 1947 Incident in Taiwan. Taichung: Historical Research Commission of Taiwan Province, 1967.

Tien, Hung-mao. *The Great Transition: Political and Social Change in the Republic of China.* Stanford: Hoover Institution Press, 1989.

Tien, Hung-mao, ed. *Taiwan□s Electoral Politics and Democratic Transition: Riding the Third Wave.* Armonk, NY: M.E. Sharpe, 1995.

Tsang, Steve, ed. *In the Shadow of China: Political Developments in Taiwan since 1949.* Honolulu: University of Hawaii Press, 1993.

Tung, William L. *The Political Institutions of Modern China.* The Hague: Martinus Nijhoff, 1968.

Wachman, Alan M. *Taiwan: National Identity and Democratization.* Armonk, NY: M.E. Sharpe, 1994.

Williams, Jack F., ed. *The Future of Hong Kong and Taiwan.* East Lansing: Asian Studies Center, Michigan State University, 1985.

----------. *The Taiwan Issue: Proceedings of the Symposium, November 6, 1975.* East Lansing: Asian Studies Center, Michigan State University, 1976.

Wu, Jaushieh J. *Taiwan□s Democratization: Forces behind the New Momentum.* Hong Kong: Oxford University Press, 1995.

Zhao, Suisheng. *Power by Design: Constitution-Making in Nationalist China.* Honolulu: University of Hawaii Press, 1996.

ARTICLES

Appleton, S.C. "Taiwan: Portents of Change," *Asian Survey,* January 1971.

----------. "Taiwan: The Year It Finally Happened," *Asian Studies,* January 1972.

Bosco, J. "Faction vs. Ideology: "Mobilization Strategies in Taiwan's Elections," *China Quarterly,* March 1994.

Brindley, Thomas A. "The China Youth Corps: Democratization in Progress," *American Journal of Chinese Studies,* October 1994.

Brown, Deborah A. "Democracy in the Republic of China on Taiwan," *American Asian Review,* Fall 1997.

Chang, David W. "Minor Parties in Recent Chinese Political Development in the PRC and the ROC on Taiwan," *American Journal of Chinese Studies,"* April 1987.

Chang, Maria Hsia. "Political Succession in the Republic of China on Taiwan," *Asian Survey,* April 1984.

Chang, Ya-yun. "A Comparative Study between the Five-power Constitution and Other Constitutions," *China Forum,* January 1975.

Chao, L., and R.H. Myers. "The First Chinese Democracy: Political Development of the Republic of China on Taiwan, 1986-1994," *Asian Survey,* March 1994.

Chao, L. et al. "Promoting Effective Democracy, Chinese Style: Taiwan's National Development Conference," *Asian Survey,* July 1997.

Chen, Lucy H. "Literary Formosa," *China Quarterly,* July-September 1963.

Chen, Theodore H.E. "Taiwan after Chiang Kai-shek," *Current History,* September 1975.

----------. "Taiwan's Future," *Current History,* September 1979.

Cheng, L. and L. White. "Elite Transformation and Modern Change in Mainland China and Taiwan: Empirical Data and the Theory of Technocracy," *China Quarterly,* March 1990.

Cheng, Peter P. "Taiwan 1975: A Year of Transition," *Asian Survey,* January 1976.

Cheng, Sheldon S.D. "A Study of the Temporary Provisions of the Constitution of the Republic of China," *Chinese Culture,* December 1972.

Cheng, T.J. "Democratizing the Quasi-Leninist Regime in Taiwan," *World Politics,* July 1989.

"Chinese Culture and Political Renewal," *Journal of Democracy,* October 1995.

Chiu, Hungdah. "Recent Constitutional Development in the Republic of China on Taiwan," *American Journal of Chinese Studies,* October 1992.

Chou, Y., and A.J. Nathan. "Democratizing Transition in Taiwan." *Asian Survey,* March 1987.

Chu, J.J. "Political Liberalization and the Rise of Taiwanese Labor Radicalism," *Journal of Contemporary Asia,* 23, no. 2, 1993.

Chu, Y.H. "Taiwan's Unique Challenges," *Journal of Democracy,* July 1996.

Chu, Y.W. "Democracy and Organized Labor in Taiwan: The 1986 Transition," *Asian Survey,* May 1996.

Clark, Cal. "Taiwan's Democratization and Political Transformation: Toward the 21st Century and Beyond," *American Asian Review,* Spring 1998.

Cole, A.B. "Political Roles of Taiwanese Enterprise," *Asian Survey,* September 1967.

Copper, John F. "Ending Martial Law in Taiwan: Implications and Prospects," *Journal of Northeast Asian Studies,* Summer 1988.

----------. "The KMT's 14th Party Congress: Toward Unity or Disunity," *American Journal of Chinese Studies,* October 1994.

----------. "Politics in Taiwan," in Hungdah Chiu, ed. *Survey of Recent Developments in China (Mainland and Taiwan), 1985-86.* Baltimore: University of Maryland School of Law, 1987.

----------. "Remembering President Chiang-kuo," *Asian Thought and Society,* January 1988.

----------. "The Role of Minor Political Parties in Taiwan," *World Affairs,* Winter 1993.

----------. "Taiwan: New Challenges to Development," *Current History,* April 1986.

----------. "Taiwan's 1985 Elections," *Asian Affairs,* Spring 1986.

----------. "Taiwan's 1986 National Election: Pushing Democracy Ahead," *Asian Thought and Society,* July 1987.

----------. "Taiwan's 1989 Elections: Pushing Democracy Ahead," *Journal of Northeast Asian Studies,* Winter 1990.

----------. "Taiwan's 1991 National Assembly Election," *Journal of Northeast Asian Studies,* Spring 1991.

----------. "Taiwan's 1992 Legislative Yuan Election," *World Affairs*, Fall 1992.

Cox, G.W. "Is the Single Nontransferable Vote Superproportional? Evidence from Japan and Taiwan," *American Journal of Political Science*, August 1996.

Cox, G.W., and E.M.S. Niou. "Seat Bonuses under the Single Nontransferable Vote System: Evidence from Japan and Taiwan," *Comparative Politics*, January 1994.

Dreyer, J.T. "Taiwan's December 1991 Election," *World Affairs*, Fall 1992.

Durdin, Tillman. "Chiang Ching-kuo and Taiwan: A Profile," *Orbis*, Winter 1975.

Dutt, V.P. "Formosa, Background Notes," *India Quarterly*, January-March 1951.

Feng, Yukon. "Changes in the Chinese Political System," *Chinese Journal of Administration*, July 1964.

Freund, Elizabeth. "Men of Steel: The Politics of Privatization for China Steel Corporation," *American Asian Review*, Summer 1996.

Gregor, A. James, and Maria Hsia Chang. "The Taiwan Independence Movement: The Failure of Political Persuasion," *Political Communication and Persuasion*, 1985.

Gurtov, Melvin. "Recent Developments on Formosa," *China Quarterly*, July-September 1967.

----------. "Taiwan in 1966: Political Rigidity, Economic Growth," *Asian Survey*, January 1967.

Harrison, Selig S. "Taiwan after Chiang Ching-kuo," *Foreign Affairs*, Spring 1988.

Heuser, Robert. "Legal Aspects of Trade with and Investment in the Republic of China: The German Experience," *International Trade Law*, Fall 1977.

Hickman, John. "Constituency Magnitude As a Determinant of Seat/Vote Proportionality and Electoral Competition in Taiwan's 1992 and 1995 Legislative Yuan Elections," *American Asian Review*, Summer 1998.

Hicks, N. "A Tale of Two Chinas," *Geographic Magazine*, January 1993.

Hood, S.J. "Political Change in Taiwan: The Rise of Kuomintang Factions," *Asian Survey*, May 1996.

Hsieh, Erh-yi. "The System of Punishment of Public Officials," *Chinese Journal of Administration*, January 1965.

Hsieh, John Fuh-sheng, Dean P. Lacy. and Emerson M.S. Niou. "Economic Voting in the 1994 Elections," *American Asian Review*, Summer 1996.

Hsu, Cheng-hsi. "The American and Chinese Legislative Systems," *Sino-American Relations*, Winter 1975.

Huang, The-fu. "Electoral Competition and the Evolution of the Kuomintang," *Issues and Studies*, May 1995.

Huang, The-fu, and Emerson M.S. Niou. "Democratic Consolidation and the Party System in Taiwan," *American Asian Review*, Fall 1996.

Ijiri, H. "Slighting Taiwan Is behind the Times," *Japan Quarterly*, January-March 1989.

Israel, John. "Politics on Formosa," *China Quarterly*, July-September 1963.

Jacobs, J. Bruce. "Paradoxes in the Politics of Taiwan: Lessons for Comparative Politics," *Politics*, November 1978.

----------. "Recent Leadership and Political Trends in Taiwan," *China Quarterly*, January-March 1971.

----------. "Taiwan's Press Political Communication Link and Research Resource," *China Quarterly*, December 1976.

Jeon, J. G. "The Political Economy of Crisis Management in the Third World: A Comparative Study of South Korea and Taiwan (1970s)," *Pacific Affairs*, Winter 1994-95.

Kagan, Richard C. "Taiwan: Another Greece," *Dissent*, January-February 1969.

Kallgren, Joyce K. "Nationalist China: Political Inflexibility and Economic Accommodation," *Asian Survey*, January 1964.

----------. "Nationalist China: Problems of a Modernizing Taiwan," *Asian Survey*, January 1965.

----------. "Vietnam and Politics in Taiwan," *Asian Survey*, January 1966.

Kuo, P. "Taiwan's News Media: Its Role in Democratization," *World Affairs*, Winter 1993.

Lashmar, P. "China Syndrome," *New Statesman and Society*, January 26, 1996.

Lavrencic, K. "Taiwan: Will Politics Spoil the Economic Miracle?" *World Today*, January 1985.

Lee, Kwo-wei. "A Study of Social Background and Recruitment Process of Local Political Decision-Makers in Taiwan," *Indian Journal of Public Administration*, April-June 1972.

Lee, T.H. "Building a Democracy for Unification," *World Affairs*, Winter 1993.

Leng, S.C., and C.Y. Lin. "Political Change on Taiwan: Transition to Democracy," *China Quarterly*, December 1993.

Lerman, Arthur J. "National Elite and Local Politicians in Taiwan," *American Political Science Review*, December 1977.

Li, Wen-lang. "Party Competition and Electoral Success in a Confucian State," *American Journal of Chinese Studies*, October 1992.

Lin, C.P., ed. "Democracy in Taiwan (symposium)," *World Affairs*, Winter 1993.

Lin, T.M. et al. "Conflict Displacement and Regime Transition in Taiwan: A Spatial Analysis," *World Politics*, July 1996.

Linebarger, Paul M.A. "Guam and Taiwan: Some Political Contrasts," *World Affairs,* April 6, 1965.

----------. "The Republic of China on Taiwan: A Descriptive Appraisal," *World Affairs,* Spring 1963.

Ling, L.H.M., and C.Y. Shih. "Confucianism with a Liberal Face: The Meaning of Democratic Politics in Postcolonial Taiwan," *The Review of Politics,* Winter 1998.

Ling, T., and R.H. Myers. "Winds of Democracy: The 1989 Taiwan Elections," *Asian Survey,* April 1990.

----------. "Surviving the Rough-and-Tumble of Presidential Politics in an Emerging Democracy: The 1990 Elections in the Republic of China on Taiwan," *China Quarterly*, March 1992.

Long, S. "Taiwan's National Assembly Elections," *China Quarterly*, March 1992.

Lu, Shumin. "Chinese Embassy Position: U.S. Should Honor Its Commitments by Deeds," *Congressional Digest*, August/ September 1995.

Mancall, M. "Succession and Myth in Taiwan," *Journal of International Affairs,* 1964.

McBeath, Gerald A. "Transformation of the Chinese Nationalist Party (KMT): Adjusting to Liberalization," *American Journal of Chinese Studies*, October 1997.

Meisner, Maurice. "The Development of Formosan Nationalism," *China Quarterly,* July-September 1963.

Moon, E.P. "Single Non-transferable Vote Methods in Taiwan in 1996: Effects of an Electoral System," *Asian Survey*, July 1997.

Myers, R.H. "A New Chinese Civilization: The Evolution of the Republic of China on Taiwan," *China Quarterly*, December 1996.

----------. "Political Theory and Recent Political Developments in the Republic of China," *Asian Survey,* September 1987.

Nathan, A.J. "The Legislative Yuan Elections in Taiwan: Consequences of the Electoral System," *Asian Survey*, April 1993.

Omestad, T. "Dateline Taiwan: A Dynasty Ends," *Foreign Policy,* Summer 1988.

Ong, Joktik. "A Formosan's View of the Formosan Independence Movement," *China Quarterly,* July-September 1963.

Peng, Ming-min. "Political Offenses in Taiwan: Laws and Problems," *China Quarterly*, June-September 1971.

Plummer, Mark. "Taiwan: The Other China," *Current History,* September 1966.

----------. "Taiwan's Chinese Nationalist Government," *Current History,* September 1971.

Ravenholt, A. "Formosa Today," *Foreign Affairs,* July 1952.

Rigger, Shelley. "The Risk of Reform: Factional Conflict in Taiwan's 1989 Local Elections," *American Journal of Chinese Studies,* October 1994.

----------. "Taiwan's Lee Teng-hui Complex," *Current History,* September 1996.

Robinson, James A., and Julian Baum. "Party Primaries in Taiwan: Footnote or Text in Democratization," *Asian Affairs,* Summer 1993.

Robinson, James A. "Local Elections in Taiwan, 1993-94: Appraising Steps in Democratization," *Political Chronicle,* 6 no. 2, 1994.

----------. "The KMT As a Leninist Regime: Prolegomenon to Devolutionary Leadership through Institutions," *Political Chronicle,* Vol.3, No.1, 1991.

----------. "Domestic Politics in Taiwan's U.N. Aspirations," *American Asian Review,* Fall 1995.

----------. "Lee Teng-hui and Taiwan's Political Development," *American Asian Review,* Spring 1996.

----------. "Myth and Taiwan Politics," *American Asian Review,* Summer 1996.

----------. "Taiwan's 1995 Legislative Yuan Election: Appraising Steps in Democratization," *American Asian Review,* Fall 1996.

----------. "Taiwan's 1996 National Assembly and Presidential Elections: Appraising Steps in Democratization," *American Asian Review,* Spring 1998.

Shaw, Y.M. "Taiwan: A View from Taipei," *Foreign Affairs,* Summer 1985.

Shin, D.C., and H. Shyu. "Political Ambivalence in South Korea and Taiwan," *Journal of Democracy,* July 1997.

Sicherman, H. "An Interview with President Lee Teng-hui of the Republic of China on Taiwan," *Orbis,* Fall 1995.

Solarz, Steven J. "Democracy and the Future of Taiwan," *Freedom at Issue,* March/April 1984.

Soong, J.C.Y. "Political Development in the Republic of China on Taiwan, 1985-1992: An Insider's View," *World Affairs,* Fall 1992.

Srinivasen, K. "Taiwan Is Confident of the Future," *Issues and Studies,* April 1972.

Stikker, A. "The Taiwan 2000 Study: Experiences and Impressions." *Futures,* August 1988.

Tan, Q. et al. "Local Politics in Taiwan: Democratic Consolidation," *Asian Survey,* May 1996.

Tien, Hung-mao. "Taiwan in 1986: Reforms under Adversity." In John S. Major and Anthony J. Kane, eds., *China Briefing, 1987*. Boulder, CO: Westview Press, 1987.

Tsai, Wen-hui. "A Giant Step Forward: The 1996 Presidential Election of the Republic of China on Taiwan," *American Asian Review*, *American Asian Review*, Spring 1997.

Wang, Gung-hsing. "Nationalist Government Policies, 1949-1951," *Annals of the American Academy of Political and Social Science*, September 1951.

Wei, Yung. "Political Development in the Republic of China on Taiwan," in Hungdah Chiu, ed. *China and the Question of Taiwan*. New York: Praeger, 1973.

----------. "Taiwan: A Modernizing Chinese Society," in Paul K.T. Sih, ed. *Taiwan in Modern Times*. New York: St. John's University, 1973.

Weiss, J. "'One Country, Two Systems': Beijing's Threat to the Republic of China," *Journal of Social, Political and Economic Studies*, Spring 1988.

Winckler, Edwin A. "Institutionalization and Participation in Taiwan: From Hard to Soft Authoritarianism," *China Quarterly*, September 1984.

Wu, Y.S. "Marketization of Politics: The Taiwan Experience," *Asian Survey*, April 1989

MILITARY AND SECURITY

GENERAL

BOOKS

Bullard, Monte. *The Soldier and the Citizen: The Role of the Military in Taiwan's Development*. Armonk, NY: M.E. Sharpe, 1997.

Chang, Parris, ed. *If China Crosses the Taiwan Strait: The International Response*. Lanham, MD: University Press of America, 1993.

Chiang, Wei-kuo. *The Strategic Significance of Taiwan in the Global Strategic Picture*. Taipei: Li Min Cultural Publications, 1977.

Fu, Jen-kun. *Taiwan and the Geopolitics of the Asian-American Dilemma*. Westport, CT: Greenwood Press, 1992.

Gregor, James, and Maria Hsia Chang, "The Military Defense of the Republic of China." In *Struggles for Change in Mainland China*. Taipei: Institute of International Relations, 1980.

Hickey, Dennis van Vranken. *Taiwan's Security in the Changing International System.* Boulder, CO: Lynne Rienner Publishers, 1997.

----------. *United States-Taiwan Security Ties: From Cold War to beyond Containment.* Westport, CT: Praeger, 1994.

Overholt, William H., ed. *Asia's Nuclear Future.* Boulder, CO: Westview Press, 1977.

U.S. Office of Naval Operations. *Taiwan (Formosa).* Washington, DC: Naval Department, 1944.

Wu Chen-tsai. "Role of the Republic of China in Collective Defense," in K.K. Sinha, ed. *Problems of Defense of South and East Asia.* Bombay, India: Manaktalas, 1969.

ARTICLES

Bellows, Thomas J. "Taiwan's Security and Foreign Affairs: Toward 2000 and Beyond," *American Asian Review,* Spring 1998.

Chan, S. "Defense Burden and Economic Growth: Unraveling the Taiwanese Enigma," *American Political Science Review,* September 1988.

Chang, F.K. "Conventional War across the Taiwan Strait," *Orbis,* Fall 1996.

Chang, Thomas. "Forum on Strategic Situation in the Western Pacific and Taiwan Strait," *Asian Outlook,* February 1986.

Chen, King C. "Peking's Attitude toward Taiwan," *Asian Survey,* October 1977.

Chiu, Hungdah. "Growth of the Chinese Military and Its Threat to Taiwan," *American Asian Review,* Spring 1996.

Copper, John F. "Taiwan's State Security Law: Old Wine in New Bottles," *Journal of Defense and Diplomacy,* October 1987.

Davis, D.R., and S. Chan. "The Security-Welfare Relationship: Longitudinal Evidence from Taiwan," *Journal of Peace Research,* February 1990.

Dreyer, J.T. "Regional Security Issues," *Journal of International Affairs,* Winter 1996.

----------. "The Republic of China's National Defense," *American Asian Review,* Spring 1996

----------. "The Taiwan Strait Crisis and the R.O.C.'s National Security," *American Asian Review,* Fall 1997.

Field, R.H. "Strategic Formosa," *Current History,* April 1949.

Fleming, D.F. "Our Brink of War Diplomacy in the Formosa Strait," *Western Political Quarterly,* September 1956.

Fraser, A.M. "Military Posture and Strategic Policy in the Republic of China," *Asian Affairs,* May-June 1974.

Kallgren, Joyce. "Nationalist China's Armed Forces," *China Quarterly,* July-September 1963.

----------. "Nationalist Chinese Military Strength: Its Use in Southeast Asia." In K.K. Sinha, ed. *Problems of Defense of South and East Asia.* Bombay, India: Manaktalas, 1969.

Lasater, Martin L. "The PRC's Force Modernization: Shadow over Taiwan and U.S. Policy," *Strategic Relations,* Winter 1984.

Lin, C.P. "The Military Balance in the Taiwan Straits," *China Quarterly,* June 1996.

Mowery, D.C. "The Taiwan Aerospace-McDonnell Douglas Agreement: A Modest Expansion of the Trend toward Globalization in Aerospace," *Journal of Policy Analysis and Management,* Summer 1992.

Prestowitz, C.V., Jr. "The McDonnell Douglas-Taiwan Aerospace Agreement: Selling Off Our Birthright," *Journal of Policy Analysis and Management,* Summer 1992.

Quester, George H. "Taiwan and Nuclear Proliferation," *Orbis,* Spring 1974.

Roucek, Joseph S. "The Geopolitics of Formosa," *United Asia,* April 1963.

Shambaugh, D. "Taiwan's Security: Maintaining Deterrence amid Political Accountability," *China Quarterly,* December 1996.

Shih, C.Y. "Psychological Security and National Security: The Taiwan Factor in China's U.S. Policy," *The Journal of Social, Political, and Economic Studies,* Winter 1991.

Tyson, L.D., and P.H. Chin. "McDonnell Douglas and Taiwan Aerospace: A Strategic Perspective on the National Interest in the Commercial Aircraft Industry," *Journal of Policy Analysis and Management,* Fall 1992.

Ward, D. et al. "Military Spending and Economic Growth in Taiwan," *Armed Forces and Society,* Summer 1993.

Wu, Yuan-li. "Economic Development and International Security in Northeast Asia: Some Issues of Political and Economic Interaction," *Korea and World Affairs,* Fall 1978.

SECURITY RELATIONS WITH THE U.S.

BOOKS

Clough, Ralph N. *East Asia and U.S. Security.* Washington, DC: Brookings Institution, 1975.

Frost, Michael S. *Taiwan's Security and United States Policy: Executive and Congressional Strategies.* Baltimore: University of Maryland School of Law, 1982.

Lasater, Martin L. *The Taiwan Issue in Sino-American Strategic Relations.* Boulder, CO: Westview Press, 1984.

Snyder, Edwin K., et al. *The Taiwan Relations Act and the Defense of the Republic of China.* Berkeley: Institute of International Studies, University of California, 1980.

U.S. House Committee on Foreign Affairs. *China-Taiwan: United States Policy: Hearing before the Committee on Foreign Affairs.* 97th Cong. 2nd sess., August 18, 1982.

ARTICLES

Chin, Chu-Kwang. "The U.S.-Japan Joint Declaration: Strategic Implications for Taiwan's Security," *World Affairs,* Winter 1998.

Clubb, O.E. "Formosa and the Offshore Islands in American Policy, 1950-1955," *Political Science Quarterly,* December 1959.

Gregor, A.J. "East Asian Stability and the Defense of the Republic of China on Taiwan," *Comparative Strategy,* October/December 1997.

Gregor, A.J. "U.S. Interests in Northeast Asia and the Security of Taiwan," *Strategic Relations,* Winter 1985.

Harsch, Ernest. "China: Growing Strains with Washington: Behind the Dispute over U.S. Arms Sales to Taiwan," *Intercontinental Press,* 6 September 1982.

Hickey, Dennis. "U.S. Arms Sales to Taiwan: Institutionalized Ambiguity," *Asian Survey,* December 1986.

Hsu, King-yi. "Sino-American Relations and the Security of Taiwan," *Asian Affairs,* September-October 1978.

Ku, Joseph. "Furors over U.S. Decision Denying Sales of FX Fighters to ROC," *Asian Outlook,* February 1982.

Lasater, Martin L. "Future Fighter Sales to Taiwan," *Comparative Strategy,* 1985.

Li, Victor, and John W. Lewis. "Resolving the China Dilemma: Advancing Normalization, Preserving Security," *International Security,* Summer 1977.

Sutter, Robert. "U.S. Arms Sales to Taiwan: Implications for American Interests," *Journal of Northeast Asian Studies,* September 1982.

Towell, P. "U.S. Reduces Fleet off Taiwan," *Congressional Quarterly Weekly Report,* March 30, 1996.

Tsou, Tang. "The Quemoy Imbroglio: Chiang Kai-shek and the United States," *Western Political Quarterly,* December 1959.

FOREIGN POLICY

GENERAL

BOOKS

Bachrack, Stanley D. *The Committee of One Million.* New York: Columbia University Press, 1976.

Bader, William B., and Jeffrey T. Berger, eds. *The Taiwan Relations Act: A Decade of Implementation.* Indianapolis, IN: Hudson Institute, 1989.

Chen, Frederick Tse-shyand, ed. *China Policy and National Security.* Dobbs Ferry, NY: Transnational Publishers, 1984.

Chien, Frederick F. *Faith and Residence: The Republic of China Forges Ahead.* Houston, TX: Kwang Hwa Publishing Company, 1988.

China and the United Nations. New York: Carnegie Endowment for International Peace, 1959.

Chiu, Hungdah, and Robert Downen, eds. *Multisystem Nations and International Law: The International Status of Germany, Korea, and China.* Baltimore, MD: University of Maryland School of Law, 1981.

Copper, John F. *Words Across the Taiwan Strait: A Critique of Beijing's "White Paper" on China's Reunification.* Lanham, MD: University Press of America, 1995.

Hsieh, Chiao Chiao. *Strategy for Survival: The Foreign Policy and External Relations of the Republic of China on Taiwan, 1949-79.* London: Sherwood Press, 1985.

Koenig, Louis W., James C. Hsiung, and King-yuh Chang, eds. *Congress, the Presidency and the Taiwan Relations Act.* New York: Praeger, 1985.

Lasater, Martin I. *U.S. Policy toward China's Reunification.* Washington, DC: Heritage Foundation, 1988.

Lee, David T., and Robert L. Pfaltzgraff, Jr., eds., *Taiwan in a Transformed Global Setting.* Brasseys Inc., 1995.

Lee, Lai T. *The Reunification of China: Pro-Taiwan Relations in Flux.* Westport, CT: Greenwood Press, 1991.

Mosher, Steven W., ed. *The United States and the Republic of China: Democratic Friends, Strategic Allies and Economic Partners.* New Brunswick, NJ: Transaction Publishers, 1991.

Myers, Ramon H., ed. *A Unique Relationship: The United States and the Republic of China under the Taiwan Relations Act.* Stanford: Hoover Institution Press, 1989.

Pillsbury, Michael. *Taiwan's Fate: Two Chinas but Not Forever.* Santa Monica: Rand Corporation, 1975.

Shen, James C.H. *The View from Twin Oaks: A Collection of Selected Speeches, 1971-1978.* Vols. I and II. Washington, DC: n.p., 1978.

Sutter, Robert G., and William Johnson, eds. *Taiwan in World Affairs.* Boulder, CO: Westview Press, 1994.

Wang, Yu S., ed. *Foreign Policy of the Republic of China on Taiwan: An Unorthodox Approach.* Westport, CT: Greenwood Press, 1990.

Wu, Hsin-Hsing. *Bridging the Taiwan Strait: Taiwan, China and the Prospects for Reunification.* Ohio University Press, 1994.

ARTICLES

Bellows, Thomas J. "The ROC's U.N. Strategy: Problems and Prospects," *American Asian Review*, Fall 1995.

----------. "Taiwan's Foreign Policy in the 1970s: A Case Study of Adaptation and Viability," *Asian Survey*, July 1976.

----------. "The Republic of China's International Relations," *American Journal of Chinese Studies*, October 1992.

Brands, H.W. "Testing Massive Retaliation: Credibility and Crisis Management in the Taiwan Strait," *International Security*, Spring 1988.

Broadfoot, Robert. "The Impact of PRC-Taiwan Ties on Hong Kong," *The China Business Review*, September-October 1990.

Bueler, W.M. "Taiwan: A Problem of International Law or Politics?" *World Today*, June 1971.

Carpenter, William M. "The U.S., the R.O.C. and the P.R.C.," *American Asian Review*, Spring 1997.

Chan, G. "Taiwan As an Emerging Foreign Aid Donor: Developments, Problems, and Prospects," *Pacific Affairs*, Spring 1997.

Chang, David W., and Hung-chao Tai. "The Informal Diplomacy of the Republic of China, with a Case Study of ROC's Relations with Singapore," *American Journal of Chinese Studies*, October 1996.

Chang, Maria Hsia. "Taiwan's Mainland Policy and the Reunification of China." Claremont, CA: Asian Studies Center, Claremont Institute, 1990.

Chang, Pao-min. "Choices for Taiwan," *World Today*, September 1978.

Chen, Chi-di. "On Its OwnXthe Republic of China (recent trends in foreign relations)," *Asian Affairs*, Fall 1983.

Chen, Lung-chu and W.M. Reisman. "Who Owns Taiwan? A Search for International Title," *Yale Law Journal*, March 1972.

Chen, Yu-ching. "World Situation and National Destiny," *Chinese Culture*, March 1973.

Cheng, P.P. "Taiwan and the Two Chinas," *Current History*, September 1969.

----------. "The Taiwan Triangle Today: A Taiwanese View," *Asian Profile*, December 1975.

Chien, F.F. "The Republic of China on Taiwan: Active Partner in the Pacific Rim," *Comparative Strategy*, January/March 1995.

Chien, Frederick. "A View from Taipei," *Foreign Affairs*, Winter 1991-92.

Ching, Frank. "Most Envied Province," *Foreign Policy*, Fall 1979.

Chiu, Hungdah. "The Outlook for Taiwan," *Asian Affairs*, January-February 1980.

----------. "The U.N. Membership for Taiwan," *American Asian Review*, Winter 1995.

Chuang, Richard Y. "The International Standing of the Republic of China: Achievements, Image, and Prospects," *American Journal of Chinese Studies*, October 1996.

Clark, Cal. "Taiwan's Pragmatic Diplomacy and Campaign for UN Membership," *American Asian Review*, Spring 1996.

Clough, Ralph N. "The Emerging New International Legal Order in the Western Pacific: The Status of Taiwan," *Journal of East Asian Affairs*, Winter/Spring 1994.

----------. "The ROC's International Participation: Obstacles and Strategies," *American Asian Review*, Fall 1995.

Copper, J.F. "The Future of Taiwan: An Analysis of Its Legal and Political Status, *Asian Quarterly*, Vol. 3, 1973.

----------. "Taiwan's Options," *Asian Affairs*, May-June 1979.

----------. "Taiwan's Strategy and America's China Policy," *Orbis*, Summer 1977.

Doherty, C.J. "Lawmakers Press White House for Firm Defense of Taiwan," *Congressional Quarterly Weekly Report*, March 16, 1996.

Domes, J. "Taiwan in 1991: Searching for Political Consensus," *Asian Survey*, January 1992.

----------. "Taiwan in 1992: On the Verge of Democracy," *Asian Survey*, January 1993.

Freeman, C.W., Jr. "Sino-American Relations: Back to Basics," *Foreign Policy*, Fall 1996.

Harkavy, Robert E. "The Pariah State Syndrome," *Orbis*, Fall 1977.

Hickey, D.V. "U.S. Policy and Taiwan's Bid to Rejoin the United Nations," *Asian Survey*, November 1997.

Hoge, J.F., Jr. "A Test of Wills over Taiwan," *Foreign Affairs*, November/December 1997.

Keeton, G.W. "The Problem of Formosa," *World Affairs*, January 1951.

Klatt, W. "Taiwan and the Foreign Investor," *Pacific Affairs*, Winter 1977-78.

Klein, Donald, and W. Levi. "Formosa's Diplomatic World," *China Quarterly*, July-September 1963.

Lee, T.H. "The Taiwan Experience and China's Future," *World Affairs*, Winter 1993.

Li, K.T. "Republic of China's Aid to Developing Nations," *Pacific Community*, July 1970.

Li, Thian-hok. "The China Impasse: A Formosan View," *Foreign Affairs*, April 1958.

Lin, C.Y. "Taiwan's South China Sea Policy," *Asian Survey*, April 1997.

Phillips, C.S., Jr. "International Legal Status of Formosa," *Western Political Quarterly*, June 1957.

Robinson, James A. "Democratization and Taiwan's External Relations: Pragmatic Diplomacy, the UN, and Mainland Affairs," *American Asian Review*, Spring 1997.

----------. "World Politics Confronts Respect: Implications of Taiwan's Democratization for China and the United States," *Journal of East Asian Affairs*, January 1996.

Rosen, Sumner M. "The Republic of China on Taiwan, the United Nations and the International Labor Organization," *American Asian Review*, Spring 1997.

Rowe, David. "Republic of China: Post-United Nations," *Issues and Studies*, May 1972.

Saxena, J.N. "The Legal Status of Taiwan," *Indian Journal of International Law*, January 1972.

Seymour, James D. "Taiwan and the United Nations," *American Asian Review*, Winter 1995.

Solomon, Richard H. "Thinking Through the China Problem," *Foreign Affairs*, January 1978.

Thompson, Thomas N. "Taiwan's Ambiguous Destiny," *Asian Survey*, July 1976.

Trager, Frank N. "A 'Willy Brandt' Solution for China?" *Asian Affairs*, September-October 1975.

Wang, F.L. "To Incorporate China: A New Policy for a New Era," *Washington Quarterly*, Winter 1998.

Weng, Byron S.J. "Taiwan-Hong Kong Relations, 1949-1997 and Beyond," *American Asian Review*, Winter 1997.

Wu, Chun-tsai. "Change in the World Situation and the Republic of China," *Pacific Community,* October 1970.

Yahuda, M. "The Foreign Relations of Greater China," *China Quarterly,* December 1993.

Yu, P.K.H. "Model of Democrats in Island China/Mainland Relations," *Journal of Contemporary Asia,* 1992.

Yu, Priscilla C. "Taiwan's International Exchange Program: A Study in Cultural Diplomacy," *Asian Affairs,* Summer 1985.

RELATIONS WITH CHINA

BOOKS

Chang, King-yuh. *A Framework for China's Reunification.* Taipei: Kwang Hwa Publishing, 1986.

Cheng, Tun-jen et al., eds. *Inherited Rivalry: Conflict across the Taiwan Straits.* Boulder, CO: Lynne Riener, 1995.

Chiu, Hungdah. *China and the Taiwan Issue.* New York: Praeger, 1979.

Chiu, Hungdah, and Karen Murphy. *The Chinese Connection and Normalization.* Baltimore: University of Maryland School of Law, 1979.

Wang, Yu San. *The China Question: Essays on Current Relations between Mainland China and Taiwan.* New York: Praeger Special Studies/ Praeger Publishers, 1985.

Wu, Hsin-hsing. *Bridging the Strait: Taiwan, China and the Prospects for Reunification.* Hong Kong: Oxford University Press, 1994.

ARTICLES

Arnold, T., and A. Donald. "The Unity of China (lecture to the Royal Society for Asian Affairs)," *Asian Affairs,* October 1992.

Bowles, C. "China Problem Reconsidered," *Foreign Affairs,* April 1960.

Brown, Deborah A. "Beijing and Taipei in Hong Kong: Confluence or Conflict," *American Asian Review,* Summer 1997.

Buruma, I. "Taiwan's New Nationalists," *Foreign Affairs,* July/August 1996.

Cabestan, J.P. "Taiwan's Mainland Policy: Normalization, Yes; Reunification, Later," *China Quarterly,* December 1996.

Chao, Chien-min. "David and Goliath: A Comparison of Reunification Policies between Mainland China and Taiwan," *Issues & Studies,* July 1994.

----------. "One Country, Two Systems': A Theoretical Analysis," *Asian Affairs,* Summer 1987.

Chen, George P. "Taiwan's Relations with Mainland China: Three Major Issues between Taipei and Beijing," *American Asian Review,* Spring 1996.

Chen, Qimao. "The Taiwan Issue and Sino-U.S. Relations: A PRC View," *Asian Survey,* November 1987.

Chiou, C.L. "Dilemmas in China's Reunification Policy Towards Taiwan," *Asian Survey,* April 1986.

Chiu, Hungdah. "The Current State of Divided China: New Perspectives and Policies on the Republic of China (Taiwan) Side," *American Journal of Chinese Studies,* April 1992.

----------. "Koo-Wang Talks and the Prospect of Building Constructive and Stable Relations across the Taiwan Strait," *Issues and Studies,* August 1993.

----------. "The Koo-Wang Talks and Intra-Chinese Relations," *American Journal of Chinese Studies,* October 1994.

----------. "Normalizing Relations with China: Some Practical and Legal Problems," *Asian Affairs,* November-December 1977.

Christensen, T.J. "Chinese Realpolitik," *Foreign Affairs,* September/October 1996.

Clubb, O.E. "Sino-American Relations and the Future of Formosa," *Political Science Quarterly,* March 1965.

Cohen, Marc J. "One China or Two: Facing Up to the Taiwan Question," *World Policy Journal,* Fall 1987.

Copper, John F. "Prospects for the Unification of Taiwan with China," *Pacific Community,* January 1976.

Crane, G.T. "China and Taiwan: Not Yet Greater China," *International Affairs,* October 1993.

Duncanson, Dennis. "What Is Taiwan to China?" *Asian Affairs,* October 1986.

Gilbert, Lewis. "Peking and Taipei," *China Quarterly,* July-September 1963.

Gold, T.B. "The Status Quo Is Not Static: Mainland-Taiwan Relations," *Asian Survey,* March 1987.

Halbach, Axel J. "Taiwan and the People's Republic of China, Foes or Partners?" *Intereconomics,* May-June 1979.

Hinton, Harold C. "Who Needs Peking? The Case Against Normalization," *Korea and World Affairs,* Winter 1978.

Hsiao, Frank S.T., and Laurence R. Sullivan. "The Politics of Reunification: Beijing's Initiative on Taiwan," *Asian Survey,* August 1980.

Hsiung, James C. "The Hong Kong Settlement: Effects on Taiwan and Prospects for Peking's Reunification Bid," *Asian Affairs,* Summer 1985.

Hsu, King-yi. "Taiwan's Response to Peking's United Front Tactics," *Asian Affairs,* November/December 1980.

Hu, C. "Taipei's Approach to Unification with the Mainland," *The Journal of Social, Political, and Economic Studies,* Spring 1992.

Hu, W. "China's Taiwan Policy and East Asian Security," *Journal of Contemporary Asia,* 1997. 27, No. 3.

Hu, W.J. "In Search of National Security: Strategic Concepts of the Republic of China at a Crossroads," *Comparative Strategy,* April/June 1995.

Huan, Guo-cang. "Taiwan: A View from Beijing." *Foreign Affairs,* Summer 1985.

Huebner, J.W. "The Abortive Liberation of Taiwan," *China Quarterly,* June 1987.

Jia, Qingguo. "Changing Relations across the Taiwan Strait," *Asian Survey,* March 1992.

Kraar, Louis. "Taiwan: Trading with the Enemy: Taiwan Has Become a Major Supplier of Goods to the Mainland, Just When Its Other Markets Were Beginning to Wane," *Fortune,* 17 February 1986.

Li, Shuiwang. "Review on a Year of Change and Preview," *Beijing Review,* 7 November 1988.

Lin, C.P. "Beijing and Taipei: Dialectics in Post-Tiananmen Interactions," *China Quarterly,* December 1993.

Ma, Ying-jeou. "The Republic of China's Policy toward the Chinese Mainland," *Issues and Studies,* February 1992.

Munro, R.H. "Giving Taipei a Place at the Table," *Foreign Affairs,* November/December 1994.

O'Connell, D.P. "The Status of Formosa and the Chinese Recognition Problem," *American Journal of International Law,* April 1956.

Overholt, W.H. "Would Chiang Find Mao an Unacceptable Strange Bedfellow?" *Asian Survey,* August 1974.

Pollack, Jonathan D. "China and Taiwan in 1983," Rand Corporation (report), December 1983.

Pye, L.W. "Taiwan's Development and Its Implications for Beijing and Washington," *Asian Survey,* June 1986.

Qimao, Chen. "The Taiwan Strait Crisis: Its Crux and Solutions," *Asian Survey,* November 1996.

Robinson, T.W. "America in Taiwan's Post-Cold War Foreign Relations," *China Quarterly,* December 1996.

Scobell, Andrew. "Taiwan: The Other China," *Brookings Review,* Fall 1988.

Shaw, Yu-ming. "Taiwan: A View from Taipei," *Foreign Affairs,* Summer 1985.

Simmons, Robert T. "Taiwan and China: The Delicate Courtship," *Current History,* September 1973.

Thayer, Nathaniel B. "China, the Formosa Question. In Gregory Henderson, Richard N. Lebow, and John G. Stoessinger, eds. *Divided Nations in a Divided World.* New York: David McKay, 1974.

Tien, H.M. "Taiwan in 1995: Electoral Politics and Cross-Strait Relations," *Asian Survey,* January 1996.

Tsang, S. "Target Zhou Enlai: The 'Kashmir Princess' Incident of 1955," *China Quarterly,* September 1994.

Tucker, N.B. "War or Peace in the Taiwan Strait?" *Washington Quarterly,* Winter 1996.

Wang, Shao-nan. "Why Did We Refuse the Chinese Communists' Peace Talks?" *Asian Outlook,* December 1981.

Weiss, Julian. "'One Country, Two Systems': Beijing's Threat to the Republic of China," *Journal of Political and Economic Studies,* Spring 1988.

Wu, An-chia. "The ROC's Mainland Policy in the 1990s," *Issues and Studies,* September 1991.

Wu, Hsin-hsing. "Taiwan-Mainland China Relations under the Leadership of Lee Teng-hui," *American Asian Review,* Summer 1996.

Wu, Y.S. "Taiwan in 1994: Managing a Critical Relationship," *Asian Survey,* January 1995.

Yeh, Milton D. "Taiwan-Mainland Relations: An Analysis of International and Domestic Factors," *American Journal of Chinese Studies,* October 1992.

Yu, G.T., and D.J. Longenecker. "The Beijing-Taipei Struggle for International Recognition: From the Niger Affair to the U.N.," *Asian Survey,* May 1994.

Yu, T. "Taiwanese Democracy under Threat: Impact and Limit of Chinese Military Coercion," *Pacific Affairs,* Spring 1997.

RELATIONS WITH THE UNITED STATES

BOOKS

Barnett, A. Doak. *U.S. Arms Sales: The China-Taiwan Tangle.* Washington, DC: Brookings Institution, 1982.

Bueler, William M. *U.S.-China Policy and the Problem of Taiwan.* Boulder, CO: Associated University Press, 1971.

China and U.S.-Far East Policy, 1945-1967. Washington, DC: Congressional Quarterly Service, 1967.

Chinese People's Institute of Foreign Affairs. *Oppose U.S. Occupation of Taiwan and "Two China" Plot.* Peking: Foreign Languages Press, 1958.

Chiu, Hungdah, and David Simon, eds. *Legal Aspects of U.S.- Republic of China Trade and Investment—Proceedings of a Regional Conference of the American Society of International Law.* Baltimore: University of Maryland School of Law, 1977.

Cohen, Jerome Alan, et al. *Taiwan and American Policy, the Dilemma in U.S.-China Relations.* New York: Praeger, 1971.

Copper, John F. *China Diplomacy: The Washington-Taipei-Beijing Triangle.* Boulder, CO: Westview Press, 1991.

Downen, Robert L. *The Taiwan Pawn in the China Game: Congress to the Rescue.* Washington, DC: Center for Strategic and International Studies, Georgetown University, 1979.

Goldwater, Barry M. *China and the Abrogation of Treaties.* Washington, DC: Heritage Foundation, 1978.

Gong, Gerrit W., and Bih-jaw Lin., eds. *Sino-American Relations in a Time of Change.* Washington, DC: Center for Strategic and International Studies and Institute of International Relations, 1994.

Gregor, A.J., and Maria H. Chang. *The Republic of China and U.S. Policy: A Study in Human Rights.* Washington, DC: Ethics and Public Policy Center, 1983.

Kintner, William, and John F. Copper. *A Matter of Two Chinas: The China-Taiwan Issues in U.S. Foreign Policy.* Philadelphia, PA: Foreign Policy Research Institute, 1979.

Koenig, Louis W., et al. *Congress, the Presidency, and the Taiwan Relations Act.* New York: Praeger, 1985.

Lasater, Martin L. *Policy and Evolution: The U.S. Role in China's Reunification.* Boulder, CO: Westview Press, 1988.

Li, Victor H. *Derecognizing Taiwan: The Legal Problems.* Washington, DC: Carnegie Endowment for International Peace, 1977.

Moorsteen, Richard, and Morton Abramowitz. *Remaking China Policy: U.S.-China Relations and Government Decision-making.* Cambridge: Harvard University Press, 1971.

Morgenthau, Hans J., ed. *The Impasse of American Foreign Policy.* Chicago: University of Chicago Press, 1962.

Myers, Ramon H., ed. *Two Chinese States: U.S. Foreign Policy and Interests.* Stanford: Hoover Institution Press, 1978.

Nerbonne, J.J. *A Foreign Correspondent Looks at Taiwan.* New York: W.S. Hein Imported Books, 1973.

Norma, Schroder. "Economic Costs and Benefits," in Ramon H. Myers, ed. *Two Chinese States: U.S. Foreign Policy and Interests.* Stanford: Hoover Institution Press, 1978.

Rowe, David N. *The Carter China Policy: Results and Prospects.* Branford, CT: David N. Rowe, 1980.

----------. *U.S. China Policy Today.* Washington, DC: University Professors for Academic Order, 1979.

Shen, James C.H. *The U.S. And Free China: How the U.S. Sold Out Its Ally.* Reston, VA: Acropolis, 1983.

The Taiwan Pawn in the China Game: Congress to the Rescue. New York: Unipub, 1979.

Tierney, John, Jr., ed. *About Face: The China Decision and Its Consequences.* New Rochelle, NY: Arlington House, 1979.

Senate Committee on Foreign Relations. U.S. Policy Toward China and Taiwan: Hearing before the Committee on Fsoreign Relations. 97th Cong., 2nd sess., 17 August 1982.

The Washington Lobby. Washington, DC: Congressional Quarterly Service, 1979.

U.S. Senate, Committee on Foreign Relations. Implementation of the Taiwan Relations Act: The First Year. A Staff Report, 96th Cong., 2nd sess. Washington, DC: U.S. Government Printing Office, 1980.

U.S. Senate, Committee on Foreign Relations, and Library of Congress Congressional Research Service. Taiwan: One Year after U.S.-China Normalization. A Workshop. Washington, DC: U.S. Government Printing Office, 1980.

Wheeler, Jimmy W., and Perry L. Wood. *Beyond Recrimination: Perspectives on U.S.-Taiwan Trade Tensions.* Indianapolis: Hudson Institute, 1987.

ARTICLES

Acheson, Dean. "United States Foreign Policy and Formosa," *Foreign Affairs,* April 1955.

Barnett, Robert W. "A Future for Taiwan." In Gene T. Hsiao, ed. *Sino-American Detente.* New York: Praeger, 1974.

Bellows, Thomas J. "Taiwan's U.N. Drive As an Issue between the U.S. Congress and the Administration" *American Asian Review,* Spring 1997.

Biddick, T.V. "Diplomatic Rivalry in the South Pacific: The PRC and Taiwan," *Asian Survey,* August 1989.

Brands, H.W. "Testing Massive Retaliation: Credibility and Crisis Management in the Taiwan Strait," *International Security,* Spring 1988.

Chang, J.L. J. "How Clinton Bashed Taiwan—and Why," *Orbis,* Fall 1995.

Copper, John F. "'The Taiwan Relations Act' As Viewed from Beijing and Taipei," *American Asian Review,* Winter 1992.

Cotton, J. "Redefining Taiwan: 'One Country, Two Governments,'" *World Today,* December 1989.

Gable, Carl I. "Taiwan Relations Act: Legislative Recognition," *Vanderbilt Journal of Transnational Law,* Summer 1979.

Garver, John W. "Arms Sales, the Taiwan Question, and Sino-U.S. Relations," *Orbis,* Winter 1985.

Harrison, S.S. "Taiwan after Chiang Ching-kuo," *Foreign Affairs,* Spring 1988.

Hickey, D.V.V. "America's Two-Point Policy and the Future of Taiwan," *Asian Survey,* August 1988.

Hsiung, James C. "U.S. Relations with China in the Post-Kissingerian Era: A Sensible Policy for the 1980's," *Asian Survey,* August 1977.

Hsu, King-yi. "America's National Interests and Its Continued Support of the Republic of China," *Issues and Studies,* March 1974.

Iriye, Akira. "Dilemmas of American Policy towards Formosa," *China Quarterly,* July-September 1963.

Jensen, B. "Eisenhower's Full Powers for Formosa and Their Constitutional Basis," *International Politics,* 1955.

Kau, Michael Y.M., et al. "Public Opinion and Our China Policy," *Asian Affairs,* January-February 1978.

Kim, H.N., and J.L. Hammersmith. "U.S.-China Relations in the Post-Normalization Era, 1979-1985," *Pacific Affairs,* Spring 1986.

Kindermann, Gottfried-Karl. "Washington between Beijing and Taipei: The Restructured Triangle, 1978-1980," *Asian Survey,* May 1980.

Lasater, M.L. "U.S. Interests in the New Taiwan," *Orbis,* Spring 1993.

Li, S. "What China Can Learn from Taiwan," *Orbis,* Summer 1989.

Murray, B. "Tiananmen: The View from Taipei," *Asian Survey,* April 1990.

Revenal, E.C. "Approaching China, Defending Taiwan," *Foreign Affairs,* October 1971.

Ross, Robert S. "International Bargaining and Domestic Politics: U.S.-China Relations Since 1972," *World Politics,* January 1986.

Scalapino, Robert A. "Uncertainties in Future Sino-U.S. Relations" [including problems associated with continuing differences over the future of Taiwan], *Orbis*, Fall 1982.

----------. "What Should the U.S. Do about Taiwan?" *Foreign Policy Bulletin*, 15 November 1960.

Sigur, Gaston J., Jr. "China Policy Today: Consensus, Consistence, Stability," *Department of State Bulletin*, February 1987.

Unger, L. "Derecognition Worked," *Foreign Policy*, Fall 1979.

Wachman, Alan M. "Carter's Constitutional Conundrum: An Examination of the President's Unilateral Termination of a Treaty," *Fletcher Forum*, Summer 1984.

Wang, Vincent Wei-cheng. "Rethinking U.S.-Taiwan Relations after the Cold War: Creative Ambiguity vs. Assertive Democratization," *American Asian Review*, Fall 1996.

Weiss, J. "One Country, Two Systems': Beijing's Threat to the Republic of China," *Journal of Social, Political, and Economic Studies*, Spring 1988.

Weiss, Thomas, "Taiwan and U.S. Policy," *Orbis*, Winter 1969.

Whiting, Allen S. "Sino-American Relations: The Decade Ahead," *Orbis*, Fall 1982.

Wright, Quincy. "The Chinese Recognition Problem," *American Journal of International Law*, July 1955.

Zagoria, Donald S. "Normalizing Relations with China by 'Abandoning' Taiwan," *Pacific Community*, November 1977.

RELATIONS WITH OTHER COUNTRIES

BOOKS

Jui, Chen-kao. *An Assessment on the Development of Substantive and Formal Relations with African Countries by the Republic of China*. Taipei: The Commission on Research and Development Evaluation of the Executive Yuan, 1991.

Tsou, Tang. *Embroilment over Quemoy: Mao, Chiang, and Dulles*. Salt Lake City: University of Utah Press, 1959.

Wall, R.F. "Formosa and the Chinese Off-Shore Islands." In G. Barraclough, ed. *Survey of International Affairs, 1956-1958*. London: Oxford University Press, 1962.

ARTICLES

Mendel, D.H., Jr. "Japanese Policy and Views Toward Formosa," *Journal of Asian Studies,* May 1969.

----------. "Japanese Public Views on Taiwan's Future," *Asian Survey,* March 1975.

----------. "Japan's Taiwan Tangle," *Asian Survey,* October 1964.

----------. "Taiwan and Trade in Japan's Mainland Chinese Policy," *Asian Forum,* October-December 1972.

Slawecki, L.M.S. "The Two Chinas in Africa," *Foreign Affairs,* January 1963.

Stockwin, Harvey. "A Hong Kong-Macao-Taiwan Triangle?" *The Round Table,* January 1979.

ABOUT THE AUTHOR

John F. Copper is the Stanley J. Buckman Distinguished Professor of International Studies at Rhodes College in Memphis, Tennessee. He is the author of more than 20 books on China, Taiwan, and Asian affairs. His book *China's Global Role* (Stanford: Hoover Institution Press, 1980) won the Clarence Day Foundation Award for outstanding research and creative activity. Professor Copper's most recent books include *China Diplomacy: The Washington-Taipei-Beijing Triangle* (Boulder, CO: Westview Press, 1992); *Words across the Taiwan Strait: A Critique of Beijing's "White Paper" on China's Reunification* (Lanham, MD: University Press of America, 1995); *The Taiwan Political Miracle: Essays on Political Development, Elections and Foreign Relations* (Lanham, MD: University Press of America, 1997); *Taiwan's Mid-1990s Elections: Taking the Final Steps to Democracy* (Westport, CT: Praeger Publishers, 1998); and *Taiwan: Nation-State or Province?* (3rd ed.) (Boulder, CO: Westview Press, 1999). Dr. Copper has also contributed to more than 40 other books and has published over 150 articles and pieces in scholarly journals and newspapers. Professor Copper has testified before the Senate Foreign Relations Committee and the House Foreign Affairs Committee. Dr. Copper received his B.A. degree from the University of Nebraska, his M.A. from the University of Hawaii, and his Ph.D. degree from the University of South Carolina. He also studied at the University of California, Berkeley and at Taiwan Normal University in Taipei. He is the recipient of the 1997 International Communications Award. Dr. Copper speaks Chinese and has lived in Asia for 13 years.

951.24   Copper, John F.,
Cop   1940-

        Historical dictionary
        of Taiwan (Republic
        of China)

DATE			